IMPERIAL MERIDIAN

STUDIES IN MODERN HISTORY

General editors: John Morrill and David Cannadine

This series, intended primarily for students, will tackle significant historical issues in concise volumes which are both stimulating and scholarly. The authors combine a broad approach, explaining the current state of our knowledge in the area, with their own research and judgements; and the topics chosen range widely in subject, period and place.

Titles already published

FRANCE IN THE AGE OF HENRY IV   *Mark Greengrass*

VICTORIAN RADICALISM   *Paul Adelman*

WHITE SOCIETY IN THE ANTEBELLUM SOUTH   *Bruce Collins*

BLACK LEADERSHIP IN AMERICA: FROM BOOKER T. WASHINGTON TO JESSE JACKSON   *(2nd Edn) John White*

THE TUDOR PARLIAMENTS   *Michael A.R. Graves*

LIBERTY AND ORDER IN EARLY MODERN EUROPE   *J.H. Shennan*

POPULAR RADICALISM   *D.G. Wright*

'PAX BRITANNICA'? BRITISH FOREIGN POLICY 1789–1914   *Muriel E. Chamberlain*

IRELAND SINCE 1800   *K. Theodore Hoppen*

IMPERIAL MERIDIAN: THE BRITISH EMPIRE AND THE WORLD 1780–1830   *C.A. Bayly*

A SYSTEM OF AMBITION? BRITISH FOREIGN POLICY 1660–1793   *Jeremy Black*

BRITANNIA OVERRULED: BRITISH POLICY AND WORLD POWER IN THE 20TH CENTURY   *David Reynolds*

POOR CITIZENS: THE STATE AND THE POOR IN TWENTIETH-CENTURY BRITAIN   *David Vincent*

THE HOUSE OF LORDS IN BRITISH POLITICS AND SOCIETY 1815–1911   *E.A. Smith*

POLITICS UNDER THE LATER STUARTS: PARTY CONFLICT IN A DIVIDED SOCIETY 1660–1715   *Tim Harris*

IMPERIAL MERIDIAN
The British Empire and the World 1780–1830

C. A. Bayly

LONGMAN
London and New York

LONGMAN GROUP UK LIMITED
Longman House, Burnt Mill, Harlow,
Essex CM20 2JE, England
and Associated Companies throughout the world.

Published in the United States of America
by Longman Inc., New York

First published 1989
Third impression 1993

BRITISH LIBRARY CATALOGUING IN PUBLICATION DATA
Bayly, C.A. (Christopher Alan), *1945–*
   Imperial Meridian: the British Empire and the world 1780–1830
(Studies in modern history).
   1. British imperialism, 1780–1830
   I. Title II. Series
   325′.32′0941

ISBN 0-582-04287-9 CSD
ISBN 0-582-49438-9 PPR

LIBRARY OF CONGRESS CATALOGING-IN-PUBLICATION DATA
Bayly, C.A. (Christopher Alan)
    Imperial meridian: the British empire and the world, 1780–1830/
C.A. Bayly.
    000 p. 000 cm. — (Studies in modern history)
    Bibliography: p.
    Includes index.
    ISBN 0-582-04287-9. ISBN 0-582-49438-9 (pbk.)
    1. Great Britain—Colonies—History—19th century. 2. Great
Britain—Colonies—History—18th century. 3. Great Britain—
Foreign relations—1760–1820. 4. Great Britain—Foreign
relations—1820–1830. 5. Imperialism—History. I. Title.
    II. Series: Studies in modern history (Longman (Firm))
DA16.B36 1989
909.7—dc19   88-8435
                                                          CP

Set in Linotron 202 10/12pt Baskerville

Produced by Longman Singapore Publishers (Pte) Ltd.
Printed in Singapore

Contents

List of Maps

Glossary

Afrikaner   the Dutch-speaking settlers of southern Africa.

ayan (Arabic; Turkish usage)   a provincial or regional notable of the Ottoman empire.

Bakhtiari   a nomadic tribal group of central Iran.

banian (Bengali)   Indian servant or intermediary of European merchant or official (*cf. dubash*).

Brahmin (Sanskrit)   the priestly caste of classical Indian civilisation. In modern times many Brahmins were not priests by occupation, (e.g. Bhumihar Brahmins, lit. 'landholding Brahmins).

Bugi   a sea-going trading community of Indonesia, originally from the Celebes.

Caliphate   *see* Khilafat.

chiftlik (Turkish)   an alienable private estate in the Ottoman empire.

Chalia   the cinnamon-picking caste of Ceylon.

creole (Portuguese)   a white settler born in a colony (mainly Caribbean and Latin America, but applied more widely).

devshirme (Turkish)   the 'levy' of boys particularly from the northern Christian lands of the Ottoman territories for service in the sultan's household.

dubash (Hindi)   lit. 'two-languages'; Indian servant or intermediary of a European officer or merchant; mainly Madras.

Ghalzai a tribe of eastern Afghanistan.

haj (Arabic) the Muslim pilgrimage to Medina and Mecca.

Hottentot *see* Khoikoi.

ijara (Persian) farming out to men of capital of the state land revenue.

iltizam (Arabic) farming out to men of capital of the state land revenue.

jagir (Persian) a grant to a state official of salary or the income from land at the Mughal emperor's pleasure.

Janissaries (Turkish) lit. 'new soldiers'; by the eighteenth century, a declining body of military corporations, once the élite of the sultan's troops in Istanbul.

Kaffir *see* Xhosa.

Khalsa a religious and military brotherhood within the Sikh community, emerging at the end of the seventeenth century.

Khilafat (Caliphate; Arabic) the spiritual succession in this world to the Prophet Muhammad.

Khoikoi the indigenous people of the Cape province (called Hottentots by the Dutch).

kraton (Javanese) a palace-complex (invested with sacred energy).

Kunbi a peasant caste of western India.

Kurds a Muslim but non-Arab tribe of northern Iraq and western Iran.

kuttab (Arabic) the scribal order of imperial servants in the Ottoman empire.

Lak a tribe of central Iran.

Maratha the warrior caste-cluster of western India.

Marwari an inhabitant of central India; often used of business people from that area.

mansabdar (Persian) an imperial office holder in the Mughal empire.

millet (Arabic; Turkish usage) a community of non-Muslim inhabitants of the Ottoman empire, constituting an inferior judicial and administrative entity.

Moplah a Muslim commercial and agricultural community of southwestern India.

mulk (Arabic) direct proprietary landed holding.

nawab (Persian) viceroy of (Mughal) emperor, later virtually independent ruler.

Parsis a commercial community of western India, Zoroastrian by religion and Persian by origin.

patriotes (French) the nationalist party of French Canada in the early nineteenth centry.

poligar (*palaiyakkarar*) (Tamil) lit. 'holder of a camp'; a warrior chieftain of south India.

Rajput the major military caste-cluster of northern India, traditionally landholders.

ryotwari (Persian) a method by which the British made land-tax arrangements in southern and western India, basing taxation directly on the peasant's fields.

Shaivism a major cult of Hinduism devoted to worship of the great God Shiva.

sharia (Arabic) Muslim law.

Shia the leading minority sect of the Islamic faith which emerged shortly after the death of the Prophet; dominant in Iran and parts of Mesopotamia.

Sikh an Indian religion emerging in the fifteenth century and consolidating itself in the Punjab.

Sufi adept of an Islamic mystical order.

Sunni the majority sect within Islam, dominant in the Arab lands and India.

Tamil a Dravidian language of south India (hence Tamils).

Telugu a Dravidian language of south and central India.

timar (Turkish usage) the military holding which supported soldiers within the Ottoman empire.

vazir (Persian) the chief minister of a Muslim empire.

Wahhabi after Abd-al Wahhab, an Arabian religious teacher; a fundamentalist sect of Sunni Islam originating in Arabia.

Xhosa a south African pastoralist tribal group (called Kaffir by the Dutch).

zamindar (Persian) lit. 'land holder'; holder of a patrimonial rental estate in India.

Abbreviations

AA	*Annals of Agriculture,* London.
CO	Colonial Office Records, PRO.
FO	Foreign Office Records, PRO.
IOL	India Office Library, London.
PRO	Public Records Office, London.
QR	*Quarterly Review,* London.

Preface

This book has emerged out of a number of years' research and writing on eighteenth- and nineteenth-century India. It is still partly about India, though much of the material and arguments here are not drawn from Indian historical writing, but from works on Britain, other parts of the British empire, or other societies outside Europe. In recent years Indian history, especially in India itself, has become more sophisticated and has distanced itself from many orientalist and colonial assumptions about the nature of Indian society. Yet it remains an introverted historiography and one that looks to Europe and North America rather than to the histories of other colonised societies for inspiration. As many of its more vigorous practitioners will admit, English history has also tended to be isolationist, stressing the 'peculiarities' of native economic and political development. Its historians have often seemed quite incurious about their Scottish and Irish neighbours, let alone the wider English world of settlement and empire overseas.

Historians of former colonial territories and historians of England have, however, concurred in their jaundiced view of British imperial history, seeing it as a hangover of the days of the Raj. Yet imperial history, broadened beyond the study of the institutions and the intentions of empire-builders to a study of the history of the colonised, could now play a critical rôle in reversing the fragmentation which has overcome the profession, and in mediating between English history and the history of other societies. This book should be regarded as a sketch of some of the themes that might be profitably investigated in bringing together and comparing these different historical traditions for the critical period of international war and overseas conquest which occurred broadly betweeen 1780 and 1830.

As always, I have benefited from discussions with my colleagues whose work is primarily on India itself. Here David Washbrook, Burton Stein, Susan Bayly and Anthony Low have made important suggestions. The two former are working in parallel on many of the issues raised in the first sections of the book; the two latter have carefully read and improved the text. Among historians of England, I have a great debt to Linda Colley and David Cannadine whose work aroused an interest in British history which has been dormant since undergraduate days but who also helped correct errors which no undergraduate should make (those that remain are not their fault). Metin Kunt courteously guided my intemperate foray into Ottoman history, while John Iliffe managed to dissent in a most constructive way from the whole project. David Reynolds and Javed Majeed also read the manuscript carefully and sympathetically. What little I know about Indonesia and 'greater India' derives from a long and convivial association with colleagues at the Kern Institute and the Centre for the Study of European Expansion at Leiden University. I profited from discussions with Jan Heesterman, André Wink, Leonard Blussé, Pieter Emmer, Dirk Kolff and Henk Wesseling. Parts of these chapters were read at the Royal Society for Asian Affairs and also at the Centre d'études de l'Inde et de l'Asie du Sud in Paris. I am very grateful to the Centre and to its Director, Dr Eric Meyer, for a stimulating visit in 1986. Finally, the Managers of the Smuts Memorial Fund and the Master and Fellows of St John's and St Catharine's colleges have contributed vital support for the author during the period when this book was being written.

C. A. Bayly
St Catharine's College
Cambridge. June 1988

Introduction

Imperial history grew out of the history of English national institutions. It was patriotism teaching by example. In the 1920s and 1930s, when colonial nationalism and economic decay at home began to erode conventional patriotism, imperial history found its most detailed expression in the multi-volume *Cambridge History of the British Empire*. The unwritten purpose of the series was to demonstrate how the English values of 'justice', 'benevolence' and 'humanity' were transformed into a universal ethos of free nations through the operation of the rule of the law and democratic government. Imperial history of this sort would not have survived the fall of the British empire and the decline of English patriotism had it not been given new life by the overlap of its subject matter with two pressing concerns of the post-war world. First, imperial history still provided a matrix within which the national histories of newly independent nations could be constructed – though in the process the rubric changed from British justice to nationalist struggle. Secondly, the growing economic disparities between the West and the 'Third World' pushed back into the centre of the stage the debate on economic imperialism which had excited liberals and Marxists at the turn of the present century.

The hybrid origins of the new, post-war imperial history are reflected in its subject matter and the moments which it emphasises. The story of the growth of free nations and the ascent of 'justice' still informs the massive studies of the peopling and liberation of North America and Australia from the sixteenth to the nineteenth centuries. The controversy over the Partition of Africa in the later nineteenth century is still haunted by the spectre of economic imperialism and underdevelopment in the Third World. The

1

study of nationalist movements and the end of empire since 1945 flourished because the ethnic and regional conflicts of the modern world can often be traced to the policies of the later colonial state.

Yet one critical moment in the emergence of the British empire and the origin of contemporary international order, the massive expansion of British dominion, of techniques of governance and exploitation between 1780 and 1830, has remained on the sidelines in these debates. The 'Old Colonial System' and American Independence have received close attention. General imperial histories build up steam again after 1830 as historians of the White Dominions search for the beginning of 'responsible government' and historians of Great Britain are alert to the extension of domestic reform and free trade into the outer world (Ward 1976). The intervening period remains curiously lacking in definition. This work seeks to reassess the importance of the period which Vincent Harlow saw as the dawn of the 'Second British Empire', though it uses the term in a rather different way from him (Harlow 1963). It also analyses from an imperial perspective some of the major changes both in British society and in the overseas world which occurred during and after the French and Napoleonic wars. First, however, we must sketch the progress of British expansion during these years and account for its neglect in the historical literature.

With the exception of the rise of Prussia to European dominance in the mid-nineteenth century and of the United States to world dominance since 1942, there is no more dramatic example of national resurgence than that of Great Britain between 1780 and 1830. To be sure, the Glorious Revolution and the creation of a flexible financial structure in the early eighteenth century had raised the national importance of Britain relative to France. However, the 1770s and 1780s were a British recessional. The American empire was lost; the infant empire in Asia racked by warfare and mismanagement. In the eastern Mediterranean, French trade greatly outstripped English trade which had been dominant at the end of the previous century (McGowan, 1981: 18). The profitability of the lucrative Caribbean islands was declining relative to the French West Indies (Ragatz 1928). Even the dependence of Ireland, the oldest colony, was in doubt. Whatever the underlying strength of the commercial economy, many Britons felt that their great days were over. In 1783, the First British Empire of American settlement and oriental trade seemed to have foundered into ruin. Worse, it seemed to attract resources and energy away from the more pressing problems of domestic development. Fresh military and diplomatic disasters dogged the years of war against revolutionary France.

By 1815 the nation could celebrate an astonishing, indeed providential, recovery of fortunes. Great Britain had finally managed to engineer a coalition of European states to oppose French power within Europe. Though her continental land power remained weak, her growing economic clout could be deployed to aid her allies with loans and armaments (Kennedy 1988: 115–58). She had sent an army to open a second front against Napoleon in Iberia. Meanwhile, British naval strength had allowed her to destroy and annex the greater part of her enemies' colonial empires. In the year of Waterloo, Patrick Colquhoun attempted to itemise the feeling of national resurgence in his influential *Treatise on the Wealth, Power and Resources of the British Empire*. His figures are often suspect but they can be corrected with modern ones to give a truer picture. In 1750 the population of British dominions including the American colonies had been, he says, at 12.5 million at most; in 1815 it was 61 million (p. 7). Both figures would need to be revised upwards. In fact, it is difficult to estimate the total population of British territories at much less than 200 million in 1820. Certainly, it must have represented about 26 per cent of the total world population by the latter date. This aggregation of dependent populations was important to contemporary Britons. Malthusian fear of numbers had not yet taken root; the British still retained an eighteenth-century concern that their population was too small to accomplish great things both at home and abroad.

More exact are figures for the total military and naval strength of the empire in 1815 which Colquhoun estimated at 1,062,020 including militias (p. 7). Of this about 179,000 were naval personnel and marines and about 160,000 were made up by the East Indian forces which had expanded fast between 1798 and 1815. This new figure represented more than a trebling of Britain's armies and navy since 1793. It put the British forces for the first time on a par with the orders of magnitude of the continental armies, navies and militias of Austria (*c.* 600,000) Russia (*c.* 1.5 million) and France (*c.* 1 million in 1811: about 200,000 after the Peace of 1815).

More significant yet was the distribution of these forces. Long dominant in the northern waters, the Royal Navy had now replaced French, Spanish and Venetian paramountcies in the western Mediterranean and was soon to destroy Ottoman supremacy, and engross the import–export trade of the eastern Mediterranean. Dutch and French shipping, once powerful in the Persian Gulf, Indian Ocean and Red Sea, had lost its teeth, and Britain ranged over the newly explored Pacific Ocean. The significance of naval dominance was increased by the new prestige of British land forces. Although the weakness of British land forces has perhaps been overplayed, their achievements during the eighteenth century were modest. At times it seemed an ignominious little army, capable only of chasing Irish peasants and seizing French sugar islands (*pace* Marlborough's shade). By 1815 the army had invaded France over the Pyrenees. It had also staked out Britain's rôle as a great Eurasian land power by using the new Indian army to intervene in Egypt in 1801 and underwriting the independence of Iran in 1809. The balance of power in Europe was now to be enforced in both East and West (Ingram 1984). Through the Indian empire, Britain could now challenge Russia on land as her naval predominance in the Mediterranean could by sea.

Even more to the taste of contemporary commentators was the celebration of Britain's economic power. The idiom was not yet generally one of free trade and new markets. The mentality was still bullionist and mercantilist. Britain had acquired enormous 'treasures' during the wars, represented by the lands and fixed capitals of the territories she had captured from her European and Asiatic enemies. Colquhoun estimated the total public and private property of the British Crown at £4,081,350,895 (Colquhoun 1815: 52), reckoning that a quarter of this value had been captured during the previous wars. The value of the territory conquered by the East India Company amounted now to about £1,000 million, while recent Asian, African and Caribbean conquests had added £150 million (ibid.: 52). These figures are unreal because no free land market existed in most Asian territories or the Cape Colony. Still, they do give us some indication of the working of the contemporary political arithmetic. In aggregate wealth, Britain now thought of itself as greatly superior to France and Russia and comparable to China, whose prosperity was regarded with exaggerated awe.

Recent and more sober assessments also confirm Great Britain's rapidly growing wealth and share of world trade. In 1825 the total Gross National Product (GNP) of the British empire may have been 2.5 times that of the French empire and double that of the Russian. However, Britain's empire was an important weight to be thrown in the balance because the aggregate GNP of metropolitan France and Russia remained about the same as Great Britain's until her great surge of industrialisation began about 1840. India provided substantial contributions to the Exchequer, besides providing a 'free' standing army. Other colonies made comparable contributions to the salaries of officials and soldiers while producing relatively cheap colonial raw materials. Even if British world trade did not massively increase in real terms between 1790 and 1830, as some contemporaries thought (Platt 1973), Britain was already the greatest international trader, accounting for about one-third of world trade by the 1830s; and the cotton textile export sector was beginning to take off. If not yet the workshop of the world, Britain was already its general trader. Though the resources used to protect the empire might actually have been used more productively within the domestic economy, few seriously advocated an imperial retreat in the second decade of the nineteenth century.

Like their later Victorian grandsons, the expansive spirit of the men of the Regency was even greater than the expansion of their trade. In the first half of the eighteenth century, Great Britain's relationship with its dependencies had largely been mediated through groups of complaisant mercantile élites and creoles (English settlers born in the colonies). This was true in Ireland, the Caribbean and the Americas; even the East India Company councils in the major stations resembled loosely controlled corporations. The wreck of North American empire had almost been accompanied by the dissolution of empire in the Caribbean and the east. A brief attempt to centralise colonial power after the Seven Years War (1756–63) had stirred to revolt powerful commercial and landed interests fortified with the rhetoric of old English 'country party' revulsion against the arbitrary power and corruption of the Court. Rich West Indian planters had declared their intention of joining the American rebels. In Ireland, the Protestant Ascendancy had declared itself on the point of dissolving the British connection during the volunteering movements of 1779–84. Only the fear of the French or of Catholic or slave revolt had tipped the balance back towards acquiescence in the meddling of a distant and mistrusted government. Even in the subcontinent, servants of the East India Company, scrambling after private fortunes, had humiliated their employers. They had drawn an unwilling Court of Directors into wars of expansion against Indian princes and fought off control from London in the name of the rights of 'freeborn' Englishmen.

The experience of the revolt of Irish peasants, slaves and non-white populations during the climacteric of the revolutionary wars wreaked great changes. In most parts of the empire the power of the colonial executive had been enhanced. Governors fortified with joint military and civil command had been raised above

5

their quarrelsome councils. The direct involvement of colonial servants in trade had been terminated and social markers had been established which subordinated expatriate commercial interests to Crown authority. A new ethos of imperial service had been created and institutions such as Haileybury College and Fort William College in Calcutta or the Anglican Universities of Canada had been established to inculcate its values. Within the 'British Empire in Europe', as contemporaries called it, the bounds had been drawn tighter. The Irish Protestant Ascendancy had been assimilated through the Act of Union of 1801 which gave Irish constituencies representation in Westminster. At the same time, the coercive forces of the Crown had been greatly increased to combat perpetual rural and Catholic dissidence. Scotland had been drawn closer to the springs of power in London as the association of Henry Dundas, Scotland's leading politician, with William Pitt had brought able lawyers and other clients from Edinburgh and the country towns flooding into politics, domestic and overseas services. The hard men of the peripheries had rushed in to the support of the centre.

The form of the colonial presence had altered as significantly. This was the period when the colonial state began seriously to discipline and control marginal groups and to create wider spheres for the exercise of state power. The separation of 'law' from 'economy' and 'government' allowed a wider range to all three. Groups of 'natives' who were thought to militate against the proper organisation of civil society were pushed to the margins. In a great mass of ordinance and legislation from the Permanent Settlement of the land revenues of Bengal, through Raffles's land rent system in Java, to the abolition of state control of land on the Cape of Good Hope and the growth of the land market in Ireland and the Highlands of Scotland, colonial authorities sought to favour fee simple, and direct alienable property tenures against more complex, shifting or communal forms of tenure. The rise of 'freedom of contract' in English law was accompanied by a virtual revolution in the concept of property in south Asia and southern Africa. Even if practice did not always follow precept because of the political dangers involved, the impact of the change in theories of property was more significant and deeper felt than the early harbingers of the industrial revolution itself. These theories did not so much westernise non-western élites as privilege indigenous magnates who had already achieved prominence in their own societies.

Social forms which could not easily be bent to the new system were repressed. Free armed traders operating out of small ports – the pattern of trade for hundreds of years – became 'pirates' and were hunted out from the Mediterranean to the Java seas. 'Free' cavalry soldiers who had been a feature of politics and warfare throughout Eurasia since before the Mongol invasions were 'ferocious banditti' to be eliminated or settled to agriculture. Nomads, slash-and-burn agriculturalists, even peasant farmers who migrated seasonally with animals and grain, were domesticated and settled wherever possible. Settlement and discipline were seen as preconditions for the expansion of civil society, the growth of civilisation, the expansion of true religion. The victory of private property and production for the market was much earlier and much more complete than ever the victory of free trade or responsible government.

The spirit which animated British relations with subject races had changed quite sharply. Whatever the promptings of Enlightenment philosophy, the English had always considered Asians and Africans inferior whether because of climate, despotic government or ignorance of Christian virtue. But these attitudes had rarely been codified or rigid and they had had only limited effect on the political hierarchies of colonial territories which perforce had included indigenous rulers and merchants. Between 1780 and 1820, however, Asians, Eurasians, Africans and even non-British and non-Protestant Europeans were widely excluded from positions of authority in government, while steps were taken to decontaminate the springs of British executive power from the influence of 'native corruption'. Ironically, the growing and orchestrated contempt for Asian, African and even European subordinates was derived in part from the very same humanitarian drives which saw the abolition of the slave trade and the beginnings of the moves for the emancipation of slaves. It was morally necessary to bring slaves back from social death into civil society. But if so, the hierarchy of civil society must be closely defined both through institutions and by an ideology which derived from the idea that cultures attained 'civilisation' by stages of moral awakening and material endeavour. The 'discovery' of the urban poor and the criminal classes in Britain were part of a very similar project and undertaken by the same civil and religious agencies.

The historical literature on this great expansion is good in detail but lacks overall cohesion. Standard textbooks on imperial history end with the death of the old colonial system in 1783 and begin again in 1815, thus relegating overseas developments in the intervening period to the category of war-time aberration. Many others choose to begin their treatment of the Victorian empire in 1830, the start of the decade which is thought to be characterised by liberal reform and the ascent of the 'imperialism of free trade'. One of the few attempts to analyse the period as a whole, and that almost exclusively from a constitutional and administrative point of view, was that of Vincent Harlow on 'The new imperial system, 1783–1815' in *The Cambridge History of the British Empire*, vol. ii (ed. J. Holland Rose *et al.*). But there is a curious paradox here. Writing at the onset of the Second World War, Harlow announced that his period saw, in the classic vision of liberal imperialism, the steady growth of 'order and justice' within the colonial system (p. 129), and implied that it led on directly to the period of Lord Durham's reforms of the government of Canada which ensured 'colonial freedom without disruption'. From his later work, *The Founding of the Second British Empire*, vol. ii, and the conclusion of his editor, A. F. Madden, it appears that he believed that the reform of the government of India in 1784 and the brief legislative independence of Ireland from 1782 to 1800 were examples of the growth of a sense of colonial 'responsibility' which reached fulfilment in the 1840s and 1850s. Yet the substance of Harlow's chapter demonstrates something quite different. This is a systematic attempt to centralise power within colonial territories, to exalt the executive above local liberties and to remove non-Europeans and non-British from positions of all but marginal political authority. This, indeed, was a system of 'authoritative rule' (Harlow could not bring himself to say 'authoritarian') which built on and enhanced the coercive methods of the old European despotisms and monopolies – Dutch, French, Spanish, Venetian, the Knights of Malta – as much as it assimilated the rigorous methods of non-European rulers such as Tipu Sultan of Mysore. Its relegation to the status of an unfortunate by-product of world war runs thin when we see these despotic or hierarchical systems not only extended but perpetuated even in European societies such as Malta, Canada and the Ionian Isles at least to the 1830s and sometimes to mid-century (Manning 1933).

This study argues that the British empire from 1780 to 1830 (and in some areas beyond) represented not simply a hiatus between the irresistible waves of liberal reform, but a series of attempts to establish overseas despotisms which mirrored in many ways the politics of neo-absolutism and the Holy Alliance of contemporary Europe. These colonial despotisms were characterised by a form of aristocratic military government supporting a viceregal autocracy, by a well-developed imperial style which emphasised hierarchy and racial subordination, and by the patronage of indigenous landed élites. Of course, constitution-making for the dependencies remained evolutionary and pragmatic; it rarely aspired to uniformity (Madden 1987: xxxiv–v). However, in the British tradition at least, the formal statements of constitutions or colonial minutes are a poor guide to real social and political change; there are distinct limitations to history based on what men tell their lawyers they are doing. If we consider the ideas which informed political arrangements, the style and direction of policies and the social context in which they operated, the argument for continuity seems inappropriate. The era between American Independence and the Great Reform Bill does indeed warrant its description as a 'Second British Empire'. Similarly, the decline of this new style of imperialism after 1830 had as much to do with indigenous resistance and international economic crisis as with the triumph of liberalism at home.

A similar crux in the historiography arises when one looks at the prevailing views of the economics of empire. Once again the starting point must be the massive scholarship of Harlow. In the *Founding of the Second British Empire,* he wrote of 'neo-mercantilism' during this era. Yet the tenor of his work seems to demonstrate that the 'swing to the east' of British imperial policy after the disappointments of the American Revolution was powered by an underswell of free-trade expansion which took British explorers and merchants into south Asia, the Far East and the Pacific. A link was thus drawn in the minds of later writers between the attempts by Shelburne and Pitt to discipline the East India Company and initiate free trade with the Americans in the 1780s, and the great assaults on monopoly – the Corn Laws and the East India Company – in the 1830s. This in turn meant that historians began to move Robinson and Gallagher's arguments on the 'imperialism of free trade' back into the late eighteenth century and advance it as a major cause of imperial expansion at that date (Nightingale 1970; Mukherjee 1982).

No-one would doubt that the rise of the rhetoric of free trade was one of the key themes of this period, or that the pressure of free trade proved an important component of imperial expansion in several areas. This can be seen in the rush to break open south American markets after 1805, in southeast Asia and in the rapid extension of the Bombay agency houses dealing in cotton and opium for China. Nevertheless, there are good reasons for doubting whether free-trade imperialism was the only, or indeed the chief, motive power behind British expansion during these years. In the major case of India, the financial and military momentum of the East India Company's army was the mainspring of expansion with free traders no more than the fly on the wheel. India's territorial revenues, not its trade, remained the chief economic prize for the British in the East. Even after 1834 the Company retained many of its features of mercantilist despotism (Stokes 1976). The Anglo-Dutch rule in Java and the British mercantilist despotism in Ceylon retained similar characteristics through to mid-century. The sale of British manufactures to India and other parts of the East was sluggish until the 1840s. Indeed, the expansion of British world trade between 1790 and 1830 can be considerably exaggerated (Platt 1973; O'Brien 1982). All this throws doubt on the argument that the leap forward of British territorial empire in Asia and Africa was primarily motivated by an irresistible expansion of the pressures of free trade.

The actual practice of colonial governments and the policies they fostered among indigenous and creole élites also cautions against the idea that this should be seen primarily as an age of dawning economic liberalism. As in several of the neo-absolutist states of Eurasia at this time, there was a conscious attempt to retain or even rebuild systems of coerced labour. Raffles had already abandoned wage labour for corvée in Java before the Dutch regained the colony in 1815. Forced labour on the cinnamon fields and other forms of servitude were maintained in Ceylon. In the vast continent of India the weight of the cash land revenue and restrictions on movement maintained in practice a system of debt bondage among the peasantry.

Above all, the institution of slavery persisted and was reconstructed after the abolition of the English slave trade in 1806. Wilberforce and Zachary Macaulay complained in 1827 that they had had hardly any success for twenty years. This sits uneasily with a historiographical perspective which sees the whole period from 1790 to 1838 as 'waiting for emancipation'. Better provision for slave populations, the intervention by colonial state to discipline but also to support slave owners and the rapid growth of new forms of servitude alongside the slave system in southern Africa and the Caribbean throws a different light on the era. Evidently, the push for the creation of landed aristocracies and land markets in areas of communal holding where land markets were poorly developed did not imply the systematic expansion of free labour.

The refurbishment of labour service during this period brings the experience of the British empire much closer to that of the southern states of America or the Russian empire. Even if we are to argue that the prevailing rhetoric of the time pointed to emancipation, it must be accepted that the very powerful arguments for caution, and for the social and religious merit of slavery – purged by 'benevolence' – must also be heard. That testimony has often gone unnoticed (Blackburn 1988).

One purpose of this book is to reconsider the Second British Empire. It attempts to view it in its own right rather than as a plateau on the ascent to liberalism. In the process it tries to put imperial history, British history and Indian history back into the same field of debate. Some historians have recently argued that Great Britain remained an *ancien régime* until as late as 1832. The ancient dignities of Crown, Church and aristocracy had been barely touched by social or economic change (Clark 1985). Even if the more extreme claims of this new Tory history of England are rejected, it must be clear that in the literature of the last two generations the rise of the 'middle classes' has been too easily tied to the Age of Reform in the 1830s and that it has been too simple to relegate the political systems of Pitt (after 1793) and that of Liverpool (prime minister 1812–27) to the status of 'wartime' or 'post-war reaction'. This fifty-year period can be viewed as a unity. It saw the emergence of a constructive conservatism which mirrored the constructive imperialism of the wider British empire. It saw an expansion of government power which predated, but was greatly enhanced by the experience of the French and Napoleonic Wars. These years transformed the concept of British nationalism, focusing it on the symbol of the once-despised monarchy and fortifying it with lower rank of military heroes such as Nelson and Wellington (Colley 1984). But because state-sponsored nationalism was always a tricky card for home administrations, imperial sentiment and, especially the notion of Britain as a Christian 'Roman Empire' became an important element of that nationalism (Colley 1986; *cf*. Koebner 1961).

The social order which maintained this surprisingly successful oligarchy of land and commerce was not quite an *ancien régime*. The Church was too decentralised and lay-controlled; the monarchy too recently reinvented; state power too dependent on the support of the gentry and merchant. Its form differed from the old continental monarchies, particularly as there was no exclusive aristocratic caste. Although the norms and organisation of the new British empire had much in common with Napoleon's meritocratic state of professional

11

lawyers and minor gentry, a clearer distinction was maintained in England between military and civil power. Nor, again, is it good enough to describe British society as one racked by a fierce struggle between a declining landed order and a rising middle class. It is better to see reflected in its policies and attitudes a remarkable consensus in national aims between a revived and prosperous landed class with an emboldened professional and business class. All these élites had the common aim of domestic, and especially agricultural, 'improvement' and national aggrandisement overseas. The norms of 'gentlemanly capitalism' prevailed (Hopkins and Cain 1986). But the continuity of this interest was ruptured as it was reconstructed through military domination and tinctured by a new national self-consciousness and visionary anglicanism.

The imperial dimension of the British state was equally important in Ireland where between 1780 and 1830 an attempt was made to modernise and purge the Protestant Ascendancy and assimilate the Catholic gentry to a Greater Britain. But historical writing has been straitjacketed by the 'English' and 'nationalist' views of Irish history. English historiography tends to see Ireland as a 'problem' to be solved by constitutional arrangements such as the Act of Union of 1801. The extent to which Ireland was the colonial society where the mechanics and ideology of imperial rule were first implemented, has often been glossed over. At the same time, nationalist historical writing unduly neglects the critical rôle of the Irish within British imperial expansion and equates nationalism with anti-imperialism. This is an anachronism. Irish patriots were desperate to reap the benefits of imperial expansion while Irish soldiers and savants were in the front line of empire-building. In short, Irish nationalism arose from Ireland's perceived exclusion from empire, not her inclusion within it.

Scottish historians have sometimes fallen prey to a whiggish nationalism also. Celtic revival in Scotland during the late eighteenth and early nineteenth centuries was as much imperialist as nationalist. In both Scotland and Ireland, pragmatic concerns, employment and salaries accelerated the drift of peasants and gentry into British and overseas service. The historiographical problem has once again been that of teleology: the attempt to draw a straight line between the later Scottish Enlightenment, the Scottish picturesque of Burns and Scott, and later nationalism. So in Ireland the disturbances of the 1790s, the land wars of the 1820s and the rise of Catholic nationalism and Irish separatism have been teased into an unambiguous sequence by the demands of creating a national history. With the exception of Bruce Lenman, modern historians of both countries have downplayed their rôle in the military and political service of the British empire.

For all this, the greatest weakness of much historical writing on the first phase of what Harlow called the 'Second British Empire' is the problem of placing British expansion in the wider context of world history. It is difficult to comprehend the indigenous processes which made empire possible and to explain the timing of its creation. In a period when it is evident that European empire was still relatively vulnerable, the British were dependent on the support of indigenous capital, clerical expertise and military personnel. What were the conditions which allowed them to tap this reserve of power? Why were some regimes, such as the constituent parts of the Ottoman empire, able to regroup and hold off western power for several generations more, while others succumbed and lost their independence? This lack of broad historical context is nowhere near as glaring for later periods of the history of British expansion. The Partition of Africa has long been seen as the outcome of 'local crisis'. In fact, the Africanisation of the Partition is now so complete that Europeans seem almost to have disappeared from the scene. In studies of the history of decolonisation, the mental histories of Third World peasantries and the strategies of their business classes and intelligentsia have received growing attention at the expense of the policies of colonial governors.

For eighteenth-century Asia and the Islamic world, the problem is now critical. Many recent studies have noted the continued strength of the economies and the sophistication of the political systems of the great Asian and Muslim empires even into the eighteenth century (Naff and Owen 1977; Wink 1986). The stereotype of the decaying and stagnant Orient has been challenged. Asia was the world's greatest textile producer. It may have accounted for 70 per cent of world industrial production and more than 60 per cent of its population. Its living standards were lower but of the same order as much of Europe in 1700; there were signs of technological development, even in agriculture. Islamic society was by no means as incapable of generating or receiving new ideas as was once thought. Yet in the course of the eighteenth century, severe political conflict developed across the whole region from the Balkans and north Africa to China. Even if European penetration and the evolution of the world economy created new stresses for Islamic and Asian societies, the conflicts which accompanied the dissolution of the great empires of the Ottomans, the Safavids of Iran and Mughals in the course of the eighteenth century were internally generated. What, then, was the nature of this change and how did it relate to the rise of European power? What, if any, was the connection between this crisis of the old regimes of Eurasia and the near-contemporary crisis of European empires in the New World which pointed forward to the European 'Age of Revolutions'? A short book such as this can only begin to answer these questions. Yet it intends to approach them as much from the Asian and Islamic perspective as from the European. By juxtaposing issues from traditions of historical writing which are generally treated separately, it will be possible at least to grasp their dimensions and importance.

Historians have recently moved away from broad generalisations and comparative studies. Some even doubt whether they are possible or useful. The vogue is for the unique experience, the moment which reveals the inwardness of a culture. What now receives emphasis is 'difference' and complexity, or decentralised and arcane circuits of power. The larger constructs of the 1960s have been abandoned, much as the global development effort which formed their practical context foundered in disillusionment. Only in the severely materialist fields concerned with world trade, disease or technology do these empires of comparison survive. What justification then is there for an essay that puts together Scotland, the Caribbean, Java and Qajar Iran?

This question can be answered both at an empirical and at a methodological level. First, this was an era when British and, to a lesser extent, French military and naval supremacy outside Europe began to impose uniform patterns of rule and uniform notions of 'law' and 'progress' on these societies distant from each other. If colonial power became less 'mystical', it also projected itself further and tried to absorb many of those domains of decentralised power and authority which had lain in villages, priesthoods or systems of gifting before the rise of Europe. This was what the contemporary British meant by the extension of the 'rule of law'. Out of the collision and accommodation between widely differing societies and these impulses to uniformity was generated much of the structure of the modern world.

Secondly, even before the final European onslaught in the period 1780 to 1830, large areas of the world were already bound into inter-regional unities not only by trade and forms of government, but by ideas, legends and beliefs. There is an important 'analytical space' between, on the one hand, very general analyses of the growing

Capitalist World System (Wallerstein 1980) and, on the other, the history of specific cultures or communities. It is an anachronism, to think of Indonesia, India, the Caribbean, let alone 'Europe' or 'Asia', as separate or separable entities. In the eighteenth century the Caribbean remained part of the wider European north Atlantic system. North India looked towards central Asia and Iran; south India towards Ceylon and Indonesia. The cultural links within these broader human communities and the interconnections of trade, learning and clerical personnel have given their histories common themes and a similar shape. Comparison helps to recover these links and common experiences which have been sundered by the later policies of empire and movement of world trade. It is a valuable heuristic tool which works constantly against the notion that there was an 'essential' India or Egypt, Jamaica or Scotland, and helps indicate how these very territorial and cultural entities were created in historical time.

The book begins, then, with an analysis of Islamic Asia before the European conquests. The analysis attempts to break away from the tradition of imperial history which works from the 'metropolis' to the 'periphery'. It was not clear in the conditions of the early eighteenth century what was the metropolis and what the periphery; it is uncertain whether the dominant influences on the nature of the British eighteenth-century empire were forces generated by the British domestic economy or by the rapid growth of ideologies and forces of production in the colonies. Yet this is not an attempt to revive a 'peripheral' as opposed to a 'eurocentric' view of British imperial expansion (Robinson 1972). Any such attempts are foredoomed to failure. The aim is to demonstrate that Britain's new empire of the period 1780 to 1830 can only be understood by taking into account both social change in Great Britain and also developments in the colonies or in the quasi-independent states that surrounded them. Again, because empire was a matter of attitudes, legends, theories and institutions, this book does not privilege economic interests in British expansion as the determining forces. Concepts of race, aristocracy, religion and patriotism emerge as of first-rate importance. Above all, empire must be seen not only as a critical phase in the history of the Americas, Asia or Africa but in the very creation of British nationalism itself.

CHAPTER ONE
Political and Social Change in the Muslim Empires, 1600–1800

During the sixteenth and seventeenth centuries, large political units flourished in Asia as they did in Europe. The Ottoman, Safavid and Mughal dynasties dominated, even if they did not control, the population and wealth of a huge territory between Algeria and the borders of Burma. In Java (considered below, pp. 67–9) the Muslim empire of Mataram emerged during the same period. As in Europe, the society of the great realms became more complex and conflict-ridden during the seventeenth century. However, their 'general crisis' reached its greatest intensity not in the seventeenth century like Europe's, but in the eighteenth century when all three empires (and Mataram) faltered or disintegrated. The demise of the Muslim land empires was a critical condition for the rise of European dominance across inland Eurasia and north Africa; it complemented the maritime ascendancy already established by France, Great Britain and the Dutch in the Mediterranean Sea and Indian Ocean. Western expansion was, of course, driven by a ruthless search for profit and was supported by a growing political and technological sophistication. But uneven economic growth and political instability within the Muslim empires and the seaboard fringes of Asia also created pressures and opportunities which encouraged European nations and trading companies to seize political power in key regions before 1800.

The beginnings of European territorial empire was most sharply demonstrated in the eastern province of the Mughal empire (Bengal) and also in its barely-consolidated southern fringes (the Deccan and Arcot) where the British were dominant by 1765. Europeans also made great inroads in Java where the Dutch East India Company had achieved supremacy by 1752; and in Egypt, an Ottoman province, which was invaded successively by

French and British forces at the very end of the century. Another former Ottoman province, Algeria, was seized by the French in 1830. Yet the Muslim empires had been hollowed out from within by complex social and economic change well before they were knocked flat by external aggression. European conquistadors, indeed, commandeered the military, administrative and financial services of the earlier states during their rise to power. For this reason, social change in Asia and the Islamic world was a critical force in the creation of European world-wide dominance of the nineteenth century and not simply its immobile background. This chapter considers the nature of that social change; chapters 3 and 4 go on to analyse the complementary process, the growth of new ideas and compulsions to expansion within the 'British Empire in Europe' and the Western Hemisphere.

STAGES OF CHANGE IN MUSLIM ASIA AND NORTH AFRICA

Over recent years, historians have begun to suggest that there were similar patterns of evolution in the political economy of these great and diverse oriental realms. Three broad eras of change seem to emerge. First, the long period of relative prosperity associated with the reigns of the great sultans and padishahs (emperors) in the sixteenth century (and in some areas on into the seventeenth century) encouraged specialisation in agriculture, the development of a rooted landed class and a flourishing commercial culture. However, these trends also encouraged the pretentions of provincial magnates and made it more difficult for the central military élites and bureaucrats to control increasingly complex and sophisticated societies.

During the second stage of change, after the mid-seventeenth century, all these regimes were faced with an escalation of internal contradictions and conflicts which arose from the uneven pace of growth between regions or from the varying economic fortunes of different groups of subjects. The emperors and their lieutenants could no longer compromise disputes over taxation, labour and status between overmighty magnates and peasants. At the same time, the expansion of the money economy and a widening of horizons also stirred the restive tribal groups on the fringes of the empires to mutiny. These tribes varied greatly among themselves, but they were all egalitarian warrior societies and they tended to seek wealth and fame either by serving or plundering the adjoining great kingdoms. Their restiveness culminated in what might be called 'tribal breakouts' in the course of the eighteenth century, a series of events which spelled the end of the 'Pax Islamica' but also put pressure on Western interests throughout Eurasia.

The third stage in this broad process of change during the eighteenth century saw regional magnates inheriting the mantle of the great emperors and constructing more compact and exclusive domains throughout the whole region from the Balkans to southeast Asia. These rulers tried to impose more severe trade 'monopolies' and regain the economic balance of power which had tipped towards peasant and landowner. This brought them into conflict with each other, damaging trade and agricultural production in some areas, but intensifying economic activity in others. It often also ranged the rulers of the regional regimes against European commercial interests which had built up protected domains on the fringes of the land empires during the heyday of Asian commercial growth. The resulting conflicts were resolved in several areas by direct European occupation.

The first stage of European expansion in Asia had coincided with the period of commercial activity following the establishment of the great land empires in the fifteenth century and the flowering of Indian Ocean trade and Chinese trade. It had facilitated this expansion through the release of silver from the New World into the Asian trading and political system (Richards 1981). In its second phase from the early seventeenth century, however, the European impact tended to become more restrictive and damaging as the Dutch and English fought to monopolise and channel trade, first in Indonesia (Villiers 1981; Reid 1975), later in India (Subrahmanyam 1987). This second, restrictive stage coincided with the wars of succession and monopoly within the Muslim empires and aggravated them. Asia was vulnerable to the European onslaught, therefore, not so much because it was impotent, decadent or stagnant, but because it was passing through a crisis in the relationship between commerce, landed wealth and patrimonial political authority comparable with that which convulsed Europe in the first half of the seventeenth century. The eighteenth-century English work which described Mir Wais Khan, a contemporary Afghan dynast, as the 'Persian Cromwell' was, perhaps, not entirely fanciful. The nature of this general crisis in Asia will now be examined in greater detail.

THE MUSLIM EMPIRES: INTEGRATION AND UNIFORMITIES

Seventeenth-century European observers tended to speak of the three great Muslim regimes in the same terms. They were absolute and terrifying Moorish despotisms in which private property and the merchant classes were crushed out under the weight of the military machine and the luxury of the court. Yet contemporaries were aware of the great contrasts between them, and modern scholarship has also emphasised the differences between their culture and government (Hodgson 1974). In the following account it will be necessary to keep in mind both the similarities and the differences. The similarities in economic and social structure across this vast area explain why a general crisis affected all three empires during the eighteenth century. But the differences help explain why the Ottomans had regrouped and survived, the Safavids had been replaced by a regional Persian kingdom (the Qajars), while the Mughals had become pensioners of the British by the early nineteenth century.

The success of the first great sixteenth-century emperors, whose courts in Delhi, Isfahan and Istanbul had dazzled their European contemporaries, rested on three great pillars. First, they were able through diplomacy, but in the last resort by deploying powerful cavalry armies, to dominate internal magnates, and to protect their territories from lethal coalitions of armed tribesmen on their fringes. The great tribal conquest-states like those of Genghis Khan or Tamburlaine were relegated to the realms of legend (until Nadir Shah of Persia tried to reconstruct one at the beginning of the eighteenth century). Secondly, the emperors were able to offer provincial élites and some outer 'barbarians' attractive rewards of service and a share in the brilliant cosmopolitan cultures of the great cities. Finally, the emperors protected and encouraged merchant families and scribal communities from the non-Muslim élites – Armenians, Greeks, Jews, Hindus. They were able to lay the basis for an international land- and sea-borne commercial culture. It was the slow erosion of these three pillars which was to bring down the house of the Muslim empires.

The similarities between the empires at their height were striking. Imperial rule was patrimonial rather than despotic (Blake 1987). The great royal households acted as patrons of peasants and merchants, tying together town and country, cultivator and herdsman. Taxation was owed predominantly in silver cash and may have accounted for as much as 30 per cent of the gross produce of the land. This in turn required the integration of markets and the spread of petty commodity production. Peasants, in short, had to sell their produce on the market in order to pay their revenue. The rulers rewarded their great commanders and cavalry soldiers with grants of the revenue owed to them by the villages. These grants, called *jagirs* in India (Habib 1963) and *timars* among the Ottomans (Shaw and Shaw 1977; *cf*. Savory, 1980), were payments for military and civil office; they were not 'landholdings' in the direct sense, and careful rulers kept moving their servants from one region to the next.

Far from being absolute and rigidly centralised, imperial rule allowed very great discretion to local leaders, tribal heads and great men of merchant corporations, although these had no formal standing in Islamic law. In the Ottoman empire, such local entities (called *millets* in the case of non-Muslim minorities) included a whole spectrum of communities from the Beduin of the deserts of Syria and Arabia to the 'Romoi', the Greek citizens of Pera, the Ionian Islands and the Peloponnese. The Safavid emperors ruled by a complicated balancing act, accommodating and sometimes chastising the powerful tribal groups of the central deserts and of the Zagros mountains. The Mughals similarly gave great discretion to the Hindu kings such as the Rajput of Rajasthan in northwest India. They ruled by patronising and overawing the deeply entrenched and predominantly Hindu magnates of the localities, the *zamindars* (lit. 'landholders').

The similarities between the great empires were refreshed by the constant flow across their borders of a stream of men, ideas and trade. The Muslim intelligentsia of this world was still linked by common assumptions and beliefs. Wherever there were Muslims, knowledge of the rational sciences of the Koran, the 'Sayings of the Prophet' and the great Arab commentarists were known and understood. Arabic and Persian operated as *linguae francae* throughout the lands from Budapest to Chittagong, and Christians and Hindus also studied them. Scholars and holy men moved in search of service, to venerate the shrines of Islamic saints and to study in the great teaching institutions. Afghans, central Asian Muslims and Persians enlisted in the Mughal armies and administration. Indian learned and holy men made their pilgrimage to the Schools of Mecca, Medina and Cairo. Istanbul, still the centre of the Caliphate and claimant to the mantle of the Prophet, retained its charisma as the exemplar of cities (Robinson, F.

1979; Hodgson 1974; Holt 1968; Lambton 1953 and Lewis 1961).

The peoples of these vast regions, Muslim and non-Muslim alike, numbering over 200 million in 1700, were also tied together by celebrated trade routes and by common patterns of consumption, which ranked nobility and signified ethnicity across the whole civilisation. Persian and Arab horses supplied the armies of all the empires. The coffee of Mocha stimulated Delhi, Istanbul and Belgrade, as did the spices of southern India and the Indonesian islands. Persian silk was brought in quantities to India and Istanbul. Cloth produced in Bengal, southern India and Gujarat found its way throughout Eurasia. As in contemporary Europe, Indian garments were an important component of the dress of wealthy families of the Ottoman empire by the seventeenth century.

A network of merchant communities, Gujarati Hindus, Jews, Syrian Muslims and Christians, Armenians, worked the trade routes, using common systems of double-entry bookkeeping, credit and trust. This economic connection had been enhanced in the sixteenth and seventeenth centuries by a great increase in the sea-borne trade of the Indian Ocean, the Red Sea and the Persian Gulf. A few big interconnected entrepots had channelled an increasing volume of manufactured goods as well as raw materials from one vast region to the next (Chaudhuri 1985: 98–118). These included Venice, Cairo, Istanbul and Aleppo, Isfahan, Surat and Delhi. Differences in forms of money and trade customs should not disguise the fact that there was considerable uniformity and integration in this Eurasian economy and that the great towns and trade routes did in fact exercise a powerful effect even on apparently isolated peasant and nomad communities (Perlin 1983). Islamic law codes sheltered a world economy and an international commercial culture pioneered by Armenians, Hindus and Greeks which was as developed as that of Europe, though lagging in technical expertise. It provided, in fact, an alternative context to Europe and China for the development of forms of capitalism, if by 'capitalism' is meant the propensity for administrators, merchants and peasant leaders to acquire capital and to devise political forms for its reproduction over generations (Gran 1978).

THE MUSLIM EMPIRES: CONTRASTS AND COMPARISONS

Some important distinctions between the empires, however, help us to explain their differing fates as all three entered the era of 'so–called decline' (Owen 1981: 5) and ultimate abasement before European power. In the first place, the centralised bureaucratic machinery of the Ottoman empire was different in intricate detail and also more highly developed than that of the Safavids or Mughals. The imperial levy and training school in Istanbul (the *devshirme*) brought generation after generation of young men from the Christian lands to the north and the Arab and African lands to the south to be trained as the sultan's personal servants. The tradition of slave bureaucracy maintained tight bonds of loyalty and aspiration between the imperial house and its dependents on into the eighteenth and nineteenth centuries. In addition, a secular bureaucracy (the *kuttab*) had emerged across the empire alongside the doctors of Islamic law *(ulama)*. By the sixteenth century, these men had a profound dedication to the principles of imperial law *(kanun)* and a model of deportment formed by the style of Istanbul (Kunt 1983).

By contrast, the centralising forces within the Safavid and Mughal empires were rather weaker. The Safavid emperors relied on their charisma as embodied religious authority within the Shia Islamic faith and also on a volatile series of alliances by which they cajoled and overawed the leaders of the great tribal and nomadic coalitions whose influence stretched to the very gates of Isfahan (Garthwaite 1983). There was a Safavid bureaucracy, but it appears to have always been weaker, more dependent on the local magnates. The Mughals, again, constructed a flexible system of 'government by contract' through great nobles who acted both as imperial officers *(mansabdars)* and often also as heads of powerful, locally resident communities. Imperial officials could dispense royal and Muslim law but the great nobles of the Mughals were always less extensions of the will and culture of the emperors than those of the Ottoman Porte. Ethnic factions of Hindu Rajputs, local Muslims, and central Asian and Persian Muslims were in evidence right from the height of the empire (Athar Ali 1968; Satish Chandra 1959). Comparatively speaking, the Ottoman sultan's servants were more homogeneous in religion and culture.

To some extent, these differences derived from the historical traditions of the empires. The Ottomans took over the bureaucratic system of the Byzantine empire and grafted on to it the 'slave' caste system of central Asian Islam. The Mughals ruled a society which was 80 per cent Hindu, and where the Muslim administrative and service class was spread thinly across north India, clustering around rural towns. But economic factors also played their part. To a much greater extent than either Delhi or Isfahan, Istanbul was a 'primate city' for its whole region. In a rain-fed economy it acted as a mart for Anatolia and Turkey in Europe but also as a great sea port and emporium for the communities and skills of the whole eastern Mediterranean. Istanbul survived as a great centre of population and trade, probably never dropping below 600,000 in population even during its eighteenth-century travails (Owen 1981: 24–5). By contrast, Delhi and Isfahan were left high and dry by the political and economic 'decentralisation' of the eighteenth century, dropping perhaps to 20,000 (Perry 1979: 238) and 80,000 respectively. For the agricultural environs of Delhi and Isfahan were more vulnerable to climatic change and invasion, dependent as they were to a much greater extent on artificial irrigation than those of Istanbul. It was obviously easier to control the Ottoman population of 30 million from a city of such size than it was to control the Indian population of 150 million from a shrunken Delhi.

THE NATURE OF 'DECLINE'

The 'decline' of these great empires has been a subject of moralising by Europeans from the seventeenth century when they already saw in the East a mirror of their own discontents with luxurious and arbitrary kings. The 'licence' and debauchery of the Ottoman Selim II (1566–74; the 'Sot') or the Mughal Muhammad Shah I (1719–48; the 'colourful') was said to have undermined the military and moral superiority of the empires in a welter of nepotism and harem faction among eunuchs. There were severe Islamic scholars to echo this view. As a Persian historian of the last days of the Safavids noted: 'The subjects all at once became rich and possessed of luxuries. The glorious sultan and the pillars of the state turned aside from the canons and traditions which past sultans . . . had followed'. (Lambton in Naff and Owen 1977: 115).

Over the last few decades, however, scholars have found this stark transition inadequate to explain the complexities of historical change which deeper archival research has brought to light. What in fact was the relationship between the 'wealth of the subjects' and the decline of the ruling house? It seems vacuous to characterise whole societies over centuries as gripped by decline and stagnation. If there were already signs of military decline in the Ottoman empire virtually from the death of Sulaiman the Magnificent, how can its longevity be explained, its continuing expansion until the early eighteenth century and finally its revival at the beginning of the nineteenth? If Mughals and Ottomans were always ruled by accommodation and bargaining with powerful local interests – if, indeed, the empires 'controlled' their subjects largely through their acquiescence – why then did powerful interests in the Ottoman, Mughal and Safavid empires decide progressively to withdraw their support during the early eighteenth century?

The problems of a simplistic model of decline are most evident when we consider the wide range of historical processes which seem to be common to the whole region and which have yet to be adequately accounted for within it. What was the significance of the growth among the Ottomans of freehold landholding, large estates and forms of 'property' in marketable tax farms and shares in village produce or labour? How are long-term processes of urbanisation and commercial expansion to be related to the decentralisation of power in the regions which gathered speed in the eighteenth century in the Ottoman empire, Iran and India? What weight is to be given to the import of Western bullion and fragmentary evidence of price inflation, by comparison with internal population growth and the spread of new styles of consumption? The feeling has emerged that the 'decline' of the central political institutions of all these empires must be related to the evolution of regional economies and the formation of classes in their societies. A simple picture of loss of control and military defeat mistakes symptom for cause. By looking at these deeper internal changes, historians might hope not only to explain the nature of the 'general crisis' of eighteenth-century Eurasia, but also to provide some explanations of why its societies fared differently. The next sections discuss the growing complexity of the Islamic land empires of the seventeenth century and the emergence of new styles of commercial power and landholding. This was to result in the decline of the centre, the emergence of regional magnates, and the 'rise of the provinces' in the eighteenth century.

POPULATION, CONSUMPTION AND COMMERCIALISATION

Several historians report the existence of population growth in the sixteenth century followed by stagnation in the seventeenth and eighteenth. There is no agreement about the relationship of population growth to the growth of acreage or general economic activity, though a sharp upswing probably went with economic growth, and demographic decline with severe economic problems. The common view is that alongside Europe, the Muslim empires saw a considerable growth in population and economic activity in the sixteenth century. The picture is more patchy for the seventeenth century. This is best demonstrated for the Ottoman empire where, having already grown in the fifteenth century, the population of Asia Minor and Anatolia may have increased by as much as 100 per cent between 1600 and 1750 (Faroqhi 1985). By contrast, the population of the European Ottoman domains, battered by poor seasons and possibly by typhus, may have fallen back quite sharply during the seventeenth century from a sixteenth-century peak, to rebound again in the eighteenth century (McGowan 1981).

The picture remains very uncertain for Egypt, the Safavid empire and India, but there appears to have been a noticeable increase here too in the course of the sixteenth century, followed by local stagnation in the seventeenth. As in contemporary Europe and China, an important feature of this early growth must have been the gradual acclimatisation of population to the plagues which had devastated so much of Eurasia in the fourteenth and fifteenth centuries. Better nutrition may have proceeded from advances in irrigation (such as the more efficient 'Persian wheel') and from new varieties of seed and food crop. Relative political stability created its own conditions for population growth. The emperors protected their subjects from the invasions of disease-bearing soldiers. The desire for new sources of taxation caused them to settle nomadic and wandering populations. Settled families are more fertile than wandering ones and the settlement of once-moving populations does indeed seem to have been an important cause of the growing population of Upper Egypt, the rim of the Persian desert or central and northwestern India. Periodic plagues brought along trade routes nevertheless appear to have held back further population growth in Syria, Egypt and Mesopotamia during the seventeenth and early eighteenth centuries.

The impact of moderate population growth on the Muslim empires was complex. On the one hand, the total volume of trade grew and patterns of regional specialisation in articles of general consumption developed. Regions such as the Punjab in India or western Anatolia or the Upper Nile basin increased production to feed the growing population of newly settled areas and the cities which sprung up along the trade routes. Urbanisation was quite rapid in Rumelia and rural Anatolia, complementing late medieval growth along the Mediterranean coasts, for the Ottomans were a great Mediterranean power as well as a Muslim land empire. In Persia and north India, large communities of scribal and merchant people grew up after 1550 around cities such as Isfahan, Shiraz, Delhi, Agra and Lahore. Military men and merchants also founded smaller towns in the interior: these served more local needs. Major centres of textile production grew up in the heartlands of all the great domains, and their produce began to be exchanged between the ruling groups of the empires.

These developments should not be seen simply as a 'natural' economic growth. An important feature was the diffusion of styles of life and definitions of community. In India the court style of the Mughal emperors was generalised across the sub-continent by Indo-Muslim gentlemen in the smaller towns and by Hindu rajas and chiefs who adjusted styles of dress and consumption to ease access to Mughal courts and councils. An aristocracy of taste had developed, signified by the term *sharif* or gentleman. Throughout the three empires this urban-based life style was exported to the countryside as landowners and jurists settled wanderers (and in India, non-believers) around their market centres. The smaller places were then tied into wider patterns of thought, and commerce, by the payments of tribute and by reciprocal royal patronage of religion, learning and service. International and interregional trade in specialist items as well as basic commodities enhanced the importance of the great entrepots and their hinterlands. Egypt flourished on its rôle as a distributor of coffee and Indian goods even after the Dutch had succeeded in diverting much of the spice trade around the Cape of Good Hope. Iran grew rich on silk exports to the Ottomans, Europe and Mughal India.

If uneven population growth and the demand of the gentry enhanced monetisation, it also contributed to growing differences between the rich and poor on the land. Pressure of population in rural Asia Minor was accompanied by a sharp drop in the average size of peasant holdings during the seventeenth and eighteenth centuries. Throughout much of India and Iran, land plenty was still the norm until well into the seventeenth century. There is nonetheless evidence of increasing rural stratification. In Rajasthan, for instance, about 10 to 12 per cent of villagers formed a peasant élite which lorded it over the rest of the village by the early eighteenth century (Singh 1975; Gupta 1986). Why was this?

In part, the answer must be that even in a situation of land plenty, peasants wanted to hold on to ancestral lands and remain in their villages rather than emigrate to fringes of the arable. They also needed protection from the élites. The spread of the use of money, combined with the need for capital to put in irrigation, buy animals or for subsistence in bad seasons, tended to reduce some peasant farmers to the status of virtual bondsmen. In India, such inequalities tended to fill out the existing categories of status embodied in the caste system, while in the Ottoman empire gradations of the earlier Byzantine agrarian organisation were maintained and extended. So localised land famines and pressure from the élites contributed to the peasant flight and periodic rebellion which was a feature of all the great empires. However, this subordination of erstwhile 'free' peasantries and the settlement of marginal and nomadic people also provided the basis for the emergence of rooted landowning classes beneath the level of the old imperial troop commanders and their revenue assignments. These rooted landowning classes, battered and transformed, were to become the keystone of the European colonial economy of the nineteenth century.

ASIAN ROUTES TO COMMERCIAL AGRICULTURE

In a more complex and more stratified society, forms of landholding and means of profiting from control of land had begun to change. It is often thought that the development of alienable property in land was something which was inaugurated, indeed forced by Western imperial rule and by nineteenth-century international trade. This view fits easily with the notion of the diffusion of the modern capitalist system from East to West. Yet in all the three realms with which we are dealing, a discernible shift towards forms of individual and marketable property in land, or its profits, took place between the fifteenth and eighteenth century. In many areas this was accompanied by the growth of great private estates or of more complex local forms of commercial profit through the 'farming out' of land taxes to local notables.

In the western parts of the Ottoman empire where the inheritance of Roman law was still in evidence, this process was clearer and the result was the consolidation of forms of freehold property which are comparable with those of western Europe. Old joint and individual forms of peasant tenure were breaking down and landlords were assimilating newly purchased holdings into their private estates. State lands for the support of military personnel or other state services were also being penetrated, bought up and turned into private freehold. Both processes seem to reflect the growing wealth and power of intermediate classes of magnates and financiers in relation to both the state and to more tightly-controlled peasantries. The development of internal and foreign markets, combined wih the close connections between local magnates and Islamic judicial authorities, helped this process on its way. There was already in Islamic law the legal concept of private dominion (or *mulk*) which had some features in common with freehold property as understood in the West. As a recent study of seventeenth-century Anatolia puts it, 'freehold property was gaining in importance long before nineteenth century legislation [inspired by the west] intervened to speed up the process' (Faroqhi 1985: 266; *cf.* Islamoglu-Inan 1987). This occurred not only in areas such as Rumelia where the export of agricultural raw materials to the West was growing in importance, but 'occurred with the growth of internal commerce as well'. Thus 'it may be surmised that the process leading towards a market in privately owned land was endogenous to the Ottoman social system as it expanded during the sixteenth and seventeenth centuries' (Faroqhi 1985: 298).

Related to this was the growth of large estates and the decline of forms of property dependent on office (prebends) in the face of heritable estates (patrimonies). At first the Ottoman empire had maintained its military preparedness by parcelling out lands to its cavalry soldiers on the basis of their need for military resources. This was called the *timar* system. *Timar* holders often resided on their holdings, but the state regularly redistributed them and they were not alienable. In the course of time, however, the cohesion of the older military nobility declined. *Timar* holders retreated from their military obligations, becoming ordinary townsmen and even traders; the 'janissaries' took their place. High officials of the state began to lose their capacity to control the land market in the provinces. By the late seventeenth and early eighteenth century, therefore, large noble estates (the so-called *chiftliks*) were springing up all over the empire. Such lands were alienable and became assimilated to the *mulki* holdings of the magnates. The emergence of a rooted landed class and of a land market went hand in hand, though the relationship between these two phenomena remains complex. Just as peasant flight and peasant stratification increased the pressure on the old imperial systems from below, so also the emergence of provincial landed classes ultimately limited the capacity of Istanbul to control its provinces.

Any attempt to generalise about tenures and social change in India is bound to be extremely hazardous. Large areas of the country were controlled by local chieftains and access to land rights was determined by complex matters of caste status and hierarchies of honour. All the same, historians working in many parts of India have recently come to discern trends which run parallel in some ways to what has been seen in the Ottoman empire. First, there is clear evidence, especially in the eighteenth century, of the decline of prebendal holdings (temporary holdings for service) and the rise of patrimonial ones (more equivalent to direct ownership). The Mughals' equivalent to the *timar* system had been the *jagirdari* system. In this case, a military leader who could raise cavalry troops was supported by a temporary grant of land (or sometimes a cash salary). Such grants were at the emperor's pleasure and could be revoked and reassigned – in theory. Beneath this level, but related to it, was the rural ruling class, the *zamindars*. *Zamindars* were sometimes indigenous (largely Hindu) magnates who saw themselves as kings of men and resources, though they were simple 'landholders' in the imperial eye. Sometimes they were soldiers or other people who had established their right to the dominion of a *zamindar* by conquest or by opening up new lands. *Zamindari* rights subsisted with the rights of peasant occupancy 'beneath' and with revenue assignments to military nobles 'above'. But the balance of rural power seemed to be tilting more and more towards the *zamindars* and their kinsmen and clients among the richer peasants (Alam 1986: 110–33; Wink 1986).

By the late seventeenth century the strain of military expansion, bad seasons (and possibly also price inflation) was putting severe pressure on the imperial system of revenue assignments. At the same time, nobles and other magnates were building up holdings of local *zamindari* land. Sometimes they assimilated revenue-free grants for religion or service to their own *zamindari;* sometimes the opening up of new land increased the power of local lineages. The emperors often connived in this process in order to strengthen their own supporters against coalitions of dissident gentry and peasants drawn mainly from the Hindu population. At all events, powerful coalitions of landed and commercial wealth consolidated themselves at the expense of imperial control; in a sense the empire had been the victim of its own success in promoting agricultural and commercial growth.

Studies of agrarian Iran during the later Safavids are few and far between. But some of these social changes have parallels there also. An important feature seems to have been the build up of *waqf* or charitable lands in the hands of groups of families descended from some original holy man or teacher. As in India, such land was being converted into ordinary holdings and by settled landlords and even merchants. Regulations for the management of trust funds allowed local managers considerable leeway; 'they began as *mutuwallis*, managers of *awaqaf* [charitable land] endowed by others, continued to amass extensive private estates of their own, and emerged as the esquires of their region with paramount local socio-economic and political powers' (Savory 1980: 186). Once again the rise of these new forms of ownership coincided with, and was often made possible by, the decline of the prebendal or office-related holdings of the old military nobility. In Iran this declining interest was represented by the Turkish *qizilbash* cavalry leaders who were the Iranian equivalents of the Mughal *mansabdars*.

So far two processes have been mentioned: the growth of large 'estates' or of patrimonial local holdings and the decline of imperial military prebends. Another process which was to provide the economic basis for the rising local notables of the eighteenth century was the extension of the practice of farming out revenues to men of capital *(iltizam/ijarah)*. This system spread rapidly within all three empires from the early seventeenth century. Since it represented a derogation from ideas of direct patronal kingship, and implied a contractual relationship between an intermediary and a ruler, possibly to the detriment of the peasant, it was denounced by the religious authorities. However, the system gave rulers the chance to project ahead revenues while moving the costs of collection on to other shoulders. Revenue farming therefore grew by leaps and bounds from the Balkans to southern India (and indeed southeast Asia) as the imperial treasuries ran into trouble. Revenue farming was the application of magnate capital for profit to the agrarian system. Sometimes it may have resulted in the destructive over-exploitation of peasantry. Revenue farming was also used to bring under cultivation marginal areas which were too poor or undeveloped to give the ordinary peasant much chance of a quick return on his investment (McGowan 1981; Wink 1986; Malik 1977; Subrahmanyam 1986).

In all the three empires, commercialisation, urbanisation and the growth of rooted landed classes were the harbingers of significant political change. These processes seem to have derived from sources of growth *within* the vast empires. However, economic links with European nations certainly speeded them up, especially in regions with significant external trade (*cf.* McGowan 1981: 171–2). Most important here was import of precious metals through European sources and the growth of trade in agricultural raw materials to Europe. The vast quantities of New World silver which made their way into the Asian economies directly through European trading companies (the Levant, Muscovy and East India Companies), or indirectly through middlemen, appears to have had an effect on both state finances and the lay of the local economy. Probably, the rapid expansion of the silver cash base of the Mughal revenue system would not have been possible without these considerable imports of bullion (Richards 1981: 285–308). They made possible the transfer of large quantities of revenue from the rich peripheral provinces such as Bengal and Gujarat to the imperial centre and fostered the development of a sophisticated merchant financier class who underpinned the operations of the imperial and noble treasuries. Like the Mughals, the Safavids also had few internal sources of silver production and relied on foreign sales of agricultural exports, notably the silk crop, to supply their wants in specie.

While they helped support the financial apparatus of empire bullion, imports from European-controlled sources may also have had distorting effects on the local economies of the empires. For instance, heavy purchases by the Levant Companies of Anatolian wool and cotton appear to have helped push up prices to the point where the local weaving guilds were forced out of business, not having adequate financial resources to control their own sources of supply (Faroqhi 1985). Again, partial dependence on export inevitably put Asian producers and middlemen at the mercy of changes in prices at a world level. For instance, the gathering crisis in Mughal north India may have reflected the decline of indigo exports as production was increased in the British and French West Indian isles. Dutch coffee production in the East and West Indies damaged the Egyptian international transit trade which provided much of the wealth of Cairo and Alexandria. So too, the declining receipts reaching the Iranian court by the end of the eighteenth century reflected both the decay of the Asia–Europe land route as the Dutch expanded international seaborne commerce and, somewhat later, the rise of Bengal silk production as a rival to Iran's own.

Still, it seems unlikely that fluctuations in European demand and external economic dependency can more than partially explain the changes in the great land-based empires. Even industries like textile production in Gujarat, Bengal and Coromandel produced largely for internal and external Asian markets rather than for European. Even where price inflation can be proved, pressure on internal resources may have been more important than bullion imports. An increase in the velocity or volume of circulating cash bullion does not *cause* commercialisation, it merely facilitates an internal reallocation of resources and the development of markets. One must therefore look again at internal changes to explain the growing difficulties which the great sovereigns were having in controlling and taxing their imperial provinces even before the end of the seventeenth century. What was the relationship between the process that some historians have called 'decentralisation' and the social changes which we have been describing?

THE RISE OF THE PROVINCIAL ELITES

Firstly and most simply, the growing complexity of provincial society made it more and more difficult for the sovereigns to control the peripheries of their domains. Local nexuses of power grew up which could not as easily be broken up as the factions among the old military aristocracies. In provincial towns throughout the Islamic world, large landlords, scribal people and administrators often connected with the religious corporations, and merchant people, who were often not Muslims, developed common interests which could frustrate the attempts at control of the state. The very success of the empires had generated this locally rooted gentry and burgher class. The influence that land, money, and the power to control the writing office generated was much greater than the power of the sword. In Iran the alliance between local merchants, the new administrative aristocracy and the families of the learned was cemented by marriage alliance (Savory 1980: 185). In India and the Ottoman empire, where a much larger extent of merchant capital was in the hands of non-Muslims, this combination was expressed more in the development of large patrimonial households. Muslim revenue farmers and magnates patronised non-Muslim merchants and scribal people, so that powerful and flexible 'private offices' grew up within the structure of the state (Holt 1973: 182–3).

It was in this way that the empires began to weaken and dissolve before they faced critical external challenges. For instance, the system of checks and balances by which the Mughals moved their great officers of state around the countryside to prevent combinations of provincial power was already failing by the mid-seventeenth century. Despite the appearance of turnover in high office there appears to have been a remarkable stability in rich provinces such as the Punjab, for instance (Singh 1988). In a province such as Egypt, the influence of the Ottoman governor was clearly on the wane by the mid-seventeenth century. Powerful 'family circles' of the local 'slave' military commanders – the mamelukes – were gradually increasing their hold on local power. These mameluke households were deeply involved in the operations of the burgeoning local economy. They had achieved a dominance over the great mercantile corporations (the *tujjar*); they invested in the production of sugar and dates (Boustany 1971: iii, 73). They employed in their ranks more and more of the Christian Coptic scribes who ran the revenue administration and developed links with the up-and-coming peasant élites of the small towns, the so-called village sheikhs (Boustany 1971: ii, 59, 74; Baer 1968).

Slowly, these provincial notables and corporate groups began to invade and suborn imperial power in the richer provinces from Tunis to Bengal. Sometimes they went into open revolt when stronger rulers attempted to recreate the basis of their kingdoms by wars of expansion or by insisting on the orthodox doctrine of their realms. The Mughal emperor Aurangzeb, 1657–1707, sought to conquer the Shia Sultanates of the central Indian plateau after 1670 and used the rhetoric of orthodox Sunnism to rally his soldiers. Severe financial problems arising from price inflation and the decline of the yields of Crown lands probably encouraged this attempt to find new sources of income. But one unforeseen result was the revolt of the Hindu Maratha soldier-peasants of western India. Again, Aurangzeb attempted to gain control of the wealthy religious corporation created by tradesmen and north Indian peasant farmers which became known as the Sikh Khalsa, sparking off a prolonged and bloody revolt which ultimately eliminated the Mughal influence from the rich province of the Punjab. Powerful magnates were often joined in revolt by those who had lost out during imperial administration and by peasant rebels (Grewal forthcoming).

In the Ottoman empire and Persia, hard-pressed emperors also tried to regain control over and tax rich tribes, corporations and magnates which had conspicuously benefited from the expansion of empire, trade and the commercial economy. Often as in

Ottoman Europe or among the Bakhtiari, Afghan or Turkik tribes of the Iranian internal or external borders, the result was fierce rebellion, infused sometimes with themes of holy war. In the meantime, rebellion or no, provinces were falling more and more under the influence of local notables and their mercantile clients. In some cases, especially in the Ottoman empire, the rulers acquiesced in this process as the only way to contain their enemies. Sometimes the decentralisation of power was forced on them. The Ottoman chroniclers called these powerful men *ayans* whether they were found in Egypt, the Balkans or Baghdad. Undoubtedly, they lumped together a vast range of local influence from small local landlords and tribal chiefs to the great mameluke (slave-ruler) households of Egypt, virtually the precursors of independent regional dynasties. Still, the amalgamation may have had some justice because all these magnates had grown rich on the wealth of the empire. Sometimes the notables were joined in revolt by impoverished peasants. Yet the great empires failed not only because of their supposedly ruthless exploitation of the peasantry but because wealthy and prideful men found less and less reason to support the myth of empire to the disadvantage of their real local interests (Naff and Owen 1977; Hourani 1961).

Finally, the very grandeur of the empires spread the notion of kingship and new techniques of power and learning to parts of society which retained a strong sense of their own identity, expressed in religious difference or regional solidarity. Magnates had seen the great display of kingship, the subtle combination of military power, money and claims to legitimacy which the imperial families had deployed. Now they also sought to be 'kings of the world' in their own regions. It was not only the spread of imperial money but the spread of the pretensions of imperial charisma which wrote the end of the empires in their very success. Thus the Sikhs turned Mughal techniques of organisation and Mughal concepts of legitimacy against Delhi, while in Arabia the puritanical religious sect of the Wahhabis were to see themselves as the true protectors of Islam in their rebellion against the sultan.

CHAPTER TWO
Crisis and Reorganisation in Muslim Asia

The slow 'hollowing out' of the Ottoman, Safavid and Mughal régimes was accompanied by a growth of faction at the centre. The seventeenth century had already seen severe fiscal and military difficulties, which may have been worsened by a widespread stagnation of trade at its end. The defeat of the Ottomans by Russia in the 1680s intensified conflict between the regional magnates of the northern borders. There were fierce struggles over the office of vazir (chief minister) of the empire as the sultans increasingly withdrew from active administration. Iran was similarly plagued by minorities and succession struggles after 1680. In India the death of the Emperor Aurangzeb (1707) was followed by two decades of fighting between factions of Indian-born notables from the localities and great imperial nobles from Iran and central Asia. Here too, the office of vazir became more autonomous. Provincial governors, basing themselves on the entrenched commercial and landholding élites which had grown up over the previous century, were gradually to assert *de facto* autonomy of Delhi.

IMPERIAL DISSOLUTION AND TRIBAL 'BREAKOUT': STAGE 2

The crumbling of the imperial centres of Isfahan and Delhi in the early eighteenth century resulted from an even more dramatic set of events. To the problems of accommodating indigenous capitalism and the sclerosis of imperial finances was added a major 'breakout' of military tribes from the restraints imposed on them by the old dominions. For the political, economic and religious life of west, central and south Asia, this was as significant as anything that happened as a consequence of the Mongol invasions of the thirteenth and fourteenth centuries. It speeded up the emergence of new domains from within the fabric of the empires. The shock it administered to trade and townsmen profoundly affected the social and ideological orientation of west and south Asia. It also provided a critical context for the rise of British territorial dominion in India and the rising influence of the European powers within the Ottoman empire and Iran.

In the short term, this second stage of imperial crisis saw attacks on all three empires by powerful but unstable coalitions of tribal warriors of Afghan, Persian or central Asian origin which overthrew or dispersed the earlier nobilities. Isfahan was sacked by the Afghans in 1722 and Delhi in 1739 by the Persian, Nadir Shah, who built his power on Iranian and Turkmen tribes. North India was again invaded by Afghans in 1747 and between 1759 and 1761. In the medium term, these invasions dispersed into the old empires several hundred thousand free, tribal cavalrymen – what were known in central Asia and north India as *kazaks* (cossacks) and in central and south India as Pindaris. Some of these free warriors founded kingdoms; some became village proprietors and what has been called 'military usurers'. In some places such tribal invasions and the migrations to which they gave rise fostered an atmosphere in which millenarian movements thrived and broke free from the controls imposed on them by 'settled' society.

The tribal 'breakout' in the north which began in 1710 was followed by an uprising of Beduin tribesmen of Arabia, who had been converted to a new, purist Islamic teaching expounded by a religious teacher of Najd in central Arabia and protected by a local ruler, Ibn Saud, who had entered a religious compact with him in 1738. This, the Wahhabi movement, named after its foremost teacher Ibn Abd al-Wahhab, expanded rapidly, putting pressure on the Ottoman provinces of the Hejaz, Iraq, Syria and Egypt. In 1801 the Shia holy place of Karbala was sacked and by 1806 Mecca and Medina, the spiritual centres of Islam, had been overrun.

Some parts of the region fared better than others. The Ottoman northern provinces mounted a strong holding operation against the assaults from Persia and Afghanistan; later the southern provinces fought back the tide of the Arabian Wahhabi tribesmen. But the Mughal and Safavid states melted away in the face of tribal breakout, lacking the political and economic cohesion of the Ottomans. The internal political economy of Eurasia was also changed by these events. The costs of widespread cavalry warfare along with the need to protect and monopolise trade and suppress millenarian and rural movements were among the forces which impelled indigenous states and European enclaves alike to create more compact and extractive states. It was the lineal descendents of such states – Muhammad Ali's realm in Egypt or the Qajars in Iran, for instance – which were incorporated into the nineteenth-century world order. This section will analyse the causes and consequences of tribal resurgence across the region.

What is striking about the tribal 'breakouts' which threatened the prosperity of the old régimes is that they were, once again, connected with the very spread of wealth and prosperity within the Safavid, Mughal and Ottoman domains. Warrior tribesmen acquired silver and position in the service of the emperors. They aspired to more elevated conceptions of kingliness or godliness as their moral and economic universe broadened. They sought higher status or even dominance within the realms of the great emperors. But they also retained communal forms of social organisation which gave them a lethal military solidarity. The 'breakouts' often occurred at the very point when tribal societies were becoming sultanates or khanates. When new rulers sought to dominate and unify the tribesmen, they often thought it politic to let egalitarian warriors have their head in plundering expeditions abroad.

In the fifteenth century the empires had come into being partly because they were able to control the great tribal coalitions from central Asia and Arabia which had racked Eurasia and thrown up leaders such as the Prophet Muhammad, Genghis Khan and Tamberlaine. Later, these empires had guaranteed their own survival by entrenching themselves on the fringes of the commercial seas: the Mediterranean, Indian Ocean and Bay of Bengal. Now they were to lose control of both their maritime and inland fringes to fierce barbarians from outside, seaborne Christian 'Franks' on the one side and Muslim free-cavalrymen on the other.

Egalitarian tribesmen and nomads had always posed military problems for the emperors. Their expansion and settlement, often called 'rebellions' by the historians, had proceeded throughout the sixteenth and seventeenth centuries. The Bakhtiari and Laks grew in strength in Persia, fattening on the rich caravan trade. Western Beduin tribes pushed into the rich lands near Fayum on the Egyptian Delta (Baer 1968: 139) and the Kurds waxed and waned in strength in their battles with the Ottoman provincial rulers in Baghdad. The Maratha Hindu soldiers acted as irregulars in the service of the sultans of the Deccan who preceded Mughal rule. Interestingly, these Marathas were also called 'tribes' by Persian commentators. The empires had some success in incorporating or domesticating these challengers. But about 1710 a series of tribal movements began in the Herat–Kandahar region of Afghanistan which confronted Mughals, Safavids and Ottomans with severe challenges. The first two empires could not absorb these challenges.

THE SEQUENCE OF 'BREAKOUTS'

This first 'breakout' began with the Ghalzai Afghans of Kandahar. Their strong tribal identity had allowed their leaders to play off Mughals and Safavids against each other throughout the seventeenth century. More important, they had grown prosperous by taxing the overland commerce between India and Iran and by trading themselves in horses, silks and dried fruits. Their leader Mir Wais was 'a man of great wealth which he had amassed through trading with India' (Lockhart 1958: 85). Attempts by the Ghalzais to assert their independence culminated in revolt when the Safavid court attempted to tax this rich fringe more rigorously. Mir Wais went to Mecca, declared himself independent of the Safavid heretics, as he now called the Shia rulers (ibid.: 86), and raised a tribal revolt which had eliminated Persian influence from much of south-eastern Afghanistan by 1720. The rise and success of the Ghalzais overthrew the long-standing balance between them and their tribal neighbours and enemies,the Abdalis of Herat. The Abdalis then invaded Iran, sacking most of the important cities of western Iran and interrupting the major trade routes between east and west.

The next step in the sequence was the rise during the 1730s of Nadir Shah Afshar who re-established a tribal alliance of Afghan and Turkik soldiers and invaded both the Ottoman empire and Mughal India. Nadir Shah seems to have seen himself as one of the great world conquerors from central Asia; he may have harboured the design of creating a new Khilafat or pan-Islamic state, overriding the distinctions between Sunni and Shia. There was probably also an economic motive for his invasions of the rich treasure cities of Delhi and Mesopotamia. The fall of the Safavids had disrupted the valuable trade in raw silk; this had drastically reduced the income of the Persian rulers and made it difficult for them to placate their soldiers. Nadir's hoard of at least £30 million captured in Delhi in 1739 not only paid the troops but also, according to a contemporary observer, helped balance Iran's now diminished trade with its partners in India and Mesopotamia (Marshall 1988: 65; *cf.* Perry 1979: 247–8).

Nadir's coalition was too disparate and unstable to survive his assassination in 1747. Their common Sunni and Afghan inheritance did, however, make it possible for Ahmed Shah Abdali to fill the power vacuum. He created a new Afghan kingdom which proceeded to consolidate its hold over western Iran and Afghanistan, Sindh and the west Punjab, unifying adventurers on horseback and tribal levies throughout the region. The Abdalis invaded India four times in the next few years, rewriting the balance of power in India by their famous defeat of the Marathas in 1761 at Panipat near Delhi. Afghan invasion continued to menace the northern part of the sub-continent as late as 1797.

The consequences for Indian politics and the Indian economy were momentous. The process of state-building and 'decentralisation' was speeded up. In time, the Afghan invasions of the 1750s allowed the Marathas, Sikhs and Jats, old enemies on the internal frontier of the Mughal empire, to recoup a position which was still quite vulnerable in 1720. The Sikhs, for instance, had been severely weakened by the Mughal defeat of the rebellion of their leader Banda Bahadur by 1714. The Persian and later Abdali invasions allowed them to move down from their hill retreat into the plains and take on the now weakened Mughal gentry. That gentry was already suffering from the decline of the trade on which their small towns depended. The invasions also confirmed the growing *de facto* independence from Delhi of Mughal provincial governors in Bengal, the Hyderabad Deccan and Awadh. These magnates and their descendants slowly created dynasties and kingdoms which were to form the enemies and later the subordinate allies of the English East India Company.

The invasions also had profound consequences for the political economy of the empires. Walter Hamilton, a contemporary English observer, noted that it was after the Persian invasion of Delhi that the economic sinews of the Mughal empire began to atrophy. The nobles at Delhi and Agra found it impossible to buy the rich produce of Bengal. This in turn made difficulties for the regular remittance of revenue from Bengal to the centre and encouraged the growing independence of the Nawabs of Bengal (Hamilton

1787: 169). Again, 'The distracted and impoverished condition of the Moghul and Persian empires both contributed considerably to lessen the great demand which was made by those states for the produce of Bengal when Delhi and Ispahan [Iran] enjoyed reigns of grandeur and vigour'. These problems, again, encouraged the British in Bengal to contemplate more aggressive schemes of military and commercial expansion. The defeat of the Marathas at Panipat by the Afghans in 1761, as every Indian schoolboy knows, was a critical precondition for the growing influence of the English East India Company in the sub-continent.

The invasions of Iran by the Afghans after 1710 had been accomplished by as few as 20,000 armed cavalrymen. But the long era of invasion and counter-invasion tended to increase the pool of free cavalry seeking service and wealth throughout the region. Afghan soldiers, who had long been filling the lower ranks of the Mughal military, now came into India in even greater numbers. They ranged wide over the whole sub-continent, altering the balance of power even in the far south. Marquis Maistre de La Tour, a French soldier working in Mysore later in the century, noted of the Mughal magnate who dominated the Deccan:

> Nizam ul-Mulk, [ruler of what was to become the state of Hyderabad] being desirous of possessing an army, which though composed of different nations become effeminate by a long peace, should nevertheless be fit for the purposes of war, had with that intention invited into his domains a great number of Pathans or inhabitants of Kandahar, the remains of those Afghans who had conquered Persia and whom Nadir Shah after having chased them out of that fertile kingdom had pursued them even to their own mountains. He had even bestowed on the chiefs among them nabobships, whence arose the Pathan nabobs of Carpet, Canour and Sunour.   (de la Tour 1784: 11)

These Afghans acted as a volatile element in south Indian politics over the next two generations, serving the pro-French party at Hyderabad and later the fiercely anti-British sultans of Mysore. Their descendants and allied military groups helped prolong local warfare and instability in south India into the third decade of the next century (Sunil Chander 1987).

THE SOCIOLOGY OF 'TRIBAL BREAKOUT'

Is it possible to postulate a broader set of causes for these momentous tribal 'breakouts'? Two processes seem to have helped determine the nature and the timing of the impact of Afghan and Turkik people on the polities of south and west Asia. First, there had been a long-term emigration by tribal soldiers of fortune which slowly built up the population of free soldiers in the sub-continent, especially by men of the tribes of central Afghanistan. These were the cavalry warriors known in the Indian sources as Rohillas ('men of the hills'). They came from clan societies in which land was regularly redistributed and marriage, faction and the organisation of property rights worked against the emergence of powerful sultans. Mountstuart Elphinstone, future governor of British Bombay, who visited the area at the very beginning of the nineteenth century, wrote that 'the disgrace of engaging in trade among the Afghans, renders land absolutely necessary to the support of each individual and whosoever is without land must quit the country' (Elphinstone 1815: ii, 34). The percentage of such Afghans in the Mughal military system appears to have increased from about 1630 onwards, and laid the way open for the creation of Afghan kingdoms in north India as the Mughal power waned at the beginning of the eighteenth century.

The second process was one by which tribal societies were transformed into military dynasties (Gellner 1983a). The key here was not so much the oppression of tribals by the state, as their closer integration into the great trading and service cultures of the empires. For instance, even in the eighteenth century it was reported by several travellers that the Afghans and the Turkmen, rich and poor alike, were dressed in Indian cloth. These cloths were not necessarily the produce of the artisans of northern India, but originated in the towns of Masulipatnam on the east coast of the sub-continent. The cloth was shipped via Karachi and Sindh or via Bushire and Iran into Afghanistan and central Asia (Elphinstone 1815: i, 385). The tribes had indeed been sharers in the wealth of the empires.

However, their growing wealth set off several sets of tensions. First, sultans and war leaders who attempted to consolidate their power within these fractious levelling societies used foreign wars as a way of taming and diverting their jealous comperes and consolidating their influence. Ahmed Shah Abdali is reported to have mentioned this as a reason for his Indian campaigns of the 1750s. Invasions of poorer west or central Asia would be counter-productive because, he is reported to have said, these were 'beehives without honey' (ibid.: ii, 247). Secondly, as seen earlier, the very wealth and prosperity of the tribals tended to attract the attention of rapacious provincial governors bringing tribesmen into conflict with the emperors. Thirdly, a disturbance in one part of this economic and political field of force had consequences in many other areas almost at once. The long-term decline of north Persia after 1714 probably forced Nadir and the Abdalis to search for 'honey' in India. In turn, the disturbance in the balance of trade and bullion flows in India incited the Maratha soldiers of the Deccan to move into rich Bengal in the north and Tanjore in the south (Sen 1928: 59). These moves in turn changed the context in which the European traders of the south operated.

This was as true of the western sector of the region as of the eastern. Nadir Shah's Pan-Islamic sultanate collapsed in 1747 but not before his wars had been accompanied by considerable movements of Turkik and Afghan peoples across the north Persian plains. While at this stage it was still the Russian 'frontier barbarians' pressing down from the north who posed the greatest challenge to the Ottomans, the tribal 'breakouts' were an extra problem. For instance, the problems of Ottoman officers in Palestine were increased in the 1740s by an influx of Turkmen, Kurdish and Beduin tribesmen who had migrated southward from the district of Rakka, crossing the Euphrates to arrive eventually in the Tiberias district of Palestine (Cohen 1973: 80). Nadir's assaults on Baghdad weakened the Ottoman military forces as far away as the Levant and the Russian borders. In the absence of powerful help from Istanbul, the Georgian slave dynasty of Baghdad consolidated itself in what is now Iraq. In Iran, meanwhile, the collapse of Nadir's tribal coalition in the north of the country and the great damage sustained by areas of *qanat* or underground canal irrigation shifted the centre of power in the whole region to the south. This paved the way for the reassertion of the more settled tribal groupings – the Zands and Qajars who successively consolidated their position and created new régimes around Isfahan.

So Nadir's campaigns and the second Afghan 'breakout' under Ahmed Shah Abdali had triggered creation of a whole range of new states throughout Eurasia: Awadh, Hyderabad and Bengal in India, the Talpur Emirs of Sindh, the Zand kingdom of Iran and the semi-independent Pashalik (governorship) of Baghdad under the Georgian, Sulaiman Pasha. In addition, the shock waves of invasion and the disruption of trade encompassed a series of minor tremors in small towns and rural hinterlands where local magnates took the opportunity of the demoralisation of the old imperial régimes to 'raise their heads in revolt'.

The eastern arm of the great Eurasian land mass was thrown

into turmoil by the breakout of the northern tribes and tribal kingdoms in the first half of the eighteenth century. It appears that contemporary tribal movements also affected the Persianised kingdoms of central Asia and set the scene for increasing Russian penetration of the region. This lies outside the scope of our study. However, an equally serious challenge was to face the central and southern wings of the Ottoman empire in the later parts of the century. This was the explosive revolt of the tribesmen of the western Arabian desert under their warleader Ibn Saud and inspired by the great fundamentalist teacher Abd-al Wahhab. The Wahhabis, and the Anzah tribes displaced by their rise, put increasing pressure on Ottoman garrisons in Syria and Iraq from the 1770s onward, rolling back the frontiers of cultivation (Lewis 1987: 8–10). At the turn of the century they captured three of the most important shrine cities of the Muslim world, Mecca, Medina and Karbala. The slaughter and destruction which followed these events sent a tremor through all Islamic societies and exposed anew the impotence of the Ottoman sultan himself, checkmated by increasingly furious conflicts between regional magnates (*ayans*) and the court in Istanbul.

This second great rash of tribal movements was not a random event. The decline of Ottoman forces in the face of pressure from both the Russians and the post-Safavid régimes in Iran had weakened their response to attack from the south. There may also have been more general changes at work which tie the Wahhabi movement into the picture of broader imperial crisis. The expansion of commerce and communication seems to have been important once again. Najd, the southwest Arabian territory from which the Wahhabi movement orginated, had become wealthier and more urbanised as trade routes grew up between the Red Sea and the Indian Ocean. Both the settled and nomadic population of Najd seems to have expanded in the sixteenth and seventeenth centuries (al-Juhany 1983: 241). As these desert regions were brought into the Islamic world economy, the spread of money-use increased economic tensions.

Ideological changes accompanied this closer communication. There had developed already puritanical movements among the pious Muslims of the Yemen against the Hindu and other infidel traders who had established themselves in their midst in the 1730s and 1740s. As the number of learned *ulama* expanded rapidly in Najd with the growth of settled society, they fanned out to the teaching schools of Cairo and Damascus. Arab desert religion was severe, despising compromise. There was already resentment against the opulence of the pilgrimage cities of the Hejaz and Mesopotamia which had benefited from the increase in pilgrim traffic from the wealthy centres of the old empires. Long before the Saudi rulers poured their tribal levies into Mecca and Medina, there had been antagonism to the opulent gilded domes which wealthy townsmen erected over the tombs of saints, contrary, it was said, to the laws of God. The increasing commercial and ideological scale of the Muslim empires had itself created the scene for more violent conflict between centre and periphery, between sect and sect. Abd al-Wahhab himself had learned his doctrines from the severe teachers of the Hanbali law in the great cities of Islam. He was no desert fanatic but a subtle scholar of the *sharia* law (*Enc. Islam*).

Finally, there appear to have been specific 'trigger' factors. After the 1760s the flow of Indian trade to Egypt and the Ottoman empire was badly disrupted (Gran 1978: 51–86). Production in eastern and western India had been damaged by Persian, Afghan, Maratha and later British invasions; consumers in Egypt and the Ottoman lands were hit by a series of economic problems, particularly in the years 1750–70 and again in the 1790s. The sudden fluctuations in this rich trade may have exacerbated the conflicts between town and town, tribesmen and pasha in southern Arabia and the Red Sea. Added to this, the decline of Ottoman authority and, later, the Napoleonic invasion of Egypt served to weaken the Ottoman military presence in Arabia. The way was open for the further expansion of Wahhabi raiding parties and the emergence of a strong theocratic and military state in central Arabia.

IDEOLOGICAL CHALLENGES AND THE RECONSTRUCTION OF ORTHODOXY

Consideration of the origins of the tribal 'breakouts' raises the question of their ideological impact on the conquered societies. Tribal people tended to an immanent form of religious belief. The word was made flesh; tribal leaders often combined mundane power with some of the characteristics of sainthood, even though tribesmen looked to townsmen for the interpretation of law and custom (Gellner 1983b). At the same time, periods of profound social disturbance also occasioned the re-emergence of millenarian and eschatological cults, and intensified conflicts between ancient and contending doctrines. The eighteenth century in Islamic Eurasia and Africa witnessed many such developments, and the shocks to trade and towns weakened the influence of the orthodox townsmen over the 'heretical' fringes.

Conflict between the great Islamic sects of Sunnism and Shiism clearly accelerated during the eighteenth century. The decline of the Mughal centre was accompanied by the establishment of a Shiite dynasty in Awadh (Cole 1984). Sunni polemicists in Delhi and other centres increased their attacks on the ancient rival (Rizvi 1982). As we have seen, the war of the Afghan tribesmen against the Safavid centre reawakened the ideological conflict between Sunni and Shia there also (Lockhart 1958: 86). The Wahhabi movement encompassed a complete rejection by the Beduin tribesmen of what they perceived as the degeneracy and luxury of the 'cities of the plain' and the claims of the Ottoman sultan to the universal Caliphate, revived after 1774. But by the same token, Muhammad Ali Pasha of Egypt, who fought the Wahhabis to a standstill from 1812 to 1818, could promote himself as protector of the real orthodoxy and enhance his fragile legitimacy in Egypt itself.

These were simply the most arresting examples of a wider change which challenged the high religions of the Islamic and Hindu world in the wake of the decline of the old empires. In India the expansion of the all-India military culture which accompanied the process of decentralisation imparted a new impetus to some of the most complex and volatile forms of Indian belief. On the fringes of the expanding faith of Sikhism, wandering and nomadic peoples spread forms of syncretic belief which assimilated together worship of Hindu warrior goddesses with Muslim states of central and south India, new generations of warrior martyrs (*pir* cults) and even in some cases the persona of Sikh gurus. Among the detritus also of the expanding Muslim states of central and south India, new generations of warrior martyrs, loosely associated with sufi mystical beliefs, were created and often assimilated into the pantheon of the rural Hindu world (Bayly forthcoming).

Devotional and sufi cults also flourished in late eighteenth-century Iran. The later Safavids, allied as they were with the orthodox Shia *mujtahids* (teachers) of the towns, had discountenanced sufi beliefs, particularly the more heterodox ones. Many sufi teachers had fled to India. Following the tribal 'breakouts' and the creation of the more tolerant and latitudinarian Zand régime in the 1760s, rural sufism appears to have revived. Notable here was the Nurbakshi sect which was actually exported from India to Iran.

The sect was associated with Shah Masum Ali, an Indian holy man of the Deccan who went to Iran in 1785. Masum Ali and his pupils propagated a faith which appears to have stressed personal devotion to an immanent deity. Movements such as this were widespread in central and southern India and were quite compatible with Hindu devotional teachings. Masum Ali soon built up a large band of supporters (Malcolm 1815: i, 414–20, says 30,000) in southern Iran. He and his disciples spent the next thirty years wandering through Iran, Afghanistan and Iraq, fighting off the attacks of the orthodox religious establishment and their royal supporters.

The decline of the empires had also been accompanied by the decimation of large towns and the trade routes on which they had flourished (though it must be remembered that smaller places sometimes grew to compensate for this deurbanisation). The result was a crisis for ancient artisan communities and guilds, particularly in the Ottoman lands and Persia, but increasingly also in India after the 1780s. Urban decline, or rapid redistributions of wealth and status among the townsmen, also formed a context for realignments of communities. Throughout the three regions, rioting between different sections of the population (Christian/Muslim, Sunni/Shia, Hindu/Muslim) went hand in hand with the emergence of popular sufi and millenarian movements. The reaction of the urban élites and learned men was profoundly to influence the shape of the Islamic religion (and the social context of colonial rule) in the nineteenth century. Sometimes élites associated themselves with sufi movements and attempted to control them, as for instance in India and Egypt. Elsewhere, and notably in Qajar Iran, élites sought to suppress and stamp out what they deemed unorthodox and undisciplined forms of belief (Algar 1969: 48–51; Arjomand 1984: 216–17).

THE NEW STATES OF THE MID-EIGHTEENTH CENTURY: STAGE 3

In the medium term, the reaction to the economic stresses and social unease caused by the great 'tribal breakouts' was a patchy reassertion of the dominance of trade, townsmen, literate urban groups and of the hegemony of political centres over tribal and agrarian populations. This took place, however, not in the context of loose hegemonies such as the Mughal or Safavid empires, but in the context of new, regional power blocs which stand, as it were, halfway between the earlier empires and modern nation states. Some of these were largely independent régimes such as the Pashalik of Baghdad or the Zand state in Iran; others were only semi-independent, such as Hyderabad or Awadh in India; yet others were colonial provinces directly ruled from London (or later, in the case of Algeria, from Paris).

These régimes adopted similar policies whether 'colonial' or 'indigenous'. They sought to monopolise and protect trade, settle wandering groups and disperse armies, to re-establish the power to tax the countryside. These régimes whether colonial or independent also became 'havens' for the protection of the commercial people, literati and religious specialists and landed magnates – social groups which had arisen within the old régimes, but whose very success had weakened the overarching military umbrella which had protected them. In examining the transitional régimes and social classes of the later eighteenth century, then, this section uncovers some of the foundations of the nineteenth-century colonial world. At the same time, the events of that transition help explain why some of the successor régimes remained independent and some became colonial provinces.

First, some basic categories of successor régimes should be established. In India the most striking were the imperial provinces which between 1720 and 1740 had secured *de facto* independence from the centre. Imperial notables in Awadh, Bengal and Hyderabad still recognised the legitimacy of the centre and, as far as possible given the warfare which followed the tribal 'breakouts', paid part of their customary revenue to Delhi. But the nobles who controlled these provinces amalgamated together fiscal, military and judicial powers which the Mughals had tried to keep separate. They transformed their offices into hereditary holdings, gradually took control of the enfeebled *jagir* system and patronised both Hindu and Muslim landholding groups which might act as intermediaries between them and the fractious countryside. In the far south of the Indian sub-continent, the expansion of Mughal state forms went ahead. Arcot consolidated itself under the aegis of the English East India Company. By contrast, the warrior state of Mysore, ruled by Haidar Ali (1761–82) and Tipu Sultan (1782–99), became an exemplar of a regional warrior state, fighting the English and disdaining the flaccid Mughal authority.

Some of the régimes of Hindu and Sikh warriors who had revolted against the Mughal rule at the end of the seventeenth and beginning of the eighteenth centuries also began to create more stable régimes. These régimes, ironically, began to adopt the Mughals' own revenue management techniques and establish themselves as landlord masters over large areas of the erstwhile empire. Thus the Hindu Marathas had established a streamlined revenue and defence system by the 1760s in areas which they had taken over from the Mughals in the 1720s and 1730s (Gordon 1977). By 1790 the Sikhs had created recognisably Mughal régimes in the rich lands of the Punjab and trade and the commercial towns had begun to revive (Grewal forthcoming). Emerging from out of the brief Afghan empire of the Durranis, magnates from tribal backgrounds in Sindh (the Talpur Emirs) had built up a viable political system by the 1790s (Lambrick 1952: ch. 1). They protected but also taxed the India–central Asia transit trade up and down the rich valley of Sindh and organised the production of their own peasantry whose grain was sold through state-run granaries.

What is striking is that comparable changes were taking place in Iran and the provinces of the Ottoman empire. Here also, the earlier atrophy of the centre and growth of provincial magnates provided the basis for new, regional régimes which emerged after ths shocks of the tribal 'breakout' and inter-provincial conflicts. By 1760, for instance, magnates of the Zand tribal group of southern Iran had been able to establish a flourishing smaller state around Shiraz in southern Iran, within what had once been the heart of the Safavid empire.

Karim Khan Zand's state of the 1770s collected from southern and central Iran a revenue which was 'quite respectable in comparison with later Safavid times' (Perry 1979: 229ff.), allowing for inflation and territories completely lost. In fact, the revenues of about 420,000 tumans were nearly equivalent to Rs. 70 lakhs. If the total revenues of south Persia were taken to be worth about Rs. 100 lakhs, this would amount to about one-third of the contemporary revenues of the last independent ruler of Bengal. The comparison is particularly interesting in view of the fact that the Zand territories probably had a population of less than a million while Bengal had a population of at least 25 and probably 30 million. Like other new rulers, Karim Khan encouraged merchant communities such as Jews, Armenians and Indians to resettle; he built and controlled state granaries to feed the people in the volatile agrarian conditions of the arid southern lands. He disciplined the surrounding tribal groups through the use of a hostage system, taking their chiefs' sons to his courts and enrolling them into his army. Indeed, Nadir

Shah had 'already shaken the effete structure of the late Safavid court into a working militaristic machine' (ibid: 279), and Karim Khan then transformed this again into a smaller, but more effective army which operated against dissident tribesmen and the Ottoman and foreign interests clustered in the great port of Basra.

The Zand monarchy fell prey to its inability to discipline the outlying tribals and in particular the Qajars. After a decade of disturbance, Aga Mahomed Khan Qajar established a new tribally-based régime in Shiraz in 1796. But the Qajars' state continued many of the policies and institutions of the Zand state such as the payment of military salaries by cash salaries rather than land grants (Lambton 1953: 133–40). The Qajars, well-established in northern Iran by the 1810s, were to remain an independent regional state through the nineteenth century, albeit heavily circumscribed by Russian pressures to the north and the British and Afghans to the east. Gradually – and not finally before the mid-nineteenth century – townsmen, orthodox religious leaders and scribal bureaucrats reasserted their authority over the great tribal coalitions.

The Ottoman empire had seen a slow process of decentralisation and the rise of the provincial magnates from the later seventeenth century. Weakness at the centre was probably less important than the growing complexity and dynamism of provincial societies, particularly in the Balkans, Egypt and Mesopotamia, all of which had benefited from the growth of production and population along the great trade routes. The problems of control centre were increased by the tendency of later sultans to bring in 'warrior slave communities' to stiffen their armies with new military skills. In Egypt the mameluke soldiers, drawn from the empire's Christian provinces and from the Sudan, were already a powerful *imperium in imperio* by the mid-seventeenth century. The change came rather later in Mesopotamia, and here it was the Islamised soldiers from Georgia who were to act as the military arbiters between competing tribal factions and as the distant arm of the sultan.

In both great regions, the slave dynasties had become dominant by the 1780s. Sulaiman Pasha had established himself in Baghdad, uniting hitherto separate offices of the state, and secure in the support of the local Arab population and merchant communities whose interest he advocated in Istanbul (Longrigg 1925: 250–8; Huart 1901: 148). In the same way, Ali Bey in Egypt had temporarily united the mameluke factions under his control and had virtually eliminated the power of the Ottoman governor from the country. Both rulers sought to settle nomads and break up nomadic alliances, to regenerate the towns and trade routes, and to hoard and monopolise trade and silver. In Syria, Palestine, the southern Balkans and ethnically Turkish territories, a similar decentralisation went ahead. But the sultans did have some power to control the *ayans* (formally abolishing them in 1786). Istanbul still remained the economic and moral centre of this circumscribed Ottoman world.

Contemporaries and historians have caught the echoes of some kind of systematic change in this very widespread process of 'decentralisation' and realm-building within the receding shadow of the old despotisms. But how far is it really possible to compare them and, indeed, what is the significance of this apparent historical convergence towards the end of the eighteenth century? It must be admitted that in culture, wealth, ecology and in the play of contingent historical events there were very great differences between India, Iran and the Ottoman empire, and also between 'successor régimes' in different regions. Yet comparable features can be highlighted in several of these states.

BUILDING REGIONAL IDENTITIES

First, there were interesting changes in the relationship between these new rulers and the types of legitimate power they were claiming. The relationship between territory, religious affiliation and ethnicity became stronger than it had been under the great empires. Thus the later eighteenth century witnessed an important stage in the creation of preconditions for the emergence of modern ethnicities and nation states in Asia as in Europe.

In Iran, the Zand kingdom appears to have been 'latitudinarian' in its attitude to religious traditions. Formally, Karim Khan was vakil or lieutenant of the now vacant Safavid throne. Nadir's seizure of religious endowments and neo-Sunnism had weakened the Shia religious establishment. Karim Khan invited some teachers back from Karbala where they had settled and built new mosques, but he also allowed sufi movements to practice again freely in the countryside. The Zand régime was also aware of particularly Persian traditions. The tombs and monuments of the great poets Saadi and Hafiz in Isfahan and Shiraz were, for instance, renovated (Malcolm 1815: ii, 151). The incoming Qajar régime, by contrast, re-established much closer connections with the Shia teachers (*mujtahids*) and in particular with those professing the *usuli* or rationalistic branch of jurisprudence (Arjomand 1984: 217; Cole 1984). Unorganised sufism and 'heretical' sects within Islam were vigorously attacked and in the towns, large areas of ad hoc and customary jurisdiction were left to the religious leaders. Shiism came to be linked quite closely to a regional régime which lacked the universalistic ambitions and religious claims of the Safavids and Nadir Shah. The Qajar régime was to become more straightforwardly 'Persian', and Shiism more like a state religion.

In the Ottoman empire some of the new rulers and élites also began to grope towards symbols of regional, ethnic or religious identity, though the charisma and power of the centre remained powerful, with few apart from the Wahhabis and northern Christians directly challenging the legitimacy of the sultan and khalifa. Emerging provincial notables in Syria began to define themselves as *awlad-Arab*, that is 'Arabs' in distinction to their Ottoman rulers (Rafeq in Owen and Naff 1977: 69–70). New élites in other parts of Syria legitimised themselves by reference to more tightly-defined religious identities (Sunni, Shia, or Alavite), though the spread of this new 'communalism' was very uneven. Even the *ayans* of Greek and Slavic parts of the realm where Orthodox Christianity recovered vigorously were not always favourable to it, while the later mameluke rulers of Egypt by pursuing specifically Egyptian policies inclined, perhaps unconsciously, to distance themselves from Istanbul. Catherine the Great of Russia tried to persuade the by no means unreceptive Ali Bey to declare 'independence' from Istanbul, while several Beys sought to implement trading links with the English East India Company which served Egyptian but not Ottoman imperial interests. The political organisation of late eighteenth-century Egypt also resembled that of pre-Ottoman Egypt rather than that of the typical imperial province. By the time Bonaparte invaded there already appears to have been an underswell of 'Egyptian' sentiment, particularly among Coptic Christians.

In India some Mughal successor states also embodied features of local culture which distanced them from the universalistic claims of the Mughal empire. In Awadh the court had begun to emphasise its Shia character by the 1790s (Cole 1984) and was already tacitly tolerant of the beliefs and practices of its powerful Hindu subjects. Maratha rulers sought status and office within the Mughal empire, but their régime's character as 'brahmin' kingdoms was also emphasised. The Sikhs under Ranjit Singh embodied a full-scale regional revolt against Mughal and Afghan supremacy but specifically Punjabi cultural elements were very much to the fore.

In every case the rôle of the regional dynasts was ambiguous. In most cases they emphasised their loyalty to the emperors and drew their legitimacy from the political culture of the old empires. Indirectly, though, they fostered the sense of regional solidarity and culture which appealed to many of the most important groups which supported their régimes. The point is that the regional ethnicities which were later seen as 'nationalism' in Europe, Asia and north Africa had already begun to form *before* the full impact of the West was felt. They were not the simple product of 'westernisation'. They were compounded out of a sense of regional interest and its embodiment in forms of local religion and tradition. Such identities were often manipulated by the colonial powers in the early nineteenth century but, ultimately, they could also provide the grounding for opposition to imperialism.

ASIAN 'MERCANTILISM'

Most important, the economic stance of these régimes bears comparison. All of them needed to forge more powerful armed forces in order to fight off the pressure of internal and external enemies. Contrary to the policies of the old empires which had supported their cavalry élites on land grants, the post-imperial régimes often moved over to cash payments and tended to recruit professional armies which were often drawn from minority groups – Circassians, Georgians, Afghans and in India armed Hindu mendicants. European military advisers and musketry were introduced by degrees, first in the Ottoman empire and Nadir's Iran, later in the Indian successor states. All this required substantial quantities of cash revenue during a period when both overland and seaborne trade were subject to serious periodic disturbance.

Using methods which were typical of the earlier empires, but which were now greatly intensified, the new régimes attempted to gain a closer control over the resources of their territories. The farming of royal rights and revenues appears to have speeded up in several regions. The practice of creating state monopolies for administration or sale was extended. During Mysore's expansion, for instance, taxes were imposed on the coconut and palmyra trees of India's southwest coast. The southwest Indian kingdom of Travancore created a more rigid monopoly of the spice trade (Das Gupta 1967: ch. 2), and began to exploit the value of its hardwood forests. This sort of policy was later adopted by the Egyptian Beys and Muhammad Ali who brought into taxation the large Beduin-controlled date orchards of the Fayum area (Baer 1968: 139; Boustany 1971: iii, 95).

While designed to generate revenue, measures such as this also had ulterior political motives. Rulers were attempting to prevent the disruptive forces of commerce (especially foreign commerce) eroding their polities. Whereas earlier emperors had encouraged bodies of traders to 'buy into' fringes of their sovereignty, potentates such as Tipu Sultan placed severe restrictions on his merchants and tried to exclude foreign competitors.

Attempts were also made to settle new areas of cultivation and secure new sources of labour supply. One method employed throughout the region was settling nomads either by imposing taxation on them, so requiring them to produce for markets, or by encouraging them with grants of land rights in marginal areas. Another method was by direct control of agricultural or artisan labour through forms of more or less direct bondage. Tipu and Haidar Ali forcibly removed cultivators from Arcot and settled them in Mysore. Afghan principalities throughout the region employed a patron–bondsman relationship (the bondsmen were called *fakhirs* and *halis* or ploughmen in north India) to ensure their labour supply. The dependent servants were provided with food, seed and clothing in return for their produce. The relationship between the new states and the landed élites of their territories varied.

In general the eighteenth century saw the continuation of the process of the emergence of large estates or 'rental holdings'. In some cases the pressure for ready cash was so great that rulers tried to penetrate through the layers of rural intermediaries and make direct contact with peasant farmers. The social organisation of the post-imperial régimes was determined by the outcome of the struggles between village and revenue entrepreneurs, between merchant and military élite. These were conflicts between the different forms of capital which had emerged from the old régimes. In several regions the new European colonial powers were to extend and enhance this newly forged power over peasant and artisan, creating the basis for the nineteenth-century export boom in primary agricultural produce.

Of critical importance to the economic fate of the successor régimes, however, was their relationship to the flows of interregional trade. The cities and urban and landed élites of the imperial regions had grown up on the wealth and consumption generated by the flow of resources within and between the Mughal, Safavid and Ottoman empires, and to a lesser extent following the burgeoning of trade with Europe. Ironically, the growing autonomy of regions and – more importantly – the 'tribal breakout' threatened that flow of wealth. Severe imbalances therefore grew up in the external trade (and hence internal patterns of consumption) of the emerging regional entities. Iran's silver hunger has already been mentioned. The decline of the trade in raw silk to India and to Europe combined with the perpetual outflow of silver to Russia, and through the mechanism of the Islamic pilgrimage to Iraq, imperilled its economy. This may have lain behind the invasions of Iraq and India by Nadir Shah. It certainly seems to have been the trigger for Karim Khan Zand's long siege of Basra and the Pashalik of Baghdad in the 1760s.

Imbalances of trade similarly helped spark the Wahhabi incursions into the Hejaz, Syria and Iraq. In India, the failure of the Mughal revenue pump and the sharp reorientation of consumption and trade routes after 1739 also helps to explain the perpetual wars between the successor states over trade routes and revenue-bearing fiefs. The Maratha rulers of the Deccan complained of a silver famine, but looked with envy on the great flows of bullion along the Ganges in the north and the Kavery in the south. Their external policy was directed to seizing these regions.

THE ASIAN CRISIS AND EUROPEAN POWER

The shape of the cumulative crisis of the eighteenth century can now be dimly glimpsed. The sequence of historical change ran perhaps like this: commercial growth and the changing balance of power between centre and province led to growing regional autonomy. The imbalances of power and wealth so created led in turn to tribal invasion, conflict between the successor states and internal battles between élites over labour supply, trade and revenues. New rulers arose in the mid- and later half of the century who sought to create more compact armies and monopolise trade and production, which though buoyant in some regions, had been damaged by such conflicts. This pattern of change was similar in many respects to earlier cycles of change in Islamic Eurasia. However, it was at this point that the rôle of the West, previously of secondary importance, became critical.

European pressure on the old imperial regions had certainly increased. Western demand for Asian goods picked up again dramatically with the general economic growth after 1730, as calicoes, teas and, increasingly, cotton and grain from regions of the Ottoman empire rose in price on the world market. Studies of Egypt and the Levant coast have shown that French and north European merchants and their local surrogates were becoming dominant purchasers in the markets of the more accessible coastal regions (Raymond 1973: i). Dutch and, to a lesser extent, English merchants took and carried a disproportionate part of the greatly diminished external trade of Iran after Nadir Shah. In India the demand for Indian textiles met by the East India Company showed no signs of abating. Yet raw material supplies were becoming a larger and larger proportion of exports. Spices from south India remained profitable; but after 1784 increasing quantities of Indian raw cotton from Gujarat and eastern India were exported to China to finance the China tea trade to England. The growing importance of Western shipping in inter-Asian as well as inter-European trade was reinforced after the first two decades of the eighteenth century. Asian merchants increasingly loaded their own trade goods to European ships in order to seek protection from the commercial wars and 'piracy' which followed the decline of the empires.

European agents, servants of the Companies as well as private merchants or military officers, were also beginning to play a more open political rôle. They craved profits and needed local capital to finance their commercial adventures. Seizing control of monopolies of agricultural or artisan products which had been created by local rulers, Britons, Frenchmen and Dutchmen became linchpins in farms of revenue and local structures of power in the coastal regions because they commanded the movement of capital. The regional rulers also began to employ larger numbers of European mercenary soldiers to train their new model armies. The European military presence became more pressing as Europe's dynastic wars became more desperate. The War of Austrian Succession (1744–8) intensified English and French attempts to find Indian clients, and led to damaging local conflicts in Persian and eastern Mediterranean waters between the armed traders of the two nations. Such conflicts became sharper during the Seven Years' War and the Wars of American Independence. Global warfare increased the military resources which the Europeans had in readiness in their colonial enclaves and also encouraged them to use force to resolve their trade disputes with Asian and African powers.

Yet Asian and north African states remained active forces in these battles to redistribute the world's resources. European imperialism might be seen as the 'highest stage of mercantilism'. Still, the European impact was moulded, even determined by the conflicts between Asian and north African élites and also by the increasingly bitter struggles of the more powerful kingdoms and states to seize their own share of trade, labour and revenues, which were now imperilled by both international and internal conflict. Several examples will help to demonstrate that Europeans as well as Asians were facing new challenges and threats to their stability, and that the preconditions for the move towards European territorial empire must be sought as much in Asia and north Africa as in changed circumstances in Europe.

The Palestine coast presents an interesting example of change within the Ottoman empire. Eighteenth-century Palestine saw the typical decline of central power with a local Shaikh, Dahir-al-Umar, becoming dominant around the rich port town of Acre (near present-day Haifa). Ottoman authority represented by the viceroys (vali) of Sidon and Damascus lost its grip on the situation (Cohen 1973). Dahir had consolidated his position as a powerful village notable and a sub-revenue farmer in an area which provided grain for the markets to the north and helped protect the rich caravan and *haj* (pilgrimage) traffic to the south. However, he also greatly increased his economic strength by acting as middleman and controller of production for cotton exports on to the French market. By mid-century, French merchants trading from Acre to Marseilles had great economic influence in the region, taking raw cotton in exchange for cash deposits at the treasury to offset revenue payments by villages. However, before his deposition by the sultan in 1775, Dahir had begun to play off the French against the British and Dutch, whose Levant interests he determinedly fostered. This made it possible for him to set his own prices and regain the political initiative from the French.

After Dahir's deposition and death, his successor as Ottoman governor, Ahmed Jezzar Pasha, the 'butcher of Acre', a Bosnian by origin, embarked on an even more successful attempt to build a centralised province within the context of the empire. He aimed at 'establishing a monopoly of his own of all the trade of Palestine'

(Cohen 1973: 22). He built granaries for state control of grain in Damascus and created a new and effective military force along with a massive personal fortune. In 1789, local factions with the apparent connivance of the French nearly managed to oust him. After defeating his enemies, Jezzar expelled all French merchants and French interests from the coast and organised his own foreign trade. The high point of his career came in 1799, when he defeated Napoleon's attempt to push against Istanbul from Egypt, by holding the port of Acre against him. Jezzar's fiefdom flourished until the 1830s; he was able to capitalise on the economic advantages which the world market presented him, while at the same time retaining his personal wealth and independence and even helping his master the sultan. Istanbul remained the magnet of power in Syria and Palestine, so Ottoman authority was ultimately strengthened by regional state-building.

On a larger scale, something similar was happening in later mameluke Egypt. Again, Ottoman power was weakened – and here irrevocably – by the growth of a dynamic but conflict-ridden regional culture under the mameluke beys. The beys were not only a military élite; they also supported themselves on revenue farming, ran sugar factories and monopolised trade. Their lien on local society was consolidated through patronage of merchants, Coptic Christian revenue managers and contacts with the rich peasants or village magnates, the *sheikhs* and members of the religious classes (Al-Sayyid Marsot in Naff and Owen 1977: 205–16). Egypt's wealth had been built on its through-trade in coffee, Indian textiles and the *haj* traffic, but it also benefited from the rich grain and cotton production of the lower Nile. That trade had suffered a decline in the earlier part of the century as European-controlled coffee production expanded and Indian production declined. In the years 1750–80 there was a resurgence in wealth and production, associated in part with French demand for cotton and grain. This was channelled through groups of immigrant Syrian merchants whose wealth grew at the expense of the old *tujjar* (merchant communities). At the same time, Egypt continued to reap rewards from the great inland trades within the Ottoman empire, with the Orient and with the Sudan. During this period of economic recovery the province was presided over for much of the time by the mameluke leader, Ali Bey. Ali's state monopolies and attempts to control trade and the merchant guilds were reminiscent of those of Jezzar Ahmed in Acre, but they were less dependent on trade to Europe, and did little to benefit central Ottoman finances.

Egypt of the later mamelukes was in a delicate position in regard to the interests of the Western powers. The sultan's residual influence in the area prevented the beys opening up trade with the English East India Company in the 1770s (this had possibly been a ploy to counter French commercial interests in the Mediterranean). But Ali Pasha and his successors were diversifying their European trading partners in order to keep European commercial interests at a distance. Napoleon's invasion of Egypt in 1798 was in part a geo-political military thrust against the British in the east. However, it was also an attempt to secure an accessible and regular supply of grain for the French Republic whose own ailing agriculture was unable to keep pace with the demand of Paris and other large towns, which had been fed with Egyptian grain during the allied invasion of 1792 (Gran 1978). In the case of Egypt, then, the consolidation of a regional, indigenous state, jealously monopolising its trade and resources, was incompatible with French interests, at least in the short run. Because the mamelukes for all their wealth had failed to modernise their military forces even to the extent of Jezzar Ahmed, they fell victim to Napoleon at the Battle of the Pyramids.

The British conquest of India has always been treated as a series of events *sui generis*, as an unplanned series of accidents in imperialist historiography or as a determined plundering of Indian wealth in the nationalist interpretation. Some features of the sequence of change do, however, make events in India amenable to comparison with developments in west Asia, and rescue India from its onerous status as an 'important special case'. As with the Ottomans, the 'decline of the empire' led not to formless anarchy so much as to intensified conflicts between entrepreneurs and magnates (both European and Indian) over labour and revenue. It also set the scene for more severe struggles between successor régimes over trade and silver. This presented the East India Company with the opportunity to exploit fractures within indigenous society. However, the more rigorous and hostile stance of the regional régimes, particularly in the latter part of the century, also presented the emerging colonial powers with challenges they could not ignore. It was no accident that both the great players at Waterloo, Napoleon and Wellington, had spent part of their youthful careers warring down Muslim enemies who were regarded as by-words for tyranny and 'monopoly' in Europe.

For instance, the critical events of the conquest of Bengal between 1757 and 1765 were driven by the conflicts between Indian rulers jealous of their trade and revenue privileges and Company personnel terrified at the prospect of their loss of investment. The Nawab Siraj-ud-Daulah, whose attack on Calcutta in 1756 was the *casus belli* for Company action, was seeking to consolidate his fragile authority over the élites of merchant-financiers, large landholders and military factions within his court (Marshall 1988: ch. iii). In turn, the British were able to capitalise on the hostility of the élites – particularly the Hindu bankers, the Jagat Seths – in replacing Siraj-ud-Daulah with their own nominee. The conflict which led to the direct annexation of Bengal by the Company in 1765 (although only formally as revenue manager) was also brought to a head by the desperate attempts of a later Nawab (Mir Kasim) to protect his trade and monopolies from piecemeal erosion by the private trade of Company servants and their Indian factotums. This intensification of conflict between Indian and European, it should be added, came at the end of a long period of turbulence in trade and production in north India which had commenced with Nadir's onslaught on Delhi and had been followed by Maratha invasion and Anglo-French War. The battle to redivide India's now more vulnerable resources had proceeded with even greater vigour after 1739.

Much of the motive force of British expansion after 1765 was provided by the need to pay for the British Indian army, the bulwark for trade in an era of continuing political flux. The Company sought to shift the costs of this growing military establishment on to Indian regional rulers who had been frightened or humbled into alliance with them. However, the Indians were unable to pay the 'subsidies' for the protective rôle of these troops, and large revenue-bearing areas were annexed directly or indirectly by the Company (Barnett 1980; Bayly 1988: ch. iii).

In time, Indian rulers began to understand the consequences of close commercial and diplomatic relations with the Company. The Marathas and in the south the Muslim sultans of Mysore attempted to build up more compact, European-style armies with which to fight off the Company and its demands. The economic tools which they employed in this brave attempt were, as in the Ottoman lands, those of state 'monopoly' and more rigid revenue management operated by putting a vice on local élites and chieftains and trying to become direct patrons of the peasantry. Both the Mysore rulers and the Marathas put themselves into the demonology of British imperial rhetoric by trying to exclude European trade and by acting as universal monopolists. They were examples of 'oriental despotism', 'Muslim tyranny' or 'the spirit of self-sufficiency'. Their policies were virtually a provocation in themselves at a period when free-trade rhetoric was being used to disguise the Company's own relentless drive for a monopoly of force, labour and revenue in the sub-continent. By the early 1790s it had become clear that the Company could never coexist with such more vigorous Indian régimes which sought to face down European power with its own weapons, exclusion of rivals from trade and a strong mobile army. The final defeat of these new would-be Indian enlightened despots was to await the international ideological panic generated by the Napoleonic wars. Ironically, though, British collectors in parts of Mysore, annexed from Tipu in 1792, were already operating systems of revenue collection scarcely different from those of the revived sultans. Company despotism most often pushed to its conclusion the logic of the political economy of its indigenous precursors, even while it drained kingship of its ideological meaning.

COLONIALISM OR CONSTRAINED INDEPENDENCE?

If Asia and the Near East had been subject, in the course of the eighteenth century, to similar pressures, and if the states that emerged into the nineteenth century had similar features, it was still important that some became colonial provinces and some remained independent. Why was this? Obviously, the availability of European allies was an important consideration. France could make friendly noises to Haidar, Tipu and the Marathas, but its real military power in the East had been broken before 1763. The relative superiority of the British to the French navy was important here. More so was the fact that the British had, almost by chance, latched themselves on to Bengal, the most dynamic of the Mughal provinces, a century earlier. By contrast, in the Near East, the Ottoman and Egyptian régimes were always able to play off the British, French and Russians against each other. Only in the far west of the Arab lands, Algeria and Tunisia, were the new regional states at the mercy of French intervention (Valensi 1977b).

Yet this cannot be the only answer. A second order of explanation can perhaps be found in the consideration that the great 'tribal breakouts' of the eighteenth century (even ultimately the Wahhabis) were more effectively absorbed by the Ottoman state. Only Syria and eastern Mesopotamia saw the degree of disruption which took place in Iran and north India. But why was the Ottoman state better able to resist? Undoubtedly its military institutions were in a stronger position to reform and modernise than those of the Mughals and the Safavids which had only limited experience of war against Europeans. In the *devshirme* system of administrative training and homogeneous regional scribal class, the Ottomans also had a more flexible system for recreating a disciplined and loyal bureaucracy, a true slave system, rather than the partly commercialised set of diplomatic relations between great Indian and foreign notables which characterised the Mughal court. The Emperor Aurangzeb (d. 1707) had failed to create a new state system based on Islam and personal loyalty, and Tipu Sultan, who did succeed, was small beer by comparison. The Muslim and Islamised Hindu gentry of the Indian small towns bewailed the decline of Delhi, but took service under provincial rulers who had neither the means nor the inclination to spend their resources in aiding the centre; glory and wealth was no longer there (Alam 1986; Barnett 1980). By contrast, it is striking that the administrators which the Ottoman state employed to reform itself in the 1820s and 1830s were mostly drawn from the bureaucracies of the loyal regional magnates (*ayans*) or from the palace itself. Men still saw service to the sultan as the pinnacle of their careers.

Finally, the buoyancy of the money economy and trade within the Ottoman empire continued to benefit Istanbul and the heart of the Ottoman state. Its nearby Christian provinces were among the most dynamic, while its position as a great sea-trader gave Istanbul and its commercial suburb, Pera, access to a great volume of wealth. Delhi and Isfahan by contrast lay in agriculturally vulnerable terrain; economic growth was on their fringes, and the beneficiaries – Hindu merchants, local magnates or tribal leaders – were culturally much more distant from the Mughal court than the Syrian or even Greek merchant was from the Ottoman Pasha.

WARS OF 'MONOPOLY' IN SOUTHEAST ASIA

Previous sections argued that the European rise to dominance in mainland Asia and the Near East must be located in the context of a 'general crisis' of the Muslim land empires. One aspect of this crisis was the problem of control which arose on the expanding commercial 'fringes', both internal and seaboard, of these empires. In the provinces, revenue farmers, new concentrations of landed power, and merchant financiers who were not drawn from the old Muslim élites, grew in political stature. Later, tribal warriors from beyond the land boundaries of the empires took advantage of the conflicts caused by uneven growth to resume an ancient pattern of predatory invasion of the imperial heartlands. The first round of such convulsions in the early eighteenth century resulted in the emergence across the whole region of compact regional régimes more jealously guarding trade, labour and what the Europeans called 'monopolies'. The struggle to redivide the endangered, or even diminished resources of the greater Eurasian world encouraged the commercial and military offensives of the Europeans in Asia at a time when their own world-wide struggles for monopoly were coming to a climax. The narrow victory achieved by the English East India Company in these many-sided wars gave it a further, unexpected opportunity to bail out dwindling commercial profits with the profits of direct political exploitation.

From one perspective, this can be seen as a 'crisis of Asian proto-capitalism' (*cf*. Perlin 1983), in the sense that new amalgamations of commercial, scribal and military power on the fringes of the Muslim empires proved impossible for them to control. However, we must also avoid an over-simplified argument that 'trade' or 'merchants' undermined indigenous state systems. The sequence of events was more complex and ambiguous. The experience of world empires and Islamic civilisation had also spread knowledge, military techniques and the connoisseurship of power. In the case of the Sikhs or the Wahhabis, for instance, it seems almost as if a widening sense of community and identity broke through the bounds of economic relations, rather than vice versa. Their revolts were much more than simple reactions to the intrusion of new economic relationships into the Punjab or central Arabia.

Although it lies beyond the bounds of this study, recent scholarship reveals similar patterns of change in east Asia (Naquin 1987). The Japanese and Chinese empires had both tried to seal themselves off against external trade between 1600 and 1750. While some Western historians explained this as a reaction to the 'impact of the west', the role of Portuguese and Dutch influence can be greatly exaggerated (Blussé 1979). The closure of Tokugawa Japan (*c*. 1625) and of late Ching China (from 1680 to 1740) both illustrated attempts by the emperors and shoguns to control the magnates of the ports and coastal peripheries, and to assert once again their unitary and transcendent authority. It was the petty capitalism of the coastal lords or the seaboard mandarin as much as the importunacy of the Europeans which called forth this great effort at control. Because east Asian rulers had managed to discipline their own 'barbarian fringes' and deployed a sense of cultural cohesion more effective than those of south Asia, they maintained their independence for longer. The 'crisis of uneven growth' in China did not come until the mid-nineteenth century (notably during the Taiping Rebellion of the 1850s), leaving it then as vulnerable to Western ambition as south Asia had been a century earlier. Japan, like the Ottoman empire, was able to draw on a historic sense of cohesion to weather its own 'reopening'.

Maritime southeast Asia, however, was an area where European influence was to become dominant during the age of the Second British Empire. Here the theme of wars of monopoly between the last Asian régimes and European interlopers emerges once again. Yet the time scale of crisis and response was different here from that of east and south Asia. This was because the intercontinental spice trade had attracted European intervention in the region's smaller-scale and more vulnerable societies at a much earlier period.

SOUTHEAST ASIA: A FRONTIER FOR EUROPEAN AND CHINESE EXPANSION

Southeast Asia and especially the Indonesian archipelago had long been a great transit zone for trade, culture and religion. Viewed from China, once the dominant influence of the area, it was the 'Nanyang', a frontier zone in which spices and exotic products had been procured since the days of the great Ming commercial voyages (*c.* 1350–1600). Hindu Indian influences had been important from early times, while the Muslim merchants of the Tamil and Keralan coasts maintained trading contacts with Sumatra into the eighteenth century. In many respects, coastal southern India and Sri Lanka should be seen more as part of the trading and cultural world of the eastern seas than as part of the Muslim land empires which we have been discussing, and this section will adopt such a broader definition of southeast Asia. Muslim merchants from more distant southern Arabia had also ventured to this southern Indian coast and to Malacca and beyond, bringing in their wake the Islamic religion. Islam proved a powerful unifying doctrine for the kings and merchants of the Malay world and the Archipelago. It was consolidated as they fought the aggressive trading practices of the Portuguese, who had been established in the region since they took Malacca in 1511, and later the Dutch, who replaced the Portuguese by the middle of the seventeenth century.

Despite the insistent and often ruthless attempts of both these European nations to establish monopolies in the spice trade, and the consequent damage to trade and production (Reid 1975), Western dominance in the region came late and was only firmly established between 1780 and 1830. It was then that the Europeans moved from partially effective control of the seaboard to conquest of the inland kingdoms of Java, Sumatra, Sri Lanka and southern India. In the process the unities of the region were fragmented by colonial boundaries. Related cultures were now seen as separate unities: 'India' and 'Ceylon', 'Malaya' and 'Indonesia' respectively. More important even than these territorial and economic changes was the cultural blitz which accompanied them. In a society where power, magic and legitimacy were so closely intertwined, the British storming and desecration of the palace complex of Jogjakarta in central Java in 1812 symbolised a rupture in the Javanese world view which was scarcely healed until independence from the Dutch in 1949. In Ceylon in 1818, the British destruction of the capital of Kandy and ravaging of the inland kingdom amounted to the cultural annihilation of an advanced civilisation, an act unparalleled since the Spanish conquest of the Inca and Aztec empires.

Even more important for the future was the changing relationships of Europeans with the Chinese empire, whose massive growth in population had provided much of the demand which fuelled the trade of the area. The junk-borne trade from the south China ports to Batavia declined in the second half of the eighteenth century (Blussé 1986). But by 1790 the British were looking for southeast Asian entrepots for their greatly expanded trade in Indian cottons and opium. The foundation of Singapore in 1819 initiated the long-term association of the Straits Chinese merchants with the expansion of the British trading empire in the east. It also heralded the assault on the Celestial Empire of China itself which was to be the work of the next generation of imperial shock-troops. This section will describe the broad processes which tipped the balance decisively away from indigenous powers towards the Europeans in the course of the eighteenth century and which also laid the foundations of European imperial power in the region during the nineteenth century. It will also analyse the origins of the institutions and conflicts which the British inherited in Ceylon and

Malaya, and which the Dutch inherited from the short-lived British Raj in Java and Sumatra (1811–16).

In many respects the pattern of change in 'greater southeast Asia' was related to, or ran parallel to, the developments which we have traced in the Islamic land empires. The expansion of Muslim state-building in India towards the Deccan and the south put pressure on the indigenous kingdoms of coastal south India, notably Tanjore and Travancore, and also on the European trading empires of the Dutch, French and British on the southern coast. European merchants and armies were thus embroiled in the wars and politics of these coastal kingdoms as a direct result of more distant changes in the north Indian Mughal polity. Again, there were powerful and interesting resonances in southeast Asia of the tribal 'breakouts' discussed in the previous section. For instance, the interconnections of wider Eurasian trade is demonstrated by the links between the Near East and southeast Asia. In the early eighteenth century, Safavid Iran was one of the greatest markets for the sugar produced on the north Java coast by the Dutch East India Company, using Chinese bonded labour and the good offices of the Javanese nobility. The decline of Safavid Iran after the Afghan invasions of the 1710s was a major reason for the sudden collapse of this Javanese sugar economy after 1730 (Blussé 1986; 91). Its consequences were to throw the Dutch at the throats of the Chinese, and by complex and indirect steps bring them into conflict with the inland kingdom of Mataram, so paving the way for European dominance on Java.

Not only the economic but also the religious and cultural unity of this greater Asian world was important. We cannot speak of any coherent 'Islamic revival' across the whole region, but there were wide communities of ideas and doctrine. For instance, in 1804 a number of Sumatran pilgrims were residing in Mecca when the Wahhabis took and plundered that city. The pilgrims were impressed by the vigour of the Wahhabis' Islamic purism. They took its message back to the ports of the central west coast of Sumatra. Here they initiated a religious revivalist movement which was to express the hostility of peasants and tradesmen to Dutch attempts to re-establish their coffee monopoly in the early nineteenth century following defeat by the British. That fundamentalist upsurge – the Padri movement – was to face the Dutch with a threat which could only be surmounted by the direct conquest of central Sumatra (Dobbin 1983).

While the pace of colonial conquest in the region was driven by the crises and ruptures which derived from change in the wider Eurasian world, there are some historical conditions which set greater southeast Asia apart from it. In the first place, European influence had already been more powerfully established in the region than it had in the Ottoman, Safavid or Mughal empires. This coastal influence had brought about in turn a significant transformation among the states of the hinterland. For if the Ottoman or the Mughal rulers could to some degree ignore the doings of the traders on the coast, that was not possible for the kings of Kandy and Mataram whose rice and spice sales, and hence political survival, depended on access to ports where the Dutch exercised their rigid grip, a grip which had tended to depress real incomes in the region by the mid-seventeenth century.

Secondly, plantation crop production was established firmly throughout the region, notably on the north coasts of Ceylon and Java and on the south coast of Sumatra. Conflicts over the control of recalcitrant labour, battles between European and indigenous capital and, ultimately, large-scale peasant revolt played a significant part in setting the scene for direct European control. In general, this feature determined European relations with the great land empires only *after* large colonial enclaves had been established in them, in Bengal and Egypt, for instance.

In the eighteenth century, European intervention in the economics and politics of southeast Asia began to take a particularly aggressive form. The cause was the slow financial decline of the Dutch East India Company whose efforts to force down prices and to enforce rigid monopolies were redoubled as Holland was gradually eclipsed by its powerful British rival and endangered by its weak control over the Asian hinterland (Furber 1976). In part, the reasons for Holland's decline in Asia were to be found in Europe. The Dutch were undercapitalised in comparison with the English and French Companies; their armed forces were smaller and their position in European politics made their factories easy prey in times of European war. In part, the reasons must also be sought in Asia. The Dutch were heavily invested in the wrong commodities, particularly in the spice trades whose profitability was now on the decline. They found it difficult with their limited resources to break into the growth areas of world trade, above all the trades in Indian cloths, tea and later opium. Here the British in particular were able to out-buy and out-sell them. The Dutch also faced powerful competition from their own servants trading illicitly, from other European merchants and from indigenous traders who tried to pierce their monopoly system. Most important, the Dutch were perpetually in conflict with local rulers who tried to establish 'monopolies' themselves and ensure income in a less stable world. European expansion and local state-building during the eighteenth century were dominated by 'wars of monopoly'. They represented the highest stage of mercantilism in the European world, but for Asians, something more: the building of intrusive forms of state power. These themes will now be investigated in three settings: Java, southern Malaysia, and Ceylon.

THE FALL OF MATARAM AND THE RISE OF THE COMPANIES

The history of Javanese states represents a kind of dialogue between the central rice-growing core of Java and the ports of the north coast. Powerful central kingdoms had given way to trading empires on the coast, and the cycle had then reversed itself. The central kingdoms had always needed to sell their produce and buy their supplies through the port-principalities of the coast which controlled the trade as far as Malacca or the ports of south China. The polyglot merchants and entrepreneurial rulers of the north coast posed difficulties of control for the inland kings of Java.

This dialogue continued after the Dutch had established themselves at the port of Batavia in 1624, but it was envenomed by the Europeans' determination to reserve a monopoly of seaborne trade. This inevitably brought them into conflict with the rulers of the Islamised kingdom of Mataram in central Java. By the middle of the seventeenth century the kings of Mataram could only trade with the spice islands and the western Archipelago if they held Dutch permits. This reduced their income and political independence. In response, King Amangkurat I (1646–77) had forbidden the export of rice from his territories, so hoping to force all traders including the Dutch to come to Mataram. 'He also encouraged the growth of cotton in Java to reduce dependence on Batavia as the cloth mart and made all trade a state monopoly' (Tate 1971: i, 73). Of course, the dynamism of Mataram had Javanese origins. For what the Dutch regarded as monopoly was also an aspect of Javanese state-building. Themes of Hindu–Buddhist sacred kingship had been outwardly armoured with Islamic norms; the expansion of rice agriculture and development of crop tribute systems made it easier to reduce independent chiefs to the status of court officials (*bupatis*). Yet the challenge of Dutch monopoly gave a new urgency to the drive towards sultanate.

Over the next century, coexistence between Javanese rulers and the Europeans in Batavia was undermined by the growth of commerce and the expansion of capitalist agriculture on the north coast. In the 1670s the Dutch intervened to help the Mataram ruler to suppress rebellion in the northern provinces brought about by his heavy taxation. Then, between 1730 and 1752, a series of civil wars engulfed Mataram. At each settlement, the Dutch annexed valuable tracts on the coast in return for military aid. In the 1740s the relationship between the conflicts arising from the development of commercial agriculture on the coast and turbulence in the interior were particularly clear (Nachtegaal 1986: 75–6). Severe Dutch management of sugar traders and labourers caused the Chinese of Batavia and the hinterland to revolt. This took place against the background of a depression in the sugar trade. The Dutch were wrong-footed. A rebellion of nobles and common people against Dutch demands for labour services and produce taxes gathered pace. The rebellion spread to the interior. In 1742 a combination of Chinese and Javanese rebels succeeded in expelling the Sultan of Mataram from his palace. The aristocracy of the northern coast now begged the Dutch Company for help and sought to become its vassals. But this action 'set in motion the tangled chain of events which led to the final disintegration and partitioning of Mataram ten years later' in 1752 (Tate 1971: ii, 79). The efforts of both indigenous rulers and the Dutch to contain the explosive growth of commercial agriculture thus provided the trigger and rationale for colonial intervention.

The successor states to Mataram in central Java provided sufficient political stability for a period of agricultural growth in the second half of the century. But relations with the Dutch coast remained tense. The rice tribute paid by the successor states to feed the Dutch in Batavia after 1742 was diverted into the pockets of Company officials. The subdivision and partitioning of labour and produce tributes was accompanied by an inflow of Chinese and other entrepreneurs. Effectively, inland Java had become an economic dependency of the European north coast. It only remained for the pressures of world war and a new, more aggressive generation of Dutch and, later, British officials in Batavia to dispense with the fiction that Javanese kingdoms were independent. First, Marshall Herman Daendels, Governor for the Batavian Republic (Napoleon's client state in the Netherlands) between 1807 and 1811, and then Stamford Raffles, representing British power, were to carry through in political terms the logic of the economic penetration which had already occurred.

PORT KINGS AND MERCHANTS: MALAYSIA AND SOUTH INDIA

Conflicts between 'new' Asian states and declining European companies (which were nevertheless supported with powerful military resources) provided one context for imperial expansion. In this respect, wars of expansion in Java had much in common with Dutch and British attempts to break the pepper monopoly set up by the kings of mid-eighteenth-century Travancore in south India. Even the battle between Tipu Sultan of Mysore and the English East India Company in the years 1783–99 was intensified by the struggles of these powerful rulers to regulate internal trade and create external outlets as the British tightened their stranglehold on the coast.

The attempts of both European and Asian powers to control labour, commercial communities and entrepreneurs created a second set of conflicts which encouraged colonial intervention or weakened indigenous states. For instance, British officials deplored the fierce reaction of the Hindu Nayar warriors of Kanara against the Muslim Mopilla merchants after Muslim Mysore had evacuated the area in 1793. Protection of this 'useful merchant community', still intermediaries in the spice trades, was one reason why the British formally annexed it in the following year.

Malaysia and Sumatra yield other examples of the importance of the fate of merchant communities in the politics of European expansion. Kedah in north-western Malaysia and the Johore–Riau empire of its southern tip were both exposed to long conflicts with the 'privateering' trading corporation of the Bugis (Curtin 1984). This powerful commercial community, once based on the southern Celebes, had been greatly restricted in its carrying trade by Dutch monopoly. Bugi maritime princes sought therefore to find new areas for trade, conquest and loot in the Malaysian peninsular. Wars with the Bugis led the rulers of Kedah to seek the aid of the English East India Company and ultimately to cede to it the island of Penang (1786). This became the base of British operations throughout the eastern seas. Bugi commercial and military pressure on the peninsular empire of Riau–Johore also created a power vacuum which was ultimately filled by the British with the foundation of Singapore in 1819. These examples serve to remind us that the tensions between land-based exporting kingdoms and seaborne 'middleman powers' were endemic to Asia and not simply by-products of European intervention.

MONOPOLY AND STATE-BUILDING IN CEYLON

All the most important features which characterised the European rise to dominance in this 'greater southeast Asia' were represented in the island of Ceylon. The Dutch had expelled the Portuguese power from Ceylon at the beginning of the seventeenth century and at this time they had fostered good relations with the inland Buddhist kingdom of Kandy. On the north coast, the Dutch had maintained the Portuguese system, making use of the large Eurasian Christian community, but forcing their outward conformity to the Dutch Reformed Church. They also maintained and developed the Portuguese monopoly over the island's valuable cinnamon crop, while seeking to enforce an even more rigid monopoly over items such as areca nut, elephants and over the pearl fisheries of the north coast. Tamil middlemen and village headmen with connections in south India acted as agents for Dutch power in the north of the country where they had been more firmly established following a series of treaties made with the Kandyans.

The accommodation between Dutch power and the inland kingdom was, however, gradually eroded in the course of the eighteenth century. This paved the way for Dutch and eventually British occupation of the whole island by 1818. The Dutch, again, were under financial pressure as their monopoly succumbed to the inroads of the British in south India. They were also weakened by the clandestine trade of Asian merchants and by the peculation of their own officials. The response of Amsterdam and Batavia to falling profits was to try to tighten the monopoly, drive down prices and engross new areas of trade and produce. This brought them into direct collision with the Kandyan kings and nobility. For the Ceylonese magnates wished to set high prices for their rice and tropical produce and also to expand their internal and overseas trade. Attempts by the Dutch to maintain their monopoly by closing the island's ports resulted in disaffection in the 1680s and 1690s and open rebellion in 1734. Covert support given by the court to such rebels embittered relations with the Dutch in Colombo (Pieris 1918: 57), but also encouraged the Dutch to develop their own teritorial empire in the coastal plain and the north.

Another development which set the Dutch against the Kandyans were periodic revolts and strikes by the caste of cinnamon peelers or Chalias. The chalias worked the Company's own estates and were also sent into the Kandyan heartlands to procure the Company's pepper supplies there. Fierce resistance to poor prices and conditions culminated in desertions by Chalias and other servants who fled to the hills where, to Dutch fury, they often secured the protection of the Kandyan court (Pieris 1918: 59).

Tension such as this came to a head during the rule of Governor Shreuder in the late 1750s. The Sinhalese regarded the Dutch as no more than 'powerful merchants [who had] been appointed to protect the island and to continue to perform the duties of messengers to the kings of Lanka'. The desperate Dutch sought a way to end the constant disputes over trade and labour and avoid the minor insurrections which they blamed on the kings of Kandy. In 1758 a major revolt broke out in the northern provinces which coincided with a strike by the Chalias. Dutch schools and rest-houses were destroyed and their trade interrupted. This outbreak was soon followed by a revolt against the ruling dynasty in Kandy which the Dutch certainly welcomed even if they did not inspire. The subsequent invasions and counter-invasions culminated in the sack and desecration of Kandy and the destruction of much of the annual crop of the kingdom. The Dutch were unable to secure a complete military victory but both sides were driven to a truce by exhaustion. In 1766 the Company was acknowledged sovereign of the northern parts of the island, while the king ceded to the Company the whole of the seaboard lands to the distance of four miles inland and the right to pick cinnamon in his territories (Pieris 1918: 113– 18).

Though it was hemmed in by Dutch power, the Kandyan kingdom in the final decades of the eighteenth century entered a period of consolidation not unlike that enjoyed by the Mataram successor states or Travancore. A Tamil Hindu dynasty, which had succeeded the extinct Sinhala line in 1737, sought to strengthen its links with the local nobility by reorganising the Buddhist Sangha (monastic organisation) and patronising Buddhist institutions (Dewaraja 1972: 119–49). The Buddhist revival spread to the coast and ensured that, for much of the population, their Dutch (and later British) masters could never achieve an easy legitimacy. The fierce resistance of Sinhala peasants to European intervention and the monopoly system was strengthened by their devotion to the Kandyan throne and Buddhist hierarchy. Periodic disputes over trade and the general depression of the northern coast encouraged the kings to look to the British in south India for political and military support when the two European nations were at war in the years 1780–3 and again after 1793.

While contemporaries tended to use the term 'monopoly', and 'mercantilism' may seem a useful concept to describe the trade policies of Asian rulers, they are more properly regarded as acts of state-building. Trade 'monopoly', like religious patronage, was an act of incorporation by rulers of their subjects. It was balanced by redistribution of honour and resources to tie nobility and peasant to the ruling institution. Such policies were responses not only to European intervention but to the changes in political and moral relations which proceeded from the development of Asian commerce. Commercial growth threatened to undermine the dependence of regional chiefs on their suzerains. It brought in restless foreign traders, Chinese, Tamils or Bugis. The conflicts between merchant people, royal officials and regional chiefs also threatened the power and honour of rulers. Their response was to create what Europeans saw as 'monopolies', but what were in fact much greater enhancements of both tribute-taking and gifting by Asian sovereigns. The creation of European monopolies was therefore matched by acts of Asian state-building. The struggle to redivide the resources amassed during the previous two centuries became more bitter. These acts of royal incorporation also had long-term consequences in the realms of culture and social life. The closer identification of king with sacred territory and of power with regional economy in the eighteenth century was, again, an important condition for the emergence of national consciousness in the nineteenth and the twentieth. The high court culture (*priyayi*) of later Mataram and its successors, the Buddhist revival in Ceylon, as much as the state sufism of Awadh or the Qajars, helped forge stronger regional identities. Colonial powers were to further refine these identities in their attempts to control newly conquered territories and, in time, ethnic spokesmen and nationalists were also to build on them.

As world war between 1793 and 1815 incited the British to 'purge the Orient of all their European rivals' (Minto 1834), they too became an active force in the wars of monopoly and labour in the eastern seas. Raffles in Java and Sumatra and the early Crown governors in Ceylon (from 1796) inherited the tensions between the seaboard commercial people and the inland kings and peasants. They also inherited the problem of securing a stable labour force to produce the valuable exports which alone could make their new territories pay. Contrary to the growing advocacy of free trade and free markets, the British rulers found themselves perpetuating monopolies, deploying forced labour and using all the tools which had been forged by the 'rapacious Dutch' and their opponents among 'oriental tyrants'. Early British rule in greater southeast Asia developed an absolutist temper, striking even by comparison with that of the triumphant East India Company to the north. This absolutist temper, however, was powerfully reinforced by the new ideological winds blowing from the 'British Empire in Europe' and the Western hemisphere, as later chapters will show.

'PROTO-CAPITALISM' IN ASIA AND EUROPEAN IMPERIALISM

Theories of imperialism have been the preserve of historians of the later nineteenth century which was, ironically, a period when imperial expansion was all over bar the shouting. The more limited debate about imperialism in the eighteenth century has centred on precipitating factors: notably the build-up of British and French troops in Asia as a consequence of European war (Marshall 1975b). This can help explain how the West was able to overwhelm indigenous states in some parts of Asia. Again, there has been an inconclusive debate about whether European private trade or the military and financial imperatives of the East India Companies themselves led to annexation and conquest (Marshall 1975b; Nightingale 1970; *cf.* Furber 1976).

But an adequate theory of imperialism, and one which is able to explain the *timing* of European expansion as also its form and limitations, would need to take into account social and political change in Asia, the Near East and Africa. This second chapter has tried to put the issue into such a wider context. The so-called decline of Asian states was itself the consequence of general economic change. Commercial growth throughout the Islamic empires had rendered old methods of imperial control obsolescent. In some areas where merchants and gentry had gained tight control over production and labour, the new developments might be called 'proto-capitalism'; its overt political consequence was the growing power of provincial élites.

The consolidation of Asian capitalism intensified political crisis as comparable changes had done in seventeenth-century Europe. Of course, there may have been internal economic constraints on the smooth development of Asian economies resulting, for instance, from inadequate transport, population instability and ecology. More evident, however, were the political constraints on such growth. Wealth in the peripheries tended to attract the attention of emperors and of imperial viceroys seeking to enhance imperial revenues. Wealth at the centre tended to attract the attention of forces on the periphery such as nomads and irregular soldiers. Uneven economic success within the loose structure of these Islamic polities fostered warfare which interrupted the pattern of growth itself. The conflicts which followed were also filled out and given meaning by ideological and ethnic differences which had been preserved, or even enhanced by the political style of the empires. As instability increased, commercial activity and revenues were endangered. This led both Asian regional rulers and the proxies of European states to guard their resources more jealously. The consequent militarisation of commerce and production gave the Europeans great advantages where they could deploy naval and military forces against the smaller regional states of this new, eighteenth-century order. The English East India Company, above all, had established a naval hegemony in the eastern seas before 1770. It was also able to manipulate the commercial and administrative skills which it had developed following the somewhat fortuitous conquest of Bengal. The Company became an Asian merchant, an Asian ruler and an Asian revenue-farmer. In this sense, the commercialisation of political power within Islamic empires and the eastern seas, as much as the ruthless drive of European capitalism, was a critical precondition for European world-empire.

CHAPTER THREE

War, Empire and the Colonies of Settlement to 1790

This book began with an analysis of social and political changes in Asia and north Africa in the period which immediately preceded the great expansion of British power during the Revolutionary and Napoleonic Wars. The purpose was not to present an account of European expansion driven only by events outside Europe (an 'excentric' theory of imperialism; Robinson 1972) or to describe a discrete set of 'local crises' leading to imperial takeover. Such attempts in isolation were doomed to failure because metropolitan impulses were, by definition, central to the process of expansion and to the creation of the social order of European empires. Rather, the purpose was to show that longer-term patterns of class formation and state-building in Asia and northern Africa were also central to the emergence and form of those empires.

The creation of colonies was never simply a question of domination. It involved a long process of political dialogue, of challenge and response, and of accommodation. An analysis which begins and ends with 'the metropolis' risks begging the question of the origins of historical change and of ignoring the contingent and contestatory. Such an approach would also tend to relegate much of world history, its greatest centres of trade, population and production to the margins of historical causation too early (Washbrook 1988). The preceding chapters have shown that conflicts and aspirations outside Europe set the context and sometimes provided the occasion for the emergence of European territorial empires. European mercantilist pressure in Asia and the eastern seas was matched by attempts of the rulers of Asia and the Middle East to hoard and enhance royal rights; Asian entrepreneurs in revenue and commerce helped to erode earlier polities and create the pressure for tighter methods of control of labour, capital and resources. Here the short-term interests of some Asian élites ran parallel to those of Europeans; they could be accommodated as important agents and junior partners within the framework of European colonies.

This chapter turns to a brief discussion of the 'plantation colonies' of the British empire; in particular it considers the Caribbean and those parts of North America which remained British after American independence in 1783. It puts these colonies of settlement into the context of what contemporaries were increasingly inclined to call 'the British Empire in Europe'; that is, a compact of British élites which crossed the Anglo-Celtic border and overrode the provincial interests and regional patriotisms of England, Scotland and Ireland. The final section draws together the British, colonial and Asian issues in a discussion of the British imperial crisis that accompanied the American War of Independence, and its results.

The eighteenth-century British empire was a ragged and conflict-ridden community of separate interests: English-speaking creoles – people born in the colonies but retaining English culture; virtually self-governing colonies of settlement; antique trading corporations, colonial land speculators and peasant farmers. Some of these colonies and plantations had been created before or during the economic slowdown and political conflicts of the seventeenth-century 'General Crisis in Europe'. Loose control from the centre during that period had encouraged the development of an expansive settler capitalism, secure in its own particularist attitudes and local patriotisms. These were expressed through separatist churches and recalcitrant colonial assemblies. The relations between these farmers or tradesmen and colonial governors were always tense. Creoles railed at the jobbery of the royal governors, at the taxation and restrictions on trade which they imposed; the authorities tried in vain to stop colonists expanding the frontiers of settlement or destroying royal resources of wood. Even on a tiny colony such as St Helena, the great conflicts of the Americas were mirrored in miniature as governors sought to halt the deforestation and land-grabbing indulged in by settlers (Grove 1988).

As Europe and its colonial dependencies entered another period of rapid growth at the beginning of the eighteenth century, these centrifugal forces intensified again. The runaway expansion of the North American population (perhaps 2.5 million by 1760) and of the Caribbean sugar economy made the settler communities yet more independent. From this perspective, the emergence of the

United States of America, politically separate from Great Britain, yet a major trading partner for her, seems typical of the direction of the empire for much of the eighteenth century, not the result of a violent and abhorrent partition of a centralised imperial state.

Yet the British empire was not to go in the direction of the Portuguese empire before it and become no more than an international commercial culture, largely devoid of political cohesion. For even before 1793 the strident and divergent interests of different groups of settlers and merchants could occasionally be beaten into line. The Elder Pitt and his ministry achieved this temporarily during the Seven Years' War (1756–63). Yet the acquiescence of the creoles depended on three basic conditions, and these were much the same whether the location was Ireland, Jamaica or the St Lawrence valley. From time to time the creoles needed British arms to repel the commercial and military threats of their French, Dutch or Portuguese enemies. Secondly, and more important, their fear of risings by the indigenous peasantry, tribesmen or slave populations gave rise to short-lived bursts of imperial loyalty; these were fired by the need to secure immediate military or naval assistance. Finally, the colonial leadership needed to maintain its representation in London in order to preserve or create special commercial relationships which were built into the system of preferential tariffs and shipping regulations known as the Navigation Acts. These underlying conditions, then, determined whether colonial élites opted in or out of the imperial enterprise.

As this chapter will show, in the case of Scotland the crisis in imperial relations had come early, between 1690 and 1745. But for Ireland and much of the rest of the western empire, centrifugal forces remained predominant until almost the end of the century. Though the defeat of 1783 brought change, it was not so much the fact of American independence, as the later spectre of an international threat to property from the levelling French without, and slave and peasant revolt within, which galvanised the imperial state into activity in both east and west.

THE 'BRITISH EMPIRE IN EUROPE'

From the 1690s, but notably after 1730, the economic unification of the British Isles had gathered pace. Yet even the moral and political unity of the 'British Empire in Europe' proceeded by uneven and ambiguous steps. The process came about relatively smoothly in England and Scotland. Here rapid economic growth was reinforced by the assimilationist ideal of 'agrarian improvement' which was also seen as a national moral crusade.

Between 1680 and 1780, England, whose population expanded rapidly from about 4.5 million to 8 million, developed a sophisticated marketing structure, while 'regionalism and provincialism in the home market were breaking down' (Thirsk 1984: 489). There was a great advance in the numbers and range of middlemen factors who were able to link supply and demand across a countryside now unified by better roads and canals and by a considerable growth of coastal shipping. Not only specialist items like Cheshire cheese but bulk goods such as corn and coal from Newcastle were finding their way on to the London market, itself greatly enlarged by population growth and an increase in wealth generated by the expansion of foreign trade. Newer centres of trade such as Bristol and Liverpool on the Atlantic coasts gave vitality to their hinterlands. Even if this was not yet an industrialised society as late as 1800, and even if production was still dispersed, 'the supply of raw-materials and the control of marketing were frequently concentrated in the hands of a few large manufacturers, effectively employing large sectors of the work force' (Innes 1987: 178). English people came to consider themselves denizens of a consumer society, and a national taste which extended beyond items of clothing and food to luxuries such as tea and coffee and services such as commercial horse-racing, theatre and concerts, came into being. As early as 1780, agriculture accounted for only 30 per cent of national income; the rest was made up of private wealth, trading balances and industrial capital held by 'middling people' (Langford 1976: 390).

This society was not 'stable'. On the contrary, old liberties and rights in land, old monopolies of profession and popular assumptions about the regulation of markets and debt were overridden as local élites of JPs and petty gentry lost power to an increasingly unified national élite operating through the management of Parliament. Severe social conflicts, riots over food and land rights and the control of markets became more intense. The 1720s and 1730s were particularly bad decades which started with the precipitate collapse of credit following the crisis of the speculative South Sea Bubble and proceeded through plague and disease to poor harvests. The 1760s, again, saw severe food riots and uprisings by declining artisans whose customary protected markets and trade practices were threatened. The 1770s and 1780s saw widespread extra-parliamentary agitations, and the century's disturbances culminated in the Gordon Riots of 1780 in which anti-establishment sentiment took the form of savage religious chauvinism. At all points, politically impotent Tories, religious dissenters and the victims of capricious taxation railed against the 'old corruption' of the Whig oligarchy in the language of 'country virtue', much as did their contemporaries in the colonies.

However, control of Parliament and the ability of older institutions and professions to assimilate some of the newcomers helped English society at least to escape the fierce inter-provincial disputes which plagued other European countries and had indeed riven England itself in the preceding century. Among the great families of the land there appears to have been a considerable durability in fortunes in land. Durability need not imply stagnation. Newcomers arrived and were absorbed: monied men from the city, directors of the East India Company and West Indian planters. But they were not in large enough numbers to swamp the existing social and political establishment. Old and new élites resorted once again to the great universities and public schools. The professions began grudgingly to reform and broaden themselves in line with the growth of the commercial economy. If the élite landowning families withdrew from local powerholding as JPs and magistrates, this left the way open for a more numerous and prosperous clergy to take their place. The old alliance between clergy and landowner was reconfirmed in a pattern of prosperity and accommodation. Most landowners and élite families benefited from the changes which accompanied the development of the economy, notably the rise in land values after 1750 and the great growth of the market in property. Some magnates benefited directly from their own production: those for instance, who fed the London markets, or landowners on the River Tyne whose estates sat on large reserves of coal. At all events, no severe conflicts occurred between landowners and bourgeoisie. Instead, 'By the time of the Seven Years' War in the 1750s . . . there was a clear vision of the national interest which overrode the older antagonisms between the landed and monied interest' (Stone and Stone 1984: 284) and, it should be added, between the English regions.

That interest was partly bound up with the stability and security of overseas trade and landholding in the Caribbean. Many English gentry and London merchant families who had made their money in European and Atlantic trade invested in

Jamaican plantations or the stock of the East India Company. The Elder Pitt declared he considered 'the sugar islands as the landed interest of this kingdom, and it was barbarism to consider them otherwise' (Richardson 1968: 43). Later the Scots, Irish and Dutch came to invest directly and indirectly in the colonial and Indian trades. The stability of these two great overseas operations was closely tied to that of the Bank of England and the emerging London finance market. The collapse of the South Sea Company in 1720 had been much more than a commercial crisis; it had riven the state and threatened the prosperity of large numbers of landed and commercial families in the south of England (including that of Edward Gibbon, the historian) which were central to the future of the Protestant Constitution. For this reason, ministers were always prepared, though with groaning reluctance, to go to the rescue of the Caribbean planters and the East India Company, protecting the trade of the former and guaranteeing the annual dividend of the latter by deploying of Crown naval and military forces. There was no irresistible pressure for colonial expansion on the part of eighteenth-century governments, more an awareness of the imminence of minor but costly colonial wars.

It is possible to exaggerate the importance of colonial trade and expansion to what Marx called this 'moneyocracy' of landed and commercial families. For the vision of national interest was more particularly expressed in the drive for agrarian improvement. Practical reflections of this were seen in the building and repair by landowners of roads, canals and rivers, in the creation of turnpike trusts, in the passion for enclosure and in the improvement of crop and herd species. But 'agrarianism' was more than this. It became an icon for national integration and for patriotism, which could bring together great landowners, yeoman farmers and professional people in a moral community which extended well beyond the confines of the limited politics of the unreformed Parliament and the occasional play of local elections. Even if the Church was not corrupt or decaying during this period, it was certainly laicised and passive. Agrarian improvement, by contrast, was the dominant faith of the élite much as evangelicalism was to be after 1780. From the 1730s onwards, agricultural societies and agricultural fairs spread through much of the country, their networks of corresponding members restraining the fractious tendencies of parliament faction and local connection. Agrarian improvement was a moral crusade, the inner heart of English expansion; indeed, it was seen as the domestic precondition of overseas enterprise. The Brecknockshire

Agricultural Society in provincial Wales declared its aim in 1753 of making Great Britain 'as flourishing as China', combating 'idle and expensive diversions' and 'exciting the lost spirit of industry among . . . the lower classes of our fellow creatures' (Hudson 1973: 17). Agrarianism was to become the dominant discourse of the Second British Empire, with the fostering of foreign trade as a dependent second.

INVERTED PATRIOTISM: THE CASE OF SCOTLAND

Wales, the first English colony, had been shackled to London since the Act of Union of 1536. In the eighteenth century its thoughtlessly Anglocentric and Protestant élite filtered through Oxford into London society (Jones 1984: 46–50), while English tradesmen and factors fanned out across the valleys. The incorporation of Scotland and Ireland into this 'British Empire in Europe' proceeded along similar paths. However, it was much more violent and contentious, driven by fear of revolt from below as much as by the desire for profit and status. The timing was also different. The Scottish élite had already thrown in its lot with London in 1707; the revolts of 1715 and 1745 confirmed their assimilation. The Irish Protestants were to haver until the end of the century when they were blown into legislative Union with Great Britain by Catholic peasant revolt. Thus the consolidation of an imperial state both inside and outside Europe depended on these three conditions: the distribution of benefits from economic integration; the intensity of revolt 'from below'; and the imminence of an external threat.

An important precondition for assimilation was economic integration. Population grew rapidly in both Scotland and Ireland in the eighteenth century. Irish population expanded from about 2.5 million to 4.4 million between 1753 and 1791. This brought about a considerable increase in production, some of which was directed to the English market, but it also increased demand for the more sophisticated manufactures of the new English cities. The import of Irish wool and linen into England greatly increased, while a large percentage of Scottish beef production was also directed to the south. The imperial triangle was completed by extensive imports and exports of both Scottish and Irish produce to the British West Indies and North America. After 1720, colonial demand increased in both the British and French West Indies, and by the 1760s and

1770s two-thirds to three-quarters of all the beef exported from Ireland went to the English colonies and to France for re-export to its own colonies. After 1770, when colonial demand for Irish beef and butter declined, 'the British market hungrily absorbed the surplus', as Irish agricultural produce which had been excluded since 1688 was once again admitted to the country. Indeed, by 1800 over 85 per cent of all Irish exports went to Britain, as compared with only 46 per cent 100 years earlier. This integration of the produce markets of the three kingdoms was paralleled on the financial side. Large numbers of Irish merchants settled in London, many of whom were connected with the West Indian and American trades; a few such as Lawrence Sullivan became active in the East India Company (Cullen 1977: 165). By 1790 some two-thirds of the Irish debt was held in English hands.

A similar change was gathering pace in Scotland, though the kingdom did manage to retain much more of its economic independence. After the Act of Union of 1707, many of the Scottish east coast ports and their merchant communities declined. They were damaged by competition from the English who developed new links with Scotland's former trading partners in northern Europe and the Baltic, though some few Scots did manage to break into the much smaller East India trade. By contrast, the ports of the west coast, notably Glasgow, developed hectically as import and export houses for the North American and West Indian sugar and tobacco or for the booming slave trade. Much of Glasgow's wealth by 1770 was tied up in slaves, sugar and tobacco. The crisis of the American War of Independence damaged this trade and ruined many of the 'Virginians' (including the father of Sir Thomas Munro, later governor of Madras). In 1771, 60 per cent of Scotland's imports had come from America and the West Indies, 13 per cent from Ireland. Yet in 1800, 36 per cent of Scottish imports still came from the United States and the Caribbean and 20 per cent from Ireland (Hamilton 1963: 265).

What were the social and political conditions for Scottish and Irish assimilation? Paradoxically, the Union of Scotland and England was an assertion of patriotism by assimilation (Phillipson 1974). Scottish patriotism and antipathy to England had evolved out of Presbyterian Protestantism and a long history of dynastic conflict. But at the end of the seventeenth century the force of Scottish pride had been driven towards assimilation with England by an overwhelming feeling of Scottish decline. Calvinist patriotism was transformed into an ideology of commercial success and agrarian improvement. For it had already become clear that there was little future for Scotland without economic improvement, and the facts of geography dictated that this could only come about by gaining access to new export markets. There was no alternative to participation in the now buoyant markets of England and its colonial partners in North America and the Caribbean. Much of the Scottish aristocracy and its professional hangers-on had promptly decamped to London where they became involved in the politics of the Whig oligarchy, offering a solid block of forty five MPs to the ministries of the time in return for the pickings and patronage which the expanded machinery of government could now deliver to them.

The political satisfaction of the Scottish oligarchy and a relative increase in wealth in line with the development of the English economy went quite a long way to ensure that fierce nationalism and resentment against distant government in London could be held within reasonable limits. At the end of the century, Henry Dundas, the archetypical Scottish political fixer in London, could recommend the effects of the Union to doubting Irish havering on the same decision. Scottish shipping, he said, had increased from 8,618 tons in 1692 to 162,274 tons in 1792 with an even greater increase in proportional value; Scottish linen production had increased over the same period from 1 to 23 million yards. More important than this, Scottish MPs rather than 'confining their deliberations to the affairs of Scotland . . . were empowered to take part in discussions reflecting not only the affairs of England but of the whole British Empire' (Dundas 1799: 12). Otherwise the Scots Parliament might have remained what the Irish Parliament indubitably was: little more than 'a Great Vestry or Parish meeting'. While Lord Belhaven at the time of Union had foreseen a future for the people of Scotland drinking water, not whisky and eating 'saltless porridge . . . The increase of excise in Scotland since the Time of the Union is certainly no proof that this part of the prophecy has been fulfilled.'

Socially as well as politically, the Scottish élite was quite successfully assimilated into English life. Some magnates such as the Dukes of Buccleugh built up large estates in England at a time when land values and rents were rising fast (Cannadine forthcoming). Smaller families such as the Edmonstones and the Elliots of the borders were active petty land speculators in Ulster, the West Indies and other British colonies: many Scottish lasses married English heirs so that 'the pretty daughters of our landed gentlemen . . . bear at the present moment, a high premium in the hymeneal market of the English aristocracy' (Dundas 1799: 25). An increasing number of Scottish lawyers and other professional people, products of the remarkable vitality of the Scottish universities, began to come to London in the course of the eighteenth century. There were two Scots among the small numbers of the English Bench by 1790 and a much larger number of barristers. The critical moment here was when Lord Bute, the Scottish peer, was in his ascendant during the early years of George III (Lenman, 1981: 37). Both Dundas and another Scottish legal expert Alexander Wedderburn received Bute's patronage. These men were later to bring a large number of their own connections into politics, the law and government service in London. As we shall see, the large representation of Scots in the Indian and other colonial services derived from Dundas's inexhaustible wells of patronage. One mechanism for the assimilation of Scotland into the 'British Empire in Europe' is therefore quite clear. Scots peers were absorbed into the British political system to give bottom and placement to the English ministries. Because Parliament was critical to these ministries as a source of taxation in wars, and since the collection of taxes itself generated offices and patronage, Scots were rewarded with jobs and office. Those Scots themselves generated more jobs and offices which they passed on to friends and relatives. The Scottish élite was materially, if not morally, assimilated with surprising ease. At the same time, the archaic cohesion and ruthlessness of Scottish family relationships helped pin together more firmly the structure of the British state.

The absorption of the baronage and their lawyers in London politics and the success of linen exports was not enough, however. More important was that the smaller gentry and professional people left in Edinburgh and Glasgow did not become an 'out-faction', festering into resentment in their provincial fastness. Critical here was the cultural and intellectual flowering of the Scottish universities and of the learned life of Edinburgh in what had been called the Scottish Enlightenment. Indeed, Phillipson has argued that this enlightenment provided a social and political function in that it enabled the Scottish provincial nobility and gentry who could not afford to go to London to retain their political position in Scotland and, to some extent, in relation to England too. Societies such as the Select Society which numbered among its members Hume, Smith, Ferguson and Robertson elaborated a secular deterministic philosophy which enabled Scotland to retain its position as a 'Republic of letters' while at the same time it contributed to the thriving, capitalist society of North Britain (Phillipson 1974).

One critical, and perhaps understated, aspect of the intellectual inventions of the Scottish enlightenment was the emergence of a Scottish version of agrarian patriotism, different in mentality but complementary to the English variety which had been expressed through the various agricultural societies. Paradoxically, the voracious demand by absentee Scottish landlords in London for cash forced their estate managers in north Britain to improve their estates (Campbell 1977: 214–30). But the philosophical underpinnings of improvement were expressed in that same vocabulary of international classicism and classical learning which made Scottish architects such favourites on the English scene. Here an important figure was Henry Home, Lord Kames, legal luminary and philosopher. Kames's work *The Gentleman Farmer* argued from classical and modern precepts that farming and agricultural improvement was the 'natural' condition of a gentleman which allowed the exercise of benevolence, brought him face to face with nature and religion and avoided the tension and corruption of character associated with commerce and most notably exemplified by the 'ardour of the Indian Nabob'. Society needed to improve the art of agriculture 'to which Britain is fundamentally indebted for the figure it makes all the world over' (Kames 1776: v, 25). Elaborate scientific and physiocratic ideas led on to more practical concerns. Kames believed that the best order of society was that of a prosperous yeoman farmer class, competing vigorously on a free land market. He opposed the entail of Scottish estates and stated that 'the distribution of land into many shares accords charmingly with the free spirit of the British constitution: but nothing is more repugnant to that spirit, than overgrown estates in land' (Kames 1774: ii, 488). Kames's philosophy, which was later translated into imperial policy by Scottish colonialists such as Elphinstone and Munro, emphasised the yeoman rather than the large landlord but allowed common action with English agrarianists through societies such as the Highland Society and later the Board of Agriculture. The Royal Charter of the Highland Society in 1787 pledged to 'cultivate correspondence and mutual good offices of other societies of England and Ireland, founded on similar principles' (Hudson 1973: 15–16).

All this might have been seriously jeopardised, as it was in Ireland, if the tensions arising from commercialisation, the development of a land market and the first stages of industrial capitalism had put intolerable pressures on the peasantry and urban workers. There were, indeed, numbers of riots and strikes associated with periods of depression in the Lowlands and depopulation of the Highlands.

However, sufficient extra prosperity was generated by the growth of the linen and colonial trades to absorb such discontent, while emigration to North America and England, or virtual emigration into the British armies which fought the Seven Years' War and American Wars, proved a safety valve rather earlier than it did in central or southern Ireland. Moreover, if there was a general popular reaction to the development of the commercial economy, that had come in 1714 and 1745 from the Highlands. The division between the Protestant Lowlands and the Gaelic Catholic Highlands was so sharp that the Scottish élites regarded this as an insupportable threat to their position. No society of United Scotsmen was to emerge comparable to the United Irishmen which embraced both the discontented Protestant squire and the mutinous Catholic peasant. After 1745 the destruction of the Highland communal tenures by enclosure and the attempt to evangelise the north in the name of Protestantism was an enterprise in which a dominant Scottish élite cooperated with London. The Scottish Society for the Propagation of Christian Knowledge had been active since 1709. By 1732 it had schools in 109 parishes and spinning academies for young ladies. Its early hatred of the 'Irish' language and Gaelic culture had helped batter down Highlands particularism (Pryde 1962: 105). In Ireland the Protestant landowning élite was smaller and the Gaelic peasant culture vast and resistant. The Irish economy was already stunted in its potential for growth by the English connection and the prospects for imperial assimilation were much less rosy.

ABORTED INTEGRATION: IRELAND IN THE EIGHTEENTH CENTURY

Scotland in the new age of empire after 1783 was to see an even closer assimilation of élites into the British European and colonial empires and the emergence of a Scottish romantic patriotism which reinforced rather than undermined British nationalism. Though the economic wealth and potential of Ireland was probably greater than that of Scotland in 1700, Ireland's role in the empire was to be one of relative subordination and impoverishment. There was indeed a strong movement among the élites for incorporation in Britain after 1798 and Irish peasant farmers, both Catholic and Protestant, were to play an important part in British imperial armies – a tendency greatly downplayed in conventional nationalist historiography. Yet this was not sufficient to counterbalance a powerful Catholic nationalism which was presaged in the 1780s and 1790s and was firmly grounded by the 1830s.

The first reason for Ireland's different path was that its experience of economic integration with the British economy was so much more difficult. After 1688 the products of Ireland's large and once healthy dairy and pastoral industry had been excluded from the English market to protect England's farmers. Scottish graziers and drovers, by contrast, gained access to the English market after 1701. Ireland was forced to rely more heavily on exports to the West Indies, North America and the French colonies, markets which were constantly interrupted by war in the course of the eighteenth century. Ireland was also excluded from Britain's lucrative East India trade except via English intermediaries (Cullen and Smout 1977: Introduction).

Yet the agrarian violence, which was to erupt with increasing frequency in Ireland after mid-century and which governed the attitude of Ireland's ruling groups to the British empire, had deeper causes than this. Ireland was pre-eminently an example of distorted agricultural growth. Population expanded rapidly after 1730 as plague and other diseases abated; Irish peasants benefited from better nutrition, and fertility seems to have increased very greatly. The rapid increase in the home market, the rapid urbanisation of Dublin, and re-entry into the English market after mid-century speeded up the process of commercialisation and development of the land market, setting off severe agrarian conflict (Clark and Donnelly 1983: Introduction). Old joint and communal tenures, in particular grazing rights,were under attack as commercial landlords and yeoman farmers attempted to gain control of more land on freehold tenures. A man without land remained a 'boy', a farmer's lad, often unable to marry (Knot 1984: 99). So those excluded from ownership joined a volatile generational culture bent on attacking new landlords, or incoming tenants where eviction had occurred, in order to protect their own future rights. The 'Whiteboy' movement of the 1760s, for instance, aimed to 'restore ancient commons and redress other grievances' (Knot 1984: 102). Population growth also put pressure on Irish peasants whose precarious subsistence was often derived from small areas of potato farming on insecure tenures. These agrarian grievances were given a vivid religious and communal dimension by the peasants' hostility to paying tithes to the alien Protestant clergy planted in their midst, an everyday reminder of the intrustion of the hated Protestant Ascendancy.

Social conflict was not limited to predominantly Catholic areas. In the Protestant north, settled by Scottish Presbyterian colonists during the course of the seventeenth century, problems of access to land were exacerbated by a crisis of proto-industrialisation connected with the wayward fortunes of the Ulster linen industry (Dickson 1983: 39–42). As in Scotland, there had been a massive increase of linen production for export to England, especially in east Ulster. Exports had soared from half-a-million yards in 1700 to 38 million yards in 1800. Population more than doubled in the area between 1753 and 1791, while land values increased steadily. One option of the small farmer and linen producer householders was emigration, notably to the Atlantic coast of Canada and the Thirteen Colonies. Now this combination of high rents, cyclical unemployment and demands for political power among the middle class associated with the linen industry (which had a sprinkling of Catholics) created an early predisposition to agrarian violence. The so-called Steelboy movement of the 1760s demanded a reduction of rents and an end to evictions by the large landowners. More seriously, the 1780s saw an Ulster movement called the Peep-of-Day Boys. In this case, Protestant gentry had begun to admit Catholics to tenancies (not at this time regarding them as a threat) and Catholics began themselves to enter the ranks of drapers. Protestant workers were themselves under threat as drapers increasingly reduced independent artisans to the status of employees. The stresses of economic change, therefore, combined with emerging sectarian mentalities to set Protestant and Catholic against each other, ensuring that when the Protestant gentry itself became agitated by the Catholic and Republican threat in the 1790s, rural and working-class Protestants lined up alongside them and acquiesced in the Union with Britain.

Parochial economic and social conflicts arising from rapid growth and a change in the nature of the economy during the great upswing after 1730 provided one set of conditions for relations between the Irish ruling class and the British empire. Another dimension, however, was added by the constitutional and political relations between the Irish élite and London. Up to 1790, and most particularly during the period of 1782–4 when the Irish volunteer movement was at its height, this establishment seemed set to follow a path similar to that of the American colonists. British control over the Irish Parliament (enshrined in Poyning's Law of 1494) was deeply resented, particularly since Ireland was restricted from full participation in the British colonial system, while still being expected to pay for imperial defence through excise and other taxes. On this the Protestant gentry and the Catholic middle class (itself disadvantaged by exclusion from office under anti-Catholic disabilities) were at one. The crisis of the American War of Independence allowed the Irish élite to demand from Britain parliamentary independence and various concessions in trade.

This Irish political community showed some signs of cultural assimilation before 1790. Agrarianist philosophy and a desire for the 'improvement' of the Catholic peasantry brought Anglican, Presbyterian and crypto-Catholic together in the vigorous literary and debating world of Dublin. In the 1760s and 1770s some Catholic gentry took to the practice of occasional conformity with Anglicanism to gain access to public office (MacDonagh 1984: 23). In local government, again, some Catholic gentry were admitted to shares of patronage, while both Protestant and Catholic sought service in the army of the East India Company, one division of the imperial forces where religious affiliation was regarded with indifference. All the same, the assimilation of the Catholic middle class, it soon proved, was too little and too late. Only 10 per cent of the subscriptions to the Bank of Ireland stock in the 1780s was in Catholic hands; some decades after it was made legal for Catholics to own land, there were remarkably few large Catholic estates (Lord Sheffield 1785: 373).

Nevertheless, vociferous colonial assemblies dominated by élites of commercial landowners appeared on both sides of the Atlantic. Irishmen at this time had a relatively poor chance of access to the heights of the English professions (the Bar had even decided to treat Irish barristers as no better qualified than West Indians in 1760). And whereas the political crises of the early years of George III's reign had widened the avenues of patronage for Bute's Scotland, political Ireland had, if anything, lost both patronage and informal representation in Westminster alongside their American comperes (Olson 1980). Despite the simmering religious problem, a loosening of imperial bonds was coming about as the Irish Parliament received its legislative independence in 1782.

THE ATLANTIC EMPIRE: DISINTEGRATION AND SURVIVAL

The tussle between the creoles' desire for independence and their need for imperial defence against internal and external threats was even sharper in the Americas. In Canada and the West Indies, as in the Thirteen Colonies themselves, strong provincial identities had emerged. Colonial leaders snapped angrily at the attempts of imperial statesmen to tax and control them.

The colonial élites of the Caribbean were in a somewhat similar position to the Irish. Here economic incorporation into the British empire was total, though merchants and plantation owners did a good deal of trade with the French, Dutch and Spanish colonies which was technically illicit under the terms of the Navigation Acts and other restrictive legislation. Tobacco production had declined while the sugar economy had advanced during the eighteenth century (Parry and Sherlock 1963: 117). But the growing cost of slave labour combined with lower profit margins had tilted the economic balance towards large estates, so that smallholding white farmers (often descendants of indentured white servants brought over in the seventeenth century) had lost influence except in parts of Jamaica and in some of the smaller islands of the Antilles. As in the Irish case, this strengthening oligarchy had powerful informal links with London and could influence the course of imperial legislation, yet its mentality was one of fractious provincialism. Many of the greatest Caribbean owners were non-resident and well-connected with English (and Irish) merchant or gentry families. The West Indian interest could always get its Bristol, Liverpool or Glasgow connections to mount powerful campaigns to reduce excise duties and other indirect taxation on island produce, or to fight off attempts by ministries to intervene in their parochial law-making. Too much money in England was tied up in Caribbean concerns for ministers to risk a serious contest of political wills with the creoles; that might have raised fears of an event like the collapse of the South Sea Bubble. Moreover, this informal and touchy accommodation was confused by the extensive West Indian patronage in the hands of people in London. While the British Crown did not legally sell positions, rich offices, especially in Jamaica, were patented to friends and relatives and then often sub-let to powerful local landowners or merchants. As in the case of the East India Company, ministers were hamstrung by the ramifications of their private patronage, and rigorous attempts to intervene on the islands might very well have raised a storm of protest among influential supporters of the ministry at home.

Yet if the islands could never be economically independent of London, morally they were drifting away from their British moorings. The process of 'creolisation' appears to have gone ahead quite quickly in the Caribbean itself. West Indians, unlike the Scots, found no one powerful patron who might bring over large numbers of men for English office. As in Ireland, many of the major landed magnates were permanently non-resident and did not think of themselves as West Indians except in a commercial sense. Only a small percentage of the notables of the colonial assemblies were educated in English public schools, or at Oxford or Cambridge; links with the English Bar were weak and the Church of England was entirely in the hands of local landowners or estate managers and their clients. Relatively few of the 229 Jamaicans at Oxbridge in the eighteenth century appear to have returned to the islands (Braithwaite 1971: 31).

Local society, particularly in Jamaica, appears to have developed its own points of reference beyond English gentility and its own complicated hierarchy reflected in minute differences of colour and expressed in conventions of dress, social behaviour and access to local office. A perfect involuted caste society pressing down upon a growing mass of slaves was coming into being. One further development which tended to increase the distance between English and Caribbean society was the islands' growing links with the American colonies, especially with the Carolinas, from where they imported rice, and the northern colonies which supplied naval stores and some manufactures. A large number of Carolina and New England merchants (such as John Fitch of Jamaica) resided on the islands and these men helped build up local public opinion which was suspicious of what came to be seen as the arbitary interventions of London. Indeed, there was considerable pro-American sympathy in the Caribbean in the 1770s. Marriages between Jamaican landed families and Yankee girls had become more common as the wealth and energy of the New England economies expanded and the profits of sugar became more uncertain. In 1774, for instance, the Jamaican House of Assembly passed a 'humble petition and memorial' in favour of the Americans during the crisis of the Stamp Act, and later the Continental Congress urged the islanders to turn their sugar fields over to grain to give them self-sufficiency and a basis for real independence (Braithwaite 1971: 68).

Yet, as in Ireland, the imperial connection still had a number of powerful local allies, and the interests of the landed élites and their clients pointed, ultimately, towards continued dependence on London. First, through much of the century the creoles needed the power of the Royal Navy to support them in their wars of monopoly and economic sabotage against the sugar-producing colonies of France and Spain. Opinion in favour of war was vigorous. Either, it was argued, the sugar installations of the rich and productive French islands must be ravaged and their slaves stolen to prevent intolerable competition from French sugars and rum; or, later in the century, the declining productivity of sugar lands, especially on Jamaica, counselled expansion of English cultivation on to French and Spanish islands. In either case, British naval supremacy was essential to guarantee survival.

Secondly, the fierce conflicts and resistance arising from the nature of plantation production in the islands forced the planter society to look to British arms in case of revolt or conflict. Colonial militias were weak and ill-organised; landowners were not prepared to pay very much in taxation to support them. Yet the number of slaves grew rapidly in the eighteenth century as production became more labour-intensive. Given the appalling rate of mortality among slaves, the vast majority were newly arrived from Africa, still retaining rudiments of organisation and memory of their free earlier condition. Slaves brought in from Angola and the Guinea Coast in particular were tenacious in their African culture and formed the core of fierce and bloody revolts in Jamaica, notably at the height of the crisis in 1775 (Parry and Sherlock 1963: 71, 145; Braithwaite 1971: 199–211). Equally worrying to the creoles were the large pockets of runaway and freed slaves on the islands, the so-called maroons who had built up their own quasi-colonies especially in the highland interior of Jamaica. These maroons were thought to encourage slave runaways and sabotage and to undermine the integrity of white social control. The maroon problem also exacerbated conflict between large white plantation owners and the smaller yeomen who wanted more protection and higher taxes on the large estates. Local punitive actions against the maroons took place in 1734 and 1795–9.

In short, the fast growth of the sugar economy in the second half of the century, within its protected British markets, intensified conflicts which could not be managed by the creole élites alone. Ultimately, indeed, it was to be the fear of mass slave resistance after the French Revolution which gave imperial statesmen the chance to reassert some control over the fractious islands, just as it was Irish Catholic revolts which pushed the Irish 'creoles' towards the Protestant empire. In both cases, the expansion of capitalist production and popular resistance were the underlying cause of imperial crisis. However, in time, these conditions also brought about the re-establishment of imperial power and enforced the partial acquiescence of the settlers.

There are some comparisons to be made here with the momentous events in the British colonies to the north. The fast expansion of American population and production and the ever-increasing pressure of land speculators and fur traders towards the west gave rise to conflicts between grazier and farmer, and between different groups of merchants. As is well known, the push into the Ohio valley, following the defeat of the French in North America in 1763, provoked fierce resistance from native American Indians which culminated in Pontiac's revolt of 1763–4. The urgent need for defence and of some type of frontier authority to mediate these violent disputes created a financial crisis for the lethargic imperial authorities. However, demands for a colonial contribution in the form of the Stamp Act and the Tea Duties provoked an irresistible creole response. Imperial patronage was in short supply. There were just too few offices generated out of the small imperial official class to assuage the American gentry. Those openings for representation and honour in London which Americans had held before 1750 were sacrificed to the new calls for parliamentary and ministerial supremacy. America produced no Lord Bute who could oil the way of colonial magnates into metropolitan politics. And even if one such had existed, America had already developed a powerful mentality of separatism in which the old rhetoric of Whig 'country opposition' was reinforced by a sense of economic autarchy and resentment at the flooding of America's infant production with the 'baubles of Britain' (Pocock 1980; Breen 1988). In short, the sheer size and self-confidence of the American Whig gentry made its assimilation into metropolitan politics along the lines of Scotland, or more ambiguously Ireland and the Caribbean, impossible. The flaccid collapse of North's ministry in 1782 was not so much a sign of England's weakness as a general understanding within the political nation of this fact of life. The United States of America, as Lord Shelburne (prime minister, 1782–3) realised, would serve Britain better as a vast export market and a huge western buffer state against the ambitions of the French and Spanish than as an expensive and troublesome set of colonies.

The survival of what became British Canada during these years was largely an accident of fate, a combination of the failure of supply of the American continental army and the winter of the north. Since more than half of Britain's Canadian subjects were French settlers of Quebec, suspicious of British Protestant aims, this survival seems even more paradoxical. Yet an attention to the interests of colonial élites and to the nature of local conflicts over land and production places Canada firmly within the framework of analysis developed here. Inexperienced British officials had worked hard to assimilate the Quebec oligarchy of traders and French yeoman farmers into the imperial structure after the conquest of 1763. The Quebec Act of 1774 had allowed Catholics to hold office and had recognised the French Catholic Church in Canada simply in order to consolidate Britain's new dominion. The Act had gone far farther in assuaging resentment of the settlers than the Irish Settlement of 1782 was to do; it constituted an important departure from the notion of stronger central control which held sway after Britain's victory in the Seven Years' War. Colonel Guy Carleton's Canadian settlement of 1791 also retained some principles of local self-government through colonial legislative councils, even though the paternalistic, royalist aspect of government was built up and English representatives given a permanent majority on the executive council of Quebec (Morton 1963: 180–3). Much attention has been paid to these early manifestations of British constitution-making as attempts to accommodate local and imperial interests and 'rally the moderates'.

More important, perhaps, was the way in which the interests of the colonial élites pushed them towards an imperial solution (Neatby 1966). The Quebec Chamber of Commerce which represented both British and French merchants had long been in competition with New England fur traders in the west. The imperial arrangements of 1763, 1783 and 1791 all gave much away to the Americans, but did at least preserve for Quebec some of its western hinterlands for future exploitation. The Nova Scotian and Atlantic communities benefited from the arrangements of 1783 which were designed to give them a monopoly of Caribbean trade, now that the Americans were excluded from direct provisioning of the islands. Again, the 'loyalist' refugees who swarmed into Canada after 1783 were attracted as much by the possibility of large land grants, safe from the gaze of New England land speculators, as by any emotional attachment to Monarchy. The empire's position in the Atlantic colonies after 1780 was secured by its governors' judicious use of patronage in Crown lands. Canadian white society (less than 200,000 people) was still small enough to be amenable to the sort of loose management and jobbery which characterised the Thirteen Colonies before 1757. Canadians were also happy for the empire to provide frontier protection and to help arbitrate the fierce disputes between the Hudson Bay Company and the North

Western Company which flared up following the march of trade and capital into the fur and timber lands of the western interior.

The expansion of empire throughout the first eight decades of the eighteenth century was determined, then, by three main influences. First, the degree of intervention by the imperial authorities was to some extent determined by conflicts over labour, capital and land in the developing colonial societies, and by the intensity of indigenous resistance. The second influence was the need of the settlers for protection and patronage in dealing with external rivals, or gaining access to the benefits of rapidly expanding inter-colonial and metropolitan trade, or to land and offices controlled by the Crown. A third important consideration was the extent to which these colonial societies had developed a distinct political, social and ideological identity, and whether those identities could still be accommodated to rather weak notions of British nationalism.

These issues became important during the imperial crisis of 1776–83. This was the first premonition of the wider, world conflict that was to reach its peak in Eurasia during the Revolutionary and Napoleonic Wars, but which was also to sweep through the Caribbean and renew the Anglo-American war. By the mid-1790s, the Irish, Caribbean and Canadian élites were to find themselves under irresistible pressure to join the imperial enterprise. Local economic conflict and mutinies had been intensified by international war and republican rhetoric. The vigour of imperial statesmen had been redoubled by new ideological winds at home, and their patronage greatly increased by war. At the same time, 'middling' interests – some Roman Catholic tradesmen in Ireland and Canada or free negroes and coloureds in the Caribbean - saw empire loyalism as an avenue to improve their own status in relation to the 'creoles'.

THE IMPERIAL CRISIS AND INTERNATIONAL WAR, 1776–83

The imperial crisis which accompanied the American Revolutionary War has benefited from some of the most interesting writing on the eighteenth century. J. G. A. Pocock's *Three British Revolutions* argued that the American Revolution should be understood as a revolt against Parliament, and taxation for imperial defence. This revolution was legitimised by the rhetoric of 'country versus court' which had been voiced earlier by English country gentlemen who opposed the Whig oligarchy of the early eighteenth century. Henceforth, by a 'great inversion', the country ideology of republican virtue became the official ideology of the United States; it was one which allowed a volcanic eruption of 'possessive individualism' as colonists swarmed across the new continent (Murrin 1980: 323–68). The Irish élites too accomplished a partial revolution against Parliament. But their revolution was limited by their continuing need to gain equal trading rights within the empire and also by the nagging fear that they would one day need imperial arms to discipline the Catholic peasantry. The crisis of the American war also consolidated the forces of 'economical reform' and radicalism throughout Great Britain, especially in London, the northern cities and among Welsh non-conformists. Here the resentment inspired by heavy taxation for distant ventures and the unrepresentative Parliament stirred riot and protest. As usual, the crisis of empires had a domestic dimension.

The debacle in the East arose also from the financial embarrassments of the East India Company. The Company was now hardly solvent, sunk by its faltering trading performance and the large new burdens of military protection and administration contracted since the seizure of Bengal in 1757. The way out of this problem, without calling on the English taxpayer, was the device known as the subsidiary alliance. Indian rulers were cajoled or coerced into paying a large part of their annual revenue (the 'subsidy') to procure their protection by East India Company armies stationed in their territories (Barnett 1980: ch.4). However, as in the American case, the cure was worse than the disease. The finances and internal organisation of the Indian successor states to the Mughals began to collapse under the weight of the regular payments they were forced to make to the Company. The outcome always drew the Company and its armies into further territorial expansion, expenditure and debt. In some cases, hard-pressed Indian rulers tried to expand their revenue base by conquest of their neighbours, as did the Nawab of Awadh when he conquered the Rohillas in 1774, or the Nawab of Arcot in his abortive attempt of 1773 to seize the revenues of his rich neighbour in Tanjore. In both cases, Company troops and officials were drawn into the game and Calcutta incurred the displeasure of London. In other cases, Indian rulers and subjects, goaded beyond endurance by the demands of the Governor-General and his subordinates, assigned their territories to the Company (as did Arcot in 1781–2) or flew into revolt (as did the Raja or Benares in 1781). Here again there was an inexorable extension of the

Company's ragged frontier of administration and its debts surged upwards (Bayly 1988: ch. 2). The British response to the dilemma of imperial military finance was to screw up the ratchet in all their overseas territories. The unintended consequence was to precipitate a series of conflicts which liberated the Americans, but enslaved the Indians.

Yet the problem of imperial finance was only the surface expression of a much deeper contradiction, and one common to both spheres of empire. It was on the unorganised fringe of the commercial world where the dynamic lay. In the New World, sugar producers and coastal merchants successfully evaded and undermined the imperial regulation of shipping enshrined in the Navigation Acts. New Englanders, men from the Carolinas and Jamaicans traded with French and Spanish colonies even during times of war. On the American mainland, weak governors with limited patronage proved no match for powerful cliques of land speculators and urban merchants.

In Asia the forms of commerce were different, but the results similar. European private traders, Company officials and their Indian helpers built up holdings of royal rights in revenue, monopoly farms and in bazaar perquisites. Others (as in the case of the famous Nawab of Arcot's debts) lent huge sums on high interest to indigenous states attempting to maintain their royal honour and to pay their troops. All this undermined the fabric of Indian states but it also began to hollow out the institutions of the Company in the same way that commercial growth had previously hollowed out the former empires. Here European merchants were only ruthlessly pushing forward economic changes which had deeper roots in Asian societies. The expansion of the great Islamic empires and of the maritime trade of southeast Asia had already thrown up conflicts between rulers and their commercial coadjutors, between port kings and kings of the inland agricultural realms.

But not all Eurasian rulers were prepared to be bundled so quickly through the trapdoor of history. European companies and trading networks faced not only the perennial problem of paying for their armies and preventing their own servants from eroding the fabric of allied Indian states. They also faced the power of those Indian régimes which had begun to use trade and monopoly as a weapon in their political and ideological struggles with Western penetration. Above all, it was the defeat of a British army by the Marathas in western India in 1779 and the ravaging of British Madras by Hyder Ali and Tipu Sultan of Mysore in the following year which forced ministers and Parliament to contemplate not only the loss of British America but the expulsion of the British from India also. The Mysore of the sultans went down in flames. But Jezzar Ahmed of Acre or Ranjit Singh who unified the Punjab (1799–1839) and Muhammad Ali Pasha of Egypt (1807–49) fought off the Europeans by diplomacy or arms.

The imperial defeats of 1776–83 had results which pointed in two different directions. On the one hand, the dissolution of empire into a series of 'creole states' linked only by common culture and commercial interest seemed to have speeded up. The United States survived as a great market for British industrial production. The connection with Ireland was made more tenuous by the granting of legislative independence to the Dublin Parliament. The sugar islands which had been saved by the skin of Admiral Rodney's teeth were in economic decline in the face of their rich and expanding French and Spanish competitors; Canada seemed unlikely to survive. Even in India, the Company had been stopped dead by the Indian powers. And private merchants continued to power ahead in Company markets, oblivious of the measures of reform which were now gestating in London and keen to keep Company fingers out of their business.

All the same, the interlocking effects of the imperial crisis did tie some parts of Britain's overseas enterprise together in new ways. The lines for advance during the next round of international war and conflict were laid. In a global historical perspective, the development of the China trade after 1783 was scarcely less important than the independence of the United States. Government needed to repair its battered finances by plugging gaps in excise revenue caused by smuggling and evasion. It also needed to bail the East India Company out, now that its growing United States market was forfeit to the New England merchants. The result was the 1784 Commutation Act which had momentous consequences throughout Asia. By reducing the duties on China teas from 120 per cent to 12.5 per cent, the British government strengthened its own tax basis and bailed out the Company by stimulating a vast rise in tea imports. Increased tea imports to the UK and Ireland, in turn, gave a further boost to sugar sales (and incidentally to the slave trade). It also forced India to produce and sell much more raw cotton to China and laid the foundations for the opium trade. For the Chinese would not yet take significant quantities of British manufactured goods (as Macartney's 1792 Embassy to Pekin was dismally to show).

Further consequences followed. Bombay grew rapidly and the possibility of war for trade with the Marathas who controlled the cotton-growing areas of Gujarat increased. It also became profitable for the first time to bring central Indian raw cotton down the Ganges to Calcutta for export to China. So a whole range of peasant producers and small towns between inland India and Bengal was galvanised into production and the economic foundations of British rule in central and upper India were laid. Finally, the need for an entrepot on its China trade route encouraged the East India Company to bid for Penang on the Malay coast. This was to be a harbinger of Britain's growing stake in the Indonesian Archipelago and the China coast (Tarling 1969).

A simple accounting of the destination of British exports and the origin of imports before and after the 1783 watershed will not illuminate these important developments in the history of empire and international capital. For the foundation of Penang was an event in the history of Chinese overseas enterprise as much as British. If there was continuity over the boundary of 1783, however, it was in the onward roll of international conflict. For the Eurasian wars to redivide the world's resources intensified once again after 1793. Not only did plague, poor harvest and the abrupt redirection of trade routes intensify the conflicts between states, but the cumulative effect of the crisis on townsmen and peasants over much of Eurasia brought about a remarkable convergence of movements of resistance, millenarian revolt and liberation. The Gallic Great Fear spread across Eurasia and America to merge with the moral panic of Asians convinced that religion and identity was in danger. It was against this background – the background of the first true world crisis since the Mongol invasions of the thirteenth century – that the British discovered the ideological and political will for a more vigorous world empire. It was then that those creole élites – in Ireland, Canada, Caribbean or India – which, as late as 1783 might have hoped for a future of profiteering outside the ambit of colonial governors and their taxation, moved more smartly into line.

CHAPTER FOUR
Britain's New Imperial Age

The French Wars saw the greatest expansion of British imperial dominion since the creation of the colonies of settlement in Ireland and America in the seventeenth century. Most later extensions of the empire, whether in Africa in the 1880s and 1890s or in the Middle East after the First World War, were the slowly matured consequences of policies laid down by Pitt and Dundas. British nationalism and imperialism reached maturity at the same moment, and the consolidation of empire in Europe was matched by its overseas expansion. Economic interests were an important, but not critical, incentive to the creation of this new imperial system. More important was the sharp perception of danger among the ruling class, threatened as they felt themselves to be by the dissolution of social order at home and a fearsome military and ideological challenge abroad.

LINEAMENTS OF THE NEW EMPIRE

The 'British Empire in Europe' was now secured against a host of internal dangers and made ready to act as a springboard for overseas effort. The cornucopia of patronage controlled by Dundas and the accelerated recruitment of Highland regiments during the wars laid the capstone on Scotland's assimilation into the 'British Empire in Europe'. Scottish economic incorporation also reached its culmination during these years. The Glasgow linen and cotton manufacturers flourished in response to home consumption and to the massive American demand which, ironically, soared after the loss of the Thirteen Colonies. The brutal modernisation of Scottish agriculture by enclosure and the Highland clearances stirred hatred and revolt, as witnessed by the Ross-shire revolts of the 1790s. But the tide of Lowland expansion into the Highlands and Islands was now irreversible. New strategic roads and bridges were established and along these communications flowed, according to one observer, 'liberality and expansion of mind', so the 'the heart of the Highlander, at present, glows with loyalty and patriotism' (cited in Lenman 1981: 340). This vigorously imposed moral union was soon to be made glorious by the Scottish romantic bards and the Highland Games. The royal patron, William IV, was to nurture that establishment-sponsored Scottish patriotism which had already been accommodated to empire when the debating societies of Edinburgh and London took up the song of McPherson's 'Ossian' in the 1780s and began to laud the heroic Celtic past.

The imperial principle also won out with ease in Wales. During the 1780s the Principality had spawned many radical cells, led by men such as the dissenting minister, Richard Price. They drew on the poverty of rural Wales and resentment at the economic and political dominance of the small group of Anglo-Welsh gentry; they also saw Welsh neglect by Parliament as part of a much wider, imperial problem. The outbreak of the French wars, however, signalled a rapid decline of old Welsh radicalism. Methodism had been the most vigorously expanding faith in Wales in the later eighteenth century. The Methodist leadership, now under suspicion of 'jacobin' tendencies, rallied smartly to the state, becoming 'plus royaliste que le roi'. John Elias taught his followers that it was their duty to submit to authority, while Charles of Bala wrote his *Welsh Methodists Vindicated* to celebrate their loyalty (Davies and Edwards 1939: 165). Like the Scottish tradition, the Welsh language and literature had already become a scholarly bauble for English writers and poets, and its moral centre was probably Oxford not Aberystwyth (Jones 1984: 46–9). Hereafter, Welsh dissent and nationalism became the preserve of small groups of radicals in the new manufacturing towns, Welsh emigrés to North America and isolated romantic bards.

Ireland also felt the full force of British empire-building in the Act of Union of 1801, but here the outcome was more doubtful. Economic motives played a part in the tide of support for the legislative Union (Beckett 1981: 277–83). Some Irish magnates, a few Cork and Dublin merchants and many British manufacturers saw in it the chance to create a great free trade area out of the United

Kingdom in which they would be at an instant advantage. Certainly, the linen industry of the north benefited at first from more direct access to British and colonial markets, protected by the war from the competition of German producers. Yet the headlong plunge into the Union in 1800 was spurred by geopolitical fear. Ireland could no longer be allowed to be run by 'juntos of ferocious nobles and low, jobbing politicians' (*QR*: 6, 1811, 130). The disdain of the Irish Parliament for the Catholics and for rural problems in general had nearly caused the country to fall under the 'iron despotism of France' during the great peasant and nationalist uprising against British rule in 1798–9. Legislative independence would have to be sacrificed to security. France could not be allowed to use gentry nationalism or Catholic peasant discontent as a new secret weapon against England, now that Scotland was no longer available as a second front. If this tactical conversion to empire of some sections of the ruling class could not ultimately bridge the great cultural and economic gap between the Celtic countryside and the Anglo-Irish élite, it did at least provide a generation of relative calm for British ministries as they consolidated their grip on other parts of the world.

Economics were, once again, an important though not a critical element in the redefinition of empire outside Europe. The great expansion of these years in Europe and Asia certainly moved forward in spheres marked out by earlier commercial interests. And in the long term, the retention of dominion had to be justified by the appearance of commercial profit, whether this was profit to the nation, to merchant and finance houses in London, or to private entrepreneurs in the colonies. Yet this new expansion was set in motion and powered by the ferocious reaction of the state and its military apparatus to external challenge and internal revolt. This gave British imperialism between 1790 and 1830 a degree of autonomy from economic interest in the narrow sense. Empire was the expression of a revivified nation-state operating at an international level according to general principles – the protection and glorification of Crown, Church, law and trade. Such a political and ideological character meant that the British empire had a good deal in common with the continental European empires of France or Russia, despite publicists' denunciations of 'French tyranny' and 'Russian barbarism'.

All parts of the world witnessed a growth of British power, but it was in the Mediterranean, Greater India and southern Africa that most was achieved. Britain's military impotence in continental Europe between 1793 and 1809 brought about a countervailing build-up of naval forces in the Mediterranean, as it was to do in so many later wars. Napoleon's thrust to Egypt had raised fears about the security of the East India Company's oriental dominions. After 1806 the Royal Navy maintained its strength in the area in order to help feed the army in the Peninsula with Egyptian and Levant grain, and also to implement the blockade of southern European ports. In 1803, after Britain had renewed war over the island, Nelson stated the new doctrine 'I now declare that I consider Malta as the most important outwork to India, and that it will give us great influence in the Levant and indeed in all the southern parts of Italy,' (Laferla 1938: i, 47). British occupation of Sicily (1806–15) and of Ionian Isles (1809–14) were acts of pre-emption designed to keep the Bonapartists out of the Mediterranean, and prolonged in Ionia by suspicion that Imperial Russia saw itself as a successor to the Ottoman empire as ruler of the Orthodox Greek populations of the Balkans and Levant. Britain's 'insular empire', however, soon established its own raison d'être.

There was a significant body of opinion which saw empire in the Mediterranean and the Ottoman lands as an end in its own right. It was to be an epochal extension of British dominion into a classic realm of power. G. F. Leckie, a Scottish planter with estates in Sicily, published in 1808 *An Historical Survey of the Foreign Affairs of Great Britain*. Here he argued from the classical examples of Rhodes, Athens and Rome that 'Empire of the sea will always balance that of the land' (Leckie 1808: vi) and since Great Britain's population was inadequate to prolonged war and economic prosperity, 'conquest or adoption of European nations should keep pace with the extension of our European and Indian empires' (ibid.: 12). Britain should build an 'insular empire' throughout the Mediterranean, fostering the industry of Greeks and Italians by the creation of a wealthy yeomanry. She should also introduce English laws and constitution into Sicily, southern Europe, Crete, Cyprus and Corsica, curtailing the power of the feudal barons of the Mediterranean lands. Otherwise Britain herself would sink into obscurity. The decline of the Roman empire 'may be dated from the renunciation of conquest' (ibid.: 143), so 'We must therefore Britannize every part of insular Europe which suits our purpose', and give this empire permanence rather than pursuing the old tactic of building up a German counterweight to imperial France (ibid.: 115).

The British assaults on Egypt in 1801 and 1807 and continuing pressure on the Ottoman Porte were defensive measures against

French intervention and Muhammad Ali's intransigence. Yet again, there were many who argued already for a policy of outright conquest and for early dismemberment of the Ottoman empire. After the peace was established, paramountcy if not dominion in the Mediterranean became the main aim of statesmen. Malta and the Ionian Islands were maintained as naval bases and emporia, the Ottoman Porte and the Egypt of Muhammad Ali, the new regional dynast, were gradually bent to Britain's will as far as their external policies were concerned. On the southwest coast of the Mediterranean the British position was also strengthened. Between 1814 and 1846, Colonel Hanmer Warrington, Consul-General at Tripoli, established what was virtually an informal British province. He became 'to all intents and purposes the Pasha's foreign secretary', channelled British loans to the kingdom, set afoot internal economic development and opened the way for British explorers to the Niger Valley (Boahen 1968: 46–9). In the East, attempts to peg down the outer Ottoman provinces inaugurated British naval predominance in the Persian Gulf with the seaborne defeat of the Wahhabis (1808) and growing diplomatic and military links with Beduin chieftains of the Aden area (Kelly 1980).

British merchant shipping had long been established in the Mediterranean; the English Livorno merchants and the factors of the Levant Company had supplied the British market with currants, grain and 'Turkey products'. No doubt settlers and merchant captains harboured the aim of expanding trade in the sea. The Near East was also seen as a significant if not a large market for English manufactures during the blockade when continental outlets were closed to Manchester and Glasgow. However, sales of manufactured cloth to the Ottomans were a *consequence* not a cause of the British build-up in the Near East (Inalcik 1987). The new Mediterranean empire was not a creation of economic imperialism in any simple sense. It was part of a geopolitical effort which encompassed but should not be reduced to economic motives. The British wanted the Mediterranean to be *mare nostrum*, subject to the rule of law and safe for international commerce. They also wanted to make the new colonies pay by expanding trade in British manufactures, Maltese cotton, and currants from the Greek Islands. In origin, this maritime dominion resulted from the clash of states and the desire, as Leckie put it, to construct a British empire as an 'abstract principle', expressing a 'great and philosophic view' and designed to stand forth against French republican imperialism (1808: vi).

Britain's acquisition of large parts of the old Dutch empire can be seen in the same light. South Africa, Ceylon, Java, the Dutch factories in India and the Caribbean were seized in order to deny them to the French or, as in the case of a slave island such as Trinidad (acquired 1797), to deliver them from the 'abominable tyranny of revolted negroes'. At the very least, as in the eighteenth-century wars, there was an assumption that they might form useful bargaining counters to extract concessions in continental Europe. Consequent on this military play of power, Britain secured undoubted economic advantages. The demolition of the Dutch monopoly in the eastern seas allowed them to flood southeast Asia with Indian opium, so aiding the parlous finances of the Company. They also secured staging posts on the China route and a large trading area in which Britain manufactured imports soon began to make headway. But economic advantages were generally by-products of military advance not their causes. Robert Percival's *Account of the Cape of Good Hope* contained a fairly accurate representation of the thinking of Pitt, Dundas and their successors. The Cape was important essentially as a strategic holding on the route to India and would protect Britain's dominance there since all Europeans would have to stop on the Cape when travelling to India. It would also secure Britain's control of new areas of predominance in the South Seas fisheries and Australasia. Besides, there were some potential economic advantages on the Cape itself. Its wine and sugar production would guard against 'the contingent loss of any of our West Indian sugar Islands' and of Portugal (Percival 1806: 332). Later it was appreciated that Cape stores could be used to provision not only the merchant fleet but also the plantation islands of St Helena and Mauritius. Ceylon was regarded in the same light; it buttressed British control of the Indian Ocean. Bengal shipping would be safe from the threat of an enemy establishment at Trincomalee, but there were some incidental economic advantages such as the cinnamon farms and the pearl fisheries of Manaar. As a frontier for Tamil petty capital, Ceylon was already well integrated into the economic system of the sub-continent.

The final stages of British expansion in India also indicate that a plethora of secondary economic interests were used to justify a general strategic principle. British business houses and Indian commercial men in Surat and Bombay all wanted an expansion of formal British control in Gujarat and the southwest coast. Gujarat cotton was in great demand for the dynamic China trade; pepper and cinnamon from Travancore and Kanara were still valued commodities (Nightingale 1970; Subramanian 1987). Awadh in the east was fully penetrated by British private traders working hand in hand with Indian entrepreneurs in trade and revenue.

All the same, the great surge forward of British control under Wellesley and the Marquess of Hastings was not a grab for resources or immediate commercial profit (Marshall 1975a; Mukherjee 1982). That is simple-minded economism. Dundas and Wellesley tried to create in India a great counterweight to France in Europe. They were concerned that what the British already held in revenue and trade was at risk from a further 'tribal breakout' of Afghans under Zaman Shah Durrani or, worse, from the revival of Maratha power within India. They also saw that indigenous buffer states of Awadh, Hyderabad and Arcot were being corroded by relentless demands for tribute and by the expansion of British and Indian commercial adventurers. Only formal rule could provide stability for the Indian empire. Once a territorial empire had been created in Bengal, it tended to roll forward of its own weight. The meddling of British residents or political officers and fear of the Company's geopolitical designs panicked the Maratha leaders into their final contest with British arms (1816–18). The British had decided that 'internal tranquillity' could only be guaranteed by absolute paramountcy in the sub-continent. Britain, now a 'nation in arms', was no longer hostile to such a design.

The importance of the political principle in British expansion helps to avoid some of the problems arising from economic interpretations. There was no dramatic shift in the composition of Britain's import or export schedule before the later 1820s when the build-up of manufactured goods began. Asia, the main theatre of the new imperialism, continued to provide the same commodities, and its total share of Britain's world trade actually fell between 1780 and 1820. The growth of British trade itself has probably been exaggerated, and the richest export markets for manufactured goods were North and South America and, after 1815, continental Europe, precisely those areas where empire was not contemplated or was quickly run down. Even if one looks to 'services', the export of capital and other fields for 'gentlemanly capitalism', the picture does not change much. The loans and credits provided by London's greatly expanded financial sector went to wartime allies in Europe and to the Americas. British-controlled capital in the Middle East, Africa and Asia was generated locally, often through the manipulation of political perquisites.

An explanation of the origins and nature of the new imperialism must therefore shift to other issues. First, as this chapter will suggest, ideological and institutional changes in 'the British Empire in Europe' must be brought back to the centre of the stage. Of course, there was much continuity in the interests of the British 'moneyocracy'. Gentleman capitalists remained concerned about the stability of the East India Company and the profits of world-wide commerce. Yet the continuity of Britain's imperial aims was fractured by political and ideological changes. Peasant dissidence in Ireland and working-class radicalism at home combined with boundless fear of French republicanism. This caused a considerable sharpening of the edges of the state, especially in more outlying regions. The landed gentry, already riding high on increased profits from land and commerce, became more self-conscious of its rôle as protector of Crown, Church and Constitution.

Military and imperial service provided outlets for this new sensibility. Under severe pressure, nationalism became a more vigorous object of state policy. But it was a principle to be indulged more safely in the imperial peripheries and overseas territories. Economic drives were subsumed into this principle to an extent that it becomes impossible to disentangle one from another and misleading to reduce nationalism to economic interest. A man like Henry Salt expressed this new nationalistic fusion of motives. Scholar, artist and traveller on the fringes of the Wellesley–Dundas circle, he ranged the world denouncing the depravity of natives even as he sketched them. His schemes for empire dwarfed those even of Leckie. There was a need, he said, for a great survey of east Africa and the implanting there of British influence: 'by calling forth the energies of the African Christians and showing them their true interests, the British nation might at a trifling expense, purchase a new and large commercial channel by which the manufactures of the country would reach the hands of the inland tribes and the independent states that have not been corrupted with Mahometanism' (Halls 1834: i, 279). Christianity, trade and national glory are completely merged. The man who helped embellish the imperial halls of the British museum writes:

> The World gets wiser now, a flaming star
> hath from the West its radiance shot afar
> O'er India's realms shall dissipate the cloud
> That enwraps her servile crowd.   (ibid.: 415)

British nationalism and gentry 'reaction' at home helped create and mould the new empire. The next two chapters consider several features of the new imperial state at home and abroad. These are the reinvented role of the Crown, the Church and the gentry; the creation of new institutions of control, coercion and audit; and the philosophical and aristocratic doctrine of racial superiority which informed these institutions. Chapter 6 then turns to the other side of the story: that is to the salience of revolt, rebellion and change outside Great Britain. After 1780, the conflicts and internal contradictions in Asia and the Islamic lands, which were described in the first two chapters, reached their peak. For the new British empire also represented a response to pressure from 'below' and from indigenous rulers who found the European despotism intolerable.

The following two chapters, then, concern the intensification of British nationalism and the growth of the British imperial state. The relationship between these two processes was complex. As Colley (1986) points out, British ministries were extremely ambivalent about directly fostering nationalism in a multi-ethnic polity because of the dangerous and uncontrollable sectional patriotisms that it might encourage. Bute's period had seen anti-Scottish feeling in England rise to new heights. The Gordon riots demonstrated that patriotism and religious frenzy might easily damage the stability of the state. Nevertheless, as Leckie noted, empire had to be something more than a clearing ground for the economic interest of élites. What should be the 'wide and philosophic principle' at the heart of empire?

The Crown had evidently to play an important rôle, especially in the empire. The wider Burkean formulation of the 'glories of the British constitution' was inappropriate where indigenous peoples were to be denied their own 'constitutions', and besides, Burke's conservatism had displayed a strong anti-imperialist face, at least as regards the East India Company. The established Church might also be an important resource for state- and empire-building but, again, there were problems. The accommodation of Protestant Dissenters and Catholics raised difficult issues in Europe, while direct evangelisation of Asians and Africans was suspect because it might create 'mongrel' Christian races whose loyalty to the Crown would be in doubt. During the generation after 1790 an uneasy compromise was evolved. On the one hand, the Anglican Church was projected more forcefully outside England, but mainly among people of British descent and their dependents, or among people who were already Christian. For non-Christians, the rôle of the Church was to be a glorious, but distant exemplar of national piety. On the other hand, the establishment delicately encouraged the 'nationalisation' of Methodism and the Dissenting Churches, whose prominent members already sought respectability and distance from the earlier stigma of radicalism.

The Protestant empire was also reinforced by the 'governing race' principle which emphasised the fitness of Britons to rule by virtue of their 'moral independency' and their understanding of the rule of law; an institutionalised and philosophical racism thus became an increasingly important part of the project. What has been called here 'agrarian patriotism' was an outward manifestation of the right to rule, and one which provided a serviceable unifying theory which threatened fewer vested interests than the encouragement of free trade. The divisions and contradictions with the plural British state could also be submerged in the very acts of war and empire-building themselves. Empire thus became a necessary component of British nationalism in a way that it had never been central to English patriotism.

But this was not always enough. Where strong local identities already existed a further tactic of government and élites was to foster what might be called 'tributary patriotisms' compatible with empire. We will see this happening among the Scots, the Irish and the Greeks, but also among Asians, where the rediscovery of ancient scriptures might encourage the development of civic virtue and 'independency' within the empire. Of course, this was a double-edged sword. If it worked with the Scots and the Welsh, it ultimately failed with the Irish, the Boers and the French Canadians. Here social and economic fissures reinforced unbridgeable cultural differences. First, though, the chapter turns to the role of the Crown.

CROWN AND NATION AT HOME AND ABROAD

Historians have underestimated the importance of a residual 'divine rights of kings' in eighteenth-century English political theory and practice, but Great Britain's *ancien régime* went through many evolutions. The shocks of revolution and regicide in Europe resulted in a sudden refurbishment of the symbols of royalty in the 1790s. However unpopular the royals remained on the streets of London, George III was transformed in political discourse from a scurrilous intriguer in the closet into His Sacred

Majesty, celebrated in numerous prints and serenaded by festivals and fireworks (Colley 1984). The Monarch's very withdrawal from public duties following his illness made it easier for political leaders after the Regency Crisis (1788) to enlarge the importance of royalty as the symbolic centre of a nation at war and to elaborate the idea of an Imperial Crown. Court ritual became more dramatic and the 'dignified' aspect of Crown in Parliament was enhanced by the increased representation of Scottish barons, and later of Irish peers in the House of Lords. After 1802, the Prince Regent established his own personal court in the extravagant setting of the oriental Brighton Pavilion. A new symbolic relationship was forged between royal ritual and popular patriotism – a realignment which in some ways paralleled the creation of a public drama of revolution in the contemporary French Republic (Hunt 1984). Outside the palaces and chambers, the 'patriotic' mob now rioted in defence of the king and his counsellors rather than against them. On the London stage, performances of '*Venice Preserved*', which had once acted as a focus for radical and republican sentiment, were now booed and interrupted with singing of 'God Save the King' and 'Rule Britannia!' (National Theatre 1984).

Royalism and nationalism were closely connected because for all its faults the Crown was one of the few institutions which could bring about a moral unification of the kingdom and empire beyond a purely political alliance of élites. However, the shock of war and near-invasion fostered a sense of identity broader than simple attachment to the 'British Constitution' or the principles of hierarchy lauded by Edmund Burke. Romanticism reinforced loyalism and nationalist fervour. Historical precedents were readily enlisted. Lord Minto, speaking on the Irish Union Bill in 1799, drew a parallel with early English history. Quoting Hume's *History of England*, he showed how the Heptarchy of Anglo-Saxon kingdoms had been fused into a nation under King Egbert and how this had enabled it to resist the Danes. The survival of Rome during the war against Hannibal was attributed to a unity which allowed the Senate to cede its powers to military leaders, a principle urged on Parliament. Later, the romantic vision of *patria* was to be summoned up by poets such as Coleridge and Southey. The Scottish variant of patriotism transformed the English view of Scots as much as Scots' own understanding of themselves. Robert Burns, that 'high souled plebeian . . . born a peasant', himself embodied the transition of the Scottish stereotype from the semi-barbaric porridge-eater of Dr Johnson's time to a gutsy 'North British' hero.

Nationalist display and viceregal ritual also became more common in the colonies. After 1800, many new 'Crown colonies' were created. Conquered territories such as Java or Ceylon were not annexed to the East India Company where the British Crown had an ambiguous status. In possessions both old and new, public ritual was designed to elevate the rôle of the governor and the Crown over the still recalcitrant creole élites. For this a serviceable model existed in the pageantry of the Viceregal Lodge in Dublin with its formal levées and investitures of the Order of St Patrick. These Irish ceremonies gave dignity to the annual ladling out of honours and had been invented by administrations in the 1760s and 1770s fighting to get their measures through the Irish Parliament.

Following his victory over Mysore, Cornwallis helped propagate a style of viceregal pageant which brought together themes of Roman triumph and imperial 'benevolence' with loyalty and devotion to the king (Marshall 1981: 18–19). Wellesley, the 'glorious little man', was more brazen. His determination to set Indian rule on a proper symbolic footing was to earn him royal displeasure as it seemed to verge on presumption. He openly took the Lord-Lieutenancy of Ireland as his model. In the new Palladian Government House, lavish Indian distinctions of rank were deftly intertwined with displays of European chivalry. (The building itself was modelled on Keddleston Hall as Wellesley's nineteenth-century avatar, George Nathaniel Curzon, was to find to his delight.) Over-riding the 'aristocratic republicanism' of the old East India Company forms of corporate government, the Anglo-Irish peer – now 'The Most Noble, the Governor General' – created his own patronage system, his own private office and his own band of acolytes and orientalising sycophants. The picture was spoiled, however, when Wellesley was rewarded with no more than a 'potato' (i.e. Irish) peerage. For the Governor-General tried to distance himself from his Irish background, echoing his brother's sentiments that 'being born in a stable didn't make one a horse'.

The 'colonies of settlement' followed suit. In the recently conquered Cape of Good Hope, Lord Charles Somerset, younger son of the Duke of Beaufort, exploited his Plantagenet ancestry and created his own small court (and Royal Ascot) in the severely Calvinistic surroundings of Dutch Capetown (Millar 1965: 95). In Nova Scotia between 1792 and 1808, the Governor John Wentworth, a New Hampshire loyalist, established another petty St James which was graced by the presence of the royal princes, the Duke of Kent and the Duke of Clarence. Even in Britain's new Mediterranean empire, conquered after 1802, Sir Thomas Maitland overcame his lowland Scots cynicism and orchestrated the pomp of the Grand Master of the Knights of Malta and the Doge of Venice with the neo-Gothic display now in vogue at Westminster. The Throne of the Grand Master of the Knights of St John in Valetta Cathedral was kept vacant for the absent English king (Laferla 1938: i, 69). Later Maitland founded the Order of St Michael and St George which was glorified with a splendid regalia, and designed to massage the self-esteem of the island gentry (ibid.: 116). Of course, these powerful viceregal figures emphasised nationalism and loyalty to the Crown to strengthen their position against interfering ministers in London as much as against the creole élites; empire loyalism did not yet imply centralisation. Yet this was not simply window-dressing; it reflected a changed understanding of the relationship between overseas expansion and the central values of metropolitan political life.

More important, expatriate public opinion began organising itself to express the new themes of nationalism and royalty. As late as 1785 the servants of the East India Company had ferociously opposed the India Bill with the rhetoric of country opposition and an appeal to the rights of 'freeborn Englishmen' (Harlow 1964: ii, 211). By 1794, however, the burghers of Calcutta, Bombay and Madras were organising mass petitions of loyalty on the occasion of the monarch's birthday and subscribing large sums in defence of the realm (IOL: Home Misc. 481). In the West Indies where many had supported the rebellious Americans in 1776, royal firework displays were held and patriotic medals displaying the head of the king and the naval hero, Admiral Rodney, were distributed in the early years of the revolutionary wars (Bridges 1827: ii, 190). A statue of Rodney was erected at Kingston, Jamaica, where he had once been received with studied indifference. In all these cases a new ideological wind from home fanned local patriotism which reflected social and economic cleavages within colonial life. In Britain, the merchant classes of the larger towns, together with smaller gentry unconnected with the great political families of the Old Whig oligarchy, were in the fore of nationalist display (Colley 1984). On the Caribbean islands, however, empire sentiment was strong among the 'free negroes' and people of mixed race who had much to gain from the humbling of the white planter oligarchies and embroiling royal governors in their struggles for equity. In Canada, some at least of the 'loyalists' who fled from the Thirteen Colonies after 1783 adopted high Tory and royalist principles in order to associate themselves more directly with agents of the Crown and mark themselves off from older settlers, both British and French. In India it was apparently younger civil servants and free merchants unconnected with the old East India Company of jobbery and racial miscegenation who took a prominent part in patriotic celebration and the divine honours accorded to the governor-general.

Once again, Ireland provided an interesting model. The fears and hatreds engendered by the Catholic and peasant revolts which flared up between 1796 and 1798 culminated in the emergence of Protestant Orange movements with their aggressive martial displays. In contrast to this, the viceroyalty seemed a relatively benevolent force to many Catholics. In 1798 Earl Fitzmaurice as lieutenant-governor pressed, but failed to win, the case for their full emancipation and enfranchisement. In the 1820s Lord Wellesley, who himself married a Catholic, voiced public hostility to extreme Protestant claims and urged full Catholic assimilation into political life (Brynn 1978: 84). Viceregal ritual, especially the St Patrick's Day celebrations, achieved a degree of popular Catholic support in Dublin during the years of the nineteenth century. The new patriotism quickly enshrined its heroes, so that by the end of the war, Nelson and Wellington, both the subject of fierce early criticism, stood beside the royal pedestal, along with other minor luminaries such as Rodney, and Wellesley who had built up a coterie among Anglo-Indians even while some in Parliament were still trying to prosecute him for war-mongering.

Nationalism needed its villains as well as its heroes. Here the generation of the 1790s began to grasp a parallel between the wickedness of its European enemies and the fury of its Asiatic foes. Bonaparte, the embodiment of 'French tyranny', had already achieved the status of universal ogre before 1800. It is interesting how the European enemy was mirrored in the person of an oriental enemy. Tipu Sultan of Mysore now became the embodiment of 'Muhammadan tyranny' and he was similarly accused of violation of the conventions of war and the 'intercourse of nations'. Tipu's father, Haidar Ali, had already attracted public vilification for his spirited stand against the British in the 1770s and 1780s. The young Thomas Munro, then a youth of thirteen, at his interview with the directors of the Company had been asked how he would deal with Haidar and replied, to applause, 'I would cut off his head'. Similarly, the legend of the atrocity of the Black Hole and its supposed perpetrator, Nawab Siraj-ud-Daulah, received new impetus and a new patriotic memorial in Calcutta during these years.

Yet the infamy achieved by Tipu Sultan is remarkable. Alleged ill-treatment of English prisoners of war and the timely black symbolism in which the Sultan planted a republican 'liberty tree' at his capital and donned a cap of liberty was a gift to propagandists. Expatriate children in the Caribbean acted plays on the theme of his death in battle at Seringapatam in 1799. Even a generation later the mild and learned Hindu reformer Ram Mohun Roy was pelted by urchins on the streets of Bristol who shouted 'Tipu! Tipu!'. Popular prints showed the fall of Seringapatam (Tipu's capital) and so did the murals of Dublin's Lyceum Theatre. Thomas Kemble's panorama on Tipu had the Sultan and his court skating on the frozen River Ganges. The Mysore Sultan had in fact become the first of the great 'black' bogeymen whose successors were to haunt the British consciousness down through Colonel Arabi in the 1880s to Col. Nasser and Col. Gaddhafi. The analogy between tyranny in the East and tyranny in the West (the Marathas were also described as 'Frenchmen of Asia') and the rapid growth of commercial publishing on imperial issues reinforced this notoriety. As we shall see later, this stereotyping of individual public enemies was accompanied by a more academic analysis of unpleasant racial stereotypes.

Alongside the closer definition of both the nation and its foes went the call to discipline and respectability. One powerful source of this opinion was the growth of evangelical attitudes among Anglican churchmen and the gentry which will be discussed below. Yet the closer association of patriotism and right conduct deserves attention here. The king, the nobility and leading members of the hierarchy such as Beilby Porteus, Bishop of London, associated degeneracy and immorality with political radicalism and regicide. During the 1790s a great variety of movements for the reform of public morals, the suppression of drunkenness and the preservation of the Sabbath emerged in the capital, sponsored and often supported by ministers. Painfully slowly, attempts to reform the older universities which had begun to occur in the 1770s and 1780s now gathered pace. Tutors began to push for a university-wide examination system in Cambridge and in 1801 the first Senate House Examinations were held. This, they hoped, would impose patriotic discipline on a student body which was felt to be restive and dissatisfied. Several of the Heads of Colleges who instituted this move had close contacts with Pitt's ministry. One wrote that his aim was to reinforce the prestige of Church and university and to teach the young to 'resist and refute the metaphysical subtleties which have thrown half of the nations of Europe into confusion' (Rothblatt 1974: 286).

These ideas found a ready ear among those connected with colonial administration. Haileybury College, founded in 1805 for the education of East India Company civil servants, reflected the new seriousness of the age. Once in India the young men were no longer allowed to roam free as did the drunken and licentious 'griffins' of the past. Wellesley's Fort William College was designed to complete this training of the master race in an atmosphere distant from the 'habitual dissipation and corruption of the people of India'. Here a new moral racism came to confirm the vision of disciplined Christian people which had been forged out of the fears of the French revolutionary wars. Wellesley himself saw a clear connection between radicalism and the permissive society. 'Jacobinical' editors were expelled from Calcutta using regulations which were a mirror of Pitt's anti-radical measures and Aliens Bill. The Governor-General also tried to clean up the social life of Calcutta. Notorious card-sharpers were disciplined (one was packed off to Canton), while gambling and Indian concubines were now frowned upon. Gone were the days when a senior British resident of Calcutta had had himself circumcised to meet the religious requirements of his Muslim womenfolk.

The mood of both political élite and populace is notoriously difficult to measure. And it is perhaps because British nationalism has expressed itself through changes of mood rather than through institutions and societies that it has been so inadequately studied by historians. Yet a similar problem arises if we move from the 'dignified' to the 'effective' aspects of the state, and the changes in it over these years. English historians have concentrated on politics and administrative 'reform', rather than on the expanding reach of government. Colonial historians have been concerned with the making of constitutions rather than the nature of the state. The widespread view that England was a little governed society has been reinforced by a tendency to ignore events in the wider British dominions and also to look forward expectantly to a liberal Age of Reform in the 1830s. If events in England, Ireland and India after 1780 are taken together, however, a picture emerges of a significant growth of the power and aims of the British imperial state, particularly in the peripheries. The expansion began as a result of the defeats of the American wars, but it seemed to gain new momentum with the emergence of revolutionary France and domestic disorders.

AN IMPERIAL REVOLUTION IN GOVERNMENT?

England, it is true, was a homogeneous kingdom and a relatively unified society from an early period. It required a less intrusive apparatus of political control, of intendants and inquisitions, than its continental neighbours. The rapid growth of agriculture and trade after the end of the American war also lessened the taxation problems of what should have been a defeated nation. In a sense, economic growth pre-empted the need for more vigorous political integration of the United Kingdom and Ireland. During the 1770s the Bank of England note replaced private bank notes. The number of private banks in London doubled between 1760 and 1800; English country banks increased from 150 in 1776 to 280 in the early 1790s. Scottish country banks showed remarkable growth; the Bank for Ireland was established in 1783. Significantly, the Scottish and Irish banks ultimately depended on the Bank of England's reserve of treasure and had to accept some degree of control (Clapham 1944: i, 169). The expansion of English industrial production and the Irish trade treaties of 1780 and 1801 speeded the creation of a vast free-trade area within the United Kingdom. All the same, government-sponsored administrative and political rationalisation was quite significant. The ministries of Shelburne and Pitt introduced significant changes in home and colonial government. Pitt's first ministry also engineered a modest consolidation of the national tax base in England and began moves towards a specialist and salaried public service (Roseveare 1969: 132–6). From an imperial perspective at least, the degree of innovation bears comparison with the later 'nineteenth century revolution in government'.

The Commutation Act of 1784 which reduced duties on imported Chinese tea was one of a series of measures designed to control smuggling and bring burgeoning trade within the purview of the state. It went along with the consolidation of customs in 1787 and a great expansion of indirect taxes on 'luxury' and consumption as the prospect of European war materialised (Evans 1983: 24–7). The ministry also imposed England's first consolidated income tax in 1799; this tax, an important marker in the development of the modern state, became permanent during the war. Englishmen were soon complaining that they were the most highly taxed in Europe; they faced levies on clocks and carriages and even windows. It is true that direct taxation remained surprisingly light. Even in Ireland, public hostility centred on local hearth taxes and tithes rather than on land and income tax. Yet even indirect taxation demanded a much closer knowledge of the means of individual trades and citizens. The increase in taxation, therefore, went alongside a growth in the number of statistical and sociological surveys commissioned by the government and by private individuals.

One reason why Pitt and his colleagues were unable to do more to create a coherent network of officers to staff the revamped taxation and financial system was that ministers were jealous of their patronage in 'office' which was important to them in building up a following in Parliament. Nevertheless, some important departures in the creation of a permanent civil service were made after the American fiasco and during the Revolutionary Wars. Shelburne (1782) attempted to eliminate sinecures as holders died, and he composed the taking of 'fees' into a single salary for officers (Norris 1963). A Treasury minute of 1782 stressed punctual performance of duties, put a new career structure in place and began and ordered the retention of state papers which had previously been purloined by individual officers (Baker 1973: 212ff.). Most important, the Treasury was elevated as a controlling agency above other departments of government, while the Commissioners for Examining Public Accounts were created. The pressures of the Revolutionary Wars consolidated this new financial and taxation system.

If England alone is considered, the developments in the controlling power of the state after 1780 seem significant, but not revolutionary, at least by comparison with the French empire a few years later. The wealth and influence of the late eighteenth-century aristocracy and the existence of a large reservoir of semi-skilled professional talent in guise of the clergy ensured that much of the expanded business of the state could still be managed in the localities. Even the great magnate families, whose activities in local society dwindled in the earlier part of the century, appear to have returned to politics and to local administration towards its end. Magnate families reasserted their power over parliamentary seats in town and country and began to sit more often in their ancient role as JPs (Cannadine: forthcoming). This may have complemented their increased interest in local economic 'improvement' and also the tense conditions of the 1790s when, government sources noted, 'the body of landed gentlemen . . . are thoroughly frightened' (Ehrman 1983: 139) by popular discontent and the possibility of invasion. Law reform was one of the few areas where centralisation began seriously to erode the independence of local justices. After 1808, the campaign associated with Sir Samuel Romilly had achieved some successes in setting limits to the use of capital punishment and standardising practice between courts across the country (Beattie 1986: 632). An inheritance of evangelical ideas that public hanging 'bestialised' rather than quieted the population displayed the law reform movement's common origins with other contemporary causes such as the abolition of the slave trade and foreign missions. It also seems possible that the demand for 'fairer justice' was also associated with mass conscription and the consciousness of a national war effort.

In other parts of the empire, the active rôle of the state was, however, much more in evidence. In Ireland the ruling class was too scattered and culturally remote from the populace especially in the south, for anything like the English JP system to work. The electorate was kept small by anti-Catholic laws and the poverty of the population so that local bodies were inadequate to share in the tasks of regulation and taxation discharged by their English equivalents. The state had to take a more direct rôle, and one which, in theory, stood above the interests of the great Protestant landowning families, the brewers, maltsters and linen-masters. The shock delivered to the Anglo-Irish ruling élite in the 1780s, therefore, engendered a movement towards reform or, more precisely, towards state regulation. Administrative 'reform', moreover, was a more acceptable response to crisis than any dallying with political reform which might have threatened the Protestant Ascendancy. The career of Sir J. Fitzpatrick (MacDonagh 1984) was born out of this new spirit. His public services began with the control and regulation of Irish charter schools (1785–7) and the scandalous Irish prison service (the Irish Prisons Amendment Act, 1787). Later, Fitzpatrick's concern for Irish soldiers serving in the imperial army embroiled him in a campaign for the reform of conditions of service for soldiers in England, and eventually drew his attention to the regulation of convict ships sailing from Portsmouth. While little change occurred in the fragmented army bureaucracy, Fitzpatrick's initiatives did coincide with a more general movement towards regulation. The need for this was impressed on the ministry after the usual failures at the beginning of the Revolutionary Wars. The Transport Board was created by order-in-council in 1794. The Alien Office, designed to control refugees and 'seditionists', took shape in 1793–4, while a national system of royal mails began to operate in 1792.

The imperial dimension of this should be stressed. Fitzpatrick achieved his entrée into English administration through the good offices of Lord Moira, one of the strongest advocates of patriotic union between Britain and Ireland (MacDonagh 1984: 154–5). Several other specialists, most notably the young Castlereagh (prime minister, 1808–18), also had their first taste of interventionist administration while serving Dublin Castle in the reforming 1780s and the troubled 1790s. Later the Moira connection was to prove one of the most important channels of administrative talent to India and the Cape of Good Hope. Fitzpatrick himself had some dealings with the East India Company when he attempted to set in motion moves for the regulation of their large and badly maintained fleet in 1796 (ibid.: 242).

Irish reform might have begun as a manifestation of civic virtue during the heady years of the early 1780s when Ireland seemed likely to go along the path trodden by America. But the rising tide of civil commotion in the later 1780s and 1790s sharpened the edges of the state and called forth its coercive energies. As dissidence went underground and festered into anti-tithe riots, Dublin Castle began to build an Irish police force with the Dublin Police Act of 1786 and the Irish Police Act of 1787. The resident magistracy, a body of 3,000 assorted gentlemen and Anglican clerics, were supplemented in the same year with a number of 'assistant barristers', settled in disturbed counties to act as 'constant assistant' to the Lord Lieutenant, to aid in the sessions and to hold courts for civil cases (McDowell 1979: 64–6). With the rebellion of 1797–8, the Insurrection Act built up the military presence in aid of the civil power. The mix of powerful civil administrators, para-military rural police and soldiers ready in barracks made Ireland seem like British Bengal or some newly conquered Caribbean island. Here was an extension of the arm of the British state as clear as anything contemplated by Bonaparte, though Todd James remarked that it was 'suited not to France, where it would not now be tolerated, but the meridian of Turkey' (ibid.: 62).

While it was intimately connected with the project of imperial state-building, Indian 'reform' had already developed its own momentum following the dangerous crisis of 1776–83. Pitt's India Bill of 1783 and the Commutation Act of 1784 were intended to help stabilise respectively the political and financial structures of the East India Company. Most important was the Bill's elevation of the rôle of the Governor-General over his own and subordinate councils and the establishment of a Board of Control in London to oversee the working of the whole Indian government. The intention was to avoid the conflicts of interest which had nearly brought defeat for the Company at the hands of the Marathas and Mysore and which had broken the British empire in the Thirteen Colonies. Ironically, the man put in charge of this economical reform and elevation of the public at the expense of the private was Lord Cornwallis, defeated at Yorktown but now both Governor-General and Commander-in-Chief in India. Cornwallis's main aim was to restore Company finances after the battering they had suffered during the previous war. His Permanent Settlement of the Bengal Revenues (1793) was designed to provide a secure revenue for the state and an expansion of trade and agriculture. This in turn would wipe out the Company's debt and release the home government from the necessity of bailing the Company out. Cornwallis and his successors failed to reduce Company debt. Still, by 1793 India was making a significant direct contribution to the British Exchequer (£500,000 per annum). It was also indirectly stimulating British tax revenues through the China trade and the consequent great increase in imports of tea and West Indian sugar into Britain.

The measures developed by Cornwallis for 'settling' India, often seen only in an oriental context, were typical of this period of state-building. Cornwallis's collectors (sundered from judicial responsibility), salaried, publicly accountable and eschewing involvement in private trade, were similar to the officers of Pitt's new customs department. The language of private civic virtue, which earlier in the century had been the pride of the country gentleman, was now applied to a salaried and more carefully trained bureaucracy. The form of the new civil service, its language and mores, and sometimes its personnel were later transferred to southern Africa, Ceylon, southeast Asia and even to the Mediterranean islands, as the local problems of imperial administration became more complex in the following decade.

Over and above the accountable district official, who inherited an awesome sense of natural fitness to govern from gentry exemplars of the past, stood the 'Board', a body of semi-specialist administrators and political appointees. The last few years of the century saw a proliferation of the numbers and function of such administrative boards both in Britain and the colonies. In India the great increase of official business connected with the reorganisation of Indian land revenue after 1793 expanded the rôle of executive overseeing bodies such as the Boards of Revenue which stood between collectors and distant or preoccupied governors. These inquisitorial and supervisory bodies were meant to guard the new autocratic district officials from peculation and old perquisites which were coming to be seen as corrupt. They were firmly subordinated to the now more powerful governors. In Britain, such new concentrations of specialist expertise had greater executive power. Thus the Colonial Office itself developed quite rapidly out of the Board of War and Colonies under the influence of Lord Bathurst and a number of taxation and colonial experts such as William Huskisson whose careers ran parallel to those of their peers at the newly professionalised Treasury (Madden 1987: 26–30).

'AGRARIAN PATRIOTISM' AND THE 'BRITISH EMPIRE IN EUROPE'

One of the most interesting examples of the use of boards as an arm of interventionist government was the Board of Agriculture established by Pitt's administration in 1793. The Board inherited the themes and attitudes of agrarian patriots and agricultural societies of the eighteenth century. Its members transformed them into a scientific and statistical method for the integration of state and empire. What we have called agrarian patriotism received a considerable fillip from the losses of the American and East Indian wars. Arthur Young, agronomist and political economist, quoted with approval the views of J. W. Baker, the Dublin Society's experimenter in husbandry, that only through projects 'of a domestical and oeconomical nature' could the waste of war be repaired. Arthur Young and his coadjutors, who began to have considerable influence on the government, argued that 'the future dependence of the state should settle more on the basis of internal resources than on such as experience had proved to be insecure (i.e. colonial possessions)'. Not only had the Thirteen Colonies been lost after costly wars because the 'beggars, fanaticks, felons and madmen of the Kingdom, had been encouraged in their speculation of settling in the wilds of America' (*AA*: i, 1784, 11), but the loss of India 'ought to come'; while the holdings in the Caribbean were 'precarious' and 'speculative' and, worse, tended to perpetuate the inhumanity of the slave trade and the mortality of thousands of British sailors. Instead, Arthur Young and his group argued through their journal, *The Annals of Agriculture and Other Useful Arts* and through countless speeches and pamphlets, true

121

patriotism and enlightened policy should be directed towards the reclamation of the 'wastes which disgrace this country'. Agricultural improvement, however, had a political, indeed imperial aspect. At this stage, emigration (later to be officially approved) was regarded as a dangerous diminution of the human resources of the country. Only a populous state could maintain both agriculture and a large army. Agricultural improvement also brought about economic and cultural assimilation. In Ireland, for instance, enclosure of common lands and the application of capital to farming had made 'ragged beggars' into farmers possessing good stocks of cattle.

The patriotic aspect of agrarian improvement in drawing together the 'British Empire in Europe' was stressed even more strongly by William Knox. Knox's particular target was emigration from northern and western Scotland to Canada and the United States which had speeded up considerably after the serious famine of 1782 and had been encouraged by the settlement of Scottish troops in America following the peace of 1783. Knox and improving gentlemen associated with the intellectual world of Glasgow and Edinburgh felt that the agrarian development of Scotland would stop the flow of 'indentured slaves' to 'unremitting toil and drudgery, in boundless deserts at a distance of 3,000 miles' and asked whether it would not be better that 'a permanent and valuable colony might not . . . be established in those outskirts of Britain, to the great benefit and security of the centre' (Knox 1784: ii). Scotland had an exceptionally good record of improvement of resources. Between 1750 and 1780 the gentry of Scotland had trebled their rents, and this had led to a considerable increase of English imports from £9 to £12 million per annum between 1750 and 1785. Northern and western Scotland could raise 50,000 hardy seamen for British fleets: altogether it was a better bet than India which contributed little except a drain of specie from the 'British Empire in Europe'. In fact, 'the embarrassments to be encountered, and the difficulties to be surmounted, in restoring a fallen empire, present a noble field for the exercise of Roman patriotism; that species of virtue which elevates the mind, supersedes all selfish or frivolous considerations and perseveres with enthusiastic zeal in whatever is great, useful and benevolent' (ibid.: 28).

Knox and his contemporaries began to fuse a north British patriotism to the Catonic virtues celebrated earlier by Lord Kames. However, the next generation were more practical men. The Board of Agriculture and the Committee of Trade were founded at the beginning of a long war during which feeding the towns became critical to the survival of the ministry. The problem was increased by a series of 'poor to appalling harvest' between 1791 and 1802, with an absolute shortage of grain in 1795 (Ehrman 1983: 464). Hostility to intervention in the grain markets even in the face of 'bread and peace riots' in the new industrial towns gained a sharper theoretical justification from both new Smithian political economists and Burkean Whigs. Now government was prepared actively to stimulate production through the Board of Agriculture which gave grants for extending arable and tried to disseminate knowledge of new farming techniques.

Such measures bore practical results in the Scottish Highlands and Islands. An influential figure in this context was Sir John Sinclair, a Caithness landholder active in many private and state-sponsored development schemes (Mitchison 1962): the British Fisheries Society (1786), the Highland Society of Edinburgh, experiments to improve varieties of Highland sheep and, ultimately, the Board of Agriculture and the great *Statistical Account of Scotland*. Sinclair was typical of a generation of Highland and Caithness landowners who were determined to break down impediments to efficiency such as old common tenurial forms (the runrig system) and the Highlanders' preference for black cattle over sheep. He opposed what he called 'republican farming' (Mitchison 1962: 97), advocated the consolidation of small estates and enclosure of public land. Unlike some other agrarian patriots he was also interested in imperial ventures, becoming a member of Sir Joseph Banks's African Association of 1788 which promoted Mungo Park's expeditions into the interior of West Africa.

State schemes of development in Scotland were less of an innovation, and less politically dangerous, than they had been in England. The Commissioners of Forfeited Estates had worked after the 1745 Rebellion to improve communication in the Highlands and to assimilate its Gaelic populations to Lowland and north British culture. As late as 1784, Pitt and Dundas (as Lord Advocate) had raised considerable sums of money by restoring forfeited estates to the heirs of the 1745 rebels: £90,000 of the proceeds was used to construct harbours, bridges and canals and also to support the educational activities of the Protestant Society in Scotland for the Propagation of Christian Knowledge among the Gaelic Catholics (Pryde 1962: 155). Government interest in the Highlands had also been maintained by periodic famines which raised fears of agrarian discontent like that of Ireland and also by the growing rôle of the Highlands as a recruiting ground for British soldiers after 1793.

Local initiative played an important rôle. In 1787 a convention of the Royal Boroughs of Scotland petitioned the Treasury for an extension of the Clyde fisheries to the Irish coast and a reciprocal right for Irish fishermen to exploit Scottish waters. The manufacturers of Glasgow also urged the development of a 'Canal of the Firths' to develop trade down the whole British west coast. State money was forthcoming for several of these schemes.

As important as practical development was the huge and systematic collection of facts and figures which the Board of Agriculture commissioned from seven districts of England and Scotland. The last quarter of the eighteenth century had seen a considerable increase in private topographical and statistical publications, notable among them the investigations of Arthur Young. But statistics as the word implies were a foundation of the modern state, and the first *General Report on the Agricultural State and political circumstances of Scotland* (1814) quoted Bacon to the effect that 'Knowledge is Power'. The Scottish surveys achieved their excellence partly because the kingdom was a highly educated society, but partly because Gaelic Scotland was a colonial society. The resident clergy of the Church of Scotland, alert for social changes of political importance, acted like resident magistrates in Ireland or the newly-instituted collectors of British India to amass and interpret information. The apparently objective compilations of facts on production, population and land tenures concealed a plan of assimilation and control. The clergy correspondents wrote of the 'mischievous' consequences of runrig and common lands, of the danger that entailed land held out to agricultural improvement. C. Findlater of Newlands, Peeblesshire, submitted to the *Survey* a disquisition on political economy laced with quotations from Adam Smith and Malthus which showed how the 'savage Gael' could be made civilised through the good effects of industry which would in turn deliver him from 'an unrestrained indulgence in the powers of procreation' (Sinclair 1814: ii, 189).

In Ireland the Anglican clergy were not in such a good position to act as the eyes and the ears of the new state; they had too much on hand getting in their tithes and preventing their hayricks being burnt out. All the same, agrarianism was seen as the natural policy for imperial consolidation. An *Essay on the Present State of Manners and Education among the Lower Class of the People of Ireland and of the Means of Improving Them* (1799) urged that an Agricultural Board should take a leading rôle in both the improvement of Irish agriculture and educating peasant children in 'active industry', as 'religious bigotry' derived from ignorance and idleness. Moreover, the government should try to 'engage the cooperation of catholic ministers' in providing information and leadership on the model of the Scottish clergy who had 'zealously' helped Sir John Sinclair. The notion of associating Catholic priests with an imperial project would appear bizarre even a generation later.

Interestingly, Sinclair had proposed both an English and an Indian Survey along the same lines of the Scottish one. Dundas had, however, refused this on the grounds that 'the statistical state of India is already as well understood as in any other part of His Majesty's dominions' (Mitchison 1962: 134). Indeed, the emergence of political statistics in India had proceeded with remarkable speed after 1783. Previous to that date, British collection of facts on the sub-continent had been extremely patchy and even the volume of Company papers had been small compared with that generated by the (much poorer) Dutch or French East India Companies. As the British became more concerned with the detailed administration of Indian justice and land revenues after Cornwallis's Permanent Settlement, the volume of official compilations increased markedly. Worthy of mention are Colebrooke and Lambert's *Account of the Husbandry and Internal Commerce of Bengal* and the huge statistical surveys of both north and south India carried out by Francis Buchanan between 1798 and 1815 (Vicziany 1986). Buchanan came from precisely the same intellectual tradition which was presently engaged in mapping Scotland and, to a lesser extent, Ireland. Educated at Glasgow in medicine and natural philosophy, he had heard Robertson, a pupil of Linnaeus, lecture there. Linnaeus, though best known for his biological taxonomies, had also pioneered anthropological classifications of the people of Lapland in the 1730s. Buchanan's method as it evolved in Mysore at the turn of the nineteenth century involved a minute taxonomic classification of natural habitat, political economy, peoples and customs. The method of relentless empiricism should not distract attention from its philosophical underpinnings in ideas of classificatory logic and a stage theory in the development of political and economic structures. Equivalents to Buchanan, many of them medically trained products of the later Scottish Enlightenment, were soon active in most areas of the empire, notably Ceylon, the Cape of Good Hope and the Pacific coast of Canada. A universal application of the ideas of 'agrarian patriotism' rather more than the novel and still contentious doctrines of radical free trade was the essential 'development theory' of Britain's new empire between 1780 and 1830. Yet here again the British experience was no more than part of a world-wide development of the scope and ambition of the state. The greatest of all contemporary statistical accounts was the Napoleonic *Description de l'Egypte*, ordered by Bonaparte and written in thirty-six volumes by the savants of the Académie Française.

AN IMPERIAL ARMY AND POLICE

We now turn from the regulatory to the coercive forces of the state: the army, militia, police and navy, alongside the developments in autocratic civil and military establishments abroad. Traditionally, the British army after Marlborough has been regarded as a polyglot shambles of Brunswickers, Hessians and Irish until well on in the Napoleonic Wars. Parliament's dislike of standing armies and the amateurishness of Pitt and his successors, until the time of Castlereagh's war ministry, are often cited as proof of the low esteem in which Britain's land forces were held until the victories in the Peninsular War during 1812–13. All the same, there had been some important developments towards the creation of an imperial army before this date, particularly in recruitment, provision and flexible, international deployment. At the start of the wars, British land forces amounted to 39,000 men; by 1809 the total at home and abroad was 200,000 men. An almost equal number of non-European troops served in the military forces of the East India Company and colonial governments.

Most important perhaps were the moves to expand recruitment from the subordinate peasantries of the British empire after 1793. In this, Great Britain stood comparison with the great continental autocracies. The British army, viewed globally, was not the army of the English industrial cities that it became in the Victorian period. Military pay could not generally compete with the wages to be earned in expanding industries and advanced agriculture of southern Britain. Instead, it was drawn from the younger sons of small peasant holdings in the Highlands of Scotland, Ulster and southern Ireland and north India. In all these areas, demographic pressure and agrarian distress, deepening towards the end of the eighteenth century, combined to make enlistment an attractive option. In the Highlands there had already developed a tradition of service in the British forces after 'the '45'. Scottish soldiers were among the few

British troops as such which played an important rôle in the Seven Years' and American Wars. Great Highland magnates such as the Dukes of Argyle, Athole and Breadalbane encouraged the flow of recruits during the French Wars. These lairds found difficulty in rack-renting the close-knit and independent farming clans. Military service, however, brought money into the area, relieved population pressure and established a reputation for loyalty. In 1791 it was said of Argyle 'there is perhaps no subject in Great Britain, who could bring so great a number of persons into the field in defence of his Sovereign and his country' (Lenman 1981: 243). In 1798, for instance, the Black Watch Regiment found 51 per cent of its recruits in the Highlands; by 1830–4 it was only 9 per cent. In 1830, Scots represented 13.5 per cent of the British army as a whole, and this figure had been nearer 20 per cent in 1815 (Spiers 1980: 48–9).

Most striking of all was the way in which the empire began to draw on its Irish peasantry and small gentry over these years. In 1830, Irishmen still accounted for about 43 per cent of the British Crown forces, and the figure may well have been over 50 per cent in 1815, and higher if the Irishmen in East India Company service were taken into account. Up to the time of the American War, Irish Catholics had not been numerous in the British army itself, and they were certainly not allowed to become officers. Recruitment was largely confined to the farming and linen families of Ulster; the Catholics were 'least tempted from their bogs' (cited in McDowell 1979: 61). As the need for manpower increased after 1787, all regiments were allowed to recruit in Ireland and after 1793 Catholics were allowed to take lower commissions in the British army.

The East India Company forces, composed of Hindus and Muslims, could hardly discriminate against Catholic Christians, though officers generally and ordinary soldiers in the artillery remained Protestant. By 1780 there were three Company recruiting stations in Ireland, two drawing from the South and Central Lowlands. The Bengal army from 1825–50 appears to have been about 33.7 per cent English, 10.9 per cent Scottish and 47.9 per cent Irish. Irish defensive militias (fencibles) were deployed in Egypt in 1801 while Irish gentry played a disproportionate rôle in the military annals of the Company. Sir Eyre Coote saved southern India in 1780–2. Arthur Wellesley and his brothers, of course, effectively created Britain's Second Empire in Asia. W. H. Tone, brother of Wolfe Tone, the Irish revolutionary, wrote a classic study of the Marathas of western India (Cadell 1949–53: 78); Wolfe Tone himself had once proposed a British colonisation of the Western Pacific. Both these facts serve as a reminder that a desire to participate in British imperial ventures at this time was in no way incompatible with revolutionary nationalist aims.

In a very different context, Britain's Indian army drew upon indigenous social groups which were suffering similar demographic and social pressures. As early as 1765 the Company had begun to recruit the rural Brahmins and Rajputs of the central Ganges valley into the Bengal army. The warrior peasants of this region had once served the declining Mughal empire; now service with the Company made it possible for them to maintain their position in the villages without compromising their status by taking to agricultural labour themselves. It was from this pool of recruits and similar aspiring warrior people throughout India (Telugu peasants in the south; Kunbis in the west) that Cornwallis and Wellesley raised the strength of the Company's armies from less than 90,000 in 1790 to nearly 200,000 in 1815, making of it one of the biggest European-style standing armies in the world. Ironically, the monopoly of service and status achieved by the high-caste peasantry of north India, and the equally rigid monopoly created by its complacent Anglo-Irish and Scots officers created problems which were to shake the foundations of empire two generations later, in the revolt of 1857.

British, Irish and colonial militias were also greatly expanded and played an important rôle in broadening the basis of empire and spreading its material benefits to members of those subordinate social groups who cared to enlist. Pitt's Militia Acts of 1793 began a long process of reorganisation which reached its peak during the patriotic volunteering movement of 1805–6. By this time Great Britain and Ireland may have had a total militia pool of nearly 90,000 which was drawn on to replenish the regular army during the Peninsular War. The local militias in Ireland and Scotland were paralleled by provincial scratch-forces in India which absorbed predatory warrior peoples and the military detritus of the Muslim kingdoms. Plunderers were often set to catch plunderers as paramilitary police. On the Cape after 1806, the British began to raise a Hottentot Corps made up of Africans who had been acculturated by long exposure to the Dutch and of people of mixed race (Percival 1806: 72, 93). In the Caribbean, black colonial militias were raised during the crisis of the slave revolts after 1793. Many people of mixed race and free blacks improved their social and economic status by working for British military and naval establishments (Braithwaite 1971: 292). The expanded rôle of imperial forces in these areas helped to rally inferior groups to empire by breaking the monopoly of the creole élites on employment and by loosening the bonds of racial exclusiveness.

Ministers stumbled towards the creation of a more integrated imperial military command and enhanced the power of Crown governors over the land forces. Both the Irish and Indian high commands were reorganised to eliminate jobbery (Fortescue 1910–30, iv, ii, 886). Such measures were forced on them by circumstances. The early part of the war saw gruelling conflicts in the West Indies characteristic of the eighteenth century. Fever and battle casualties there swallowed up 40,000 men between 1794 and 1798. Then came a massive push in the Middle East. Here for the first time the British and British Indian armies cooperated on an international scale outside India, against the French in Egypt. Wellesley's campaigns in India forced a reluctant ministry to commit to him a further 30,000 king's troops. All these efforts culminated in the struggle of the Peninsular War which was not simply the largest military campaign the British empire had ever fought, but also a massive exercise in logistics, diplomacy and local administration.

One important aspect of the evolving imperial army was its growing seclusion from the civil population. Colonial armies had always been housed in fort-barracks; they could hardly be quartered on indigenous populations. During the wars this policy was extended to the 'British Empire in Europe' and other 'white colonies'. Over 200 barracks were built in Britain alone between 1797 and the end of the war (Fortescue 1910–30, iv, ii, 907), so that the British army was 'imperceptibly transferred from quarters in alehouses to quarters in barracks'. Here it could not only 'protect' the civil population, but also be used against it in times of civil unrest, should that be necessary. The construction of barracks, jails and, to a lesser extent, canals marked the physical expansion of empire from Ontario to the River Ganges. It was against these manifestations of the 'military engineering school of architecture', offhandedly embellished with a few classical columns, that subject populations throughout the world were to turn their wrath over the next century. Whereas the Mughals had built mosques and tombs, an old Indian told William Sleeman the Company only built jails and barracks. War had created a two-edged weapon for the state, to be used both against 'native' enemies and working-class rebels.

Compared with the mobilisation of troops by the French empire, that of the British empire was on a small scale; but the British expansion and deployment of economic resources for military ends was on an even greater scale. The British arms trade was already the biggest in the world; it had swamped Asia and the Americas with sophisticated muskets. In the wars of the 1780s, two-thirds of the arms used by Haidar Ali and Tipu Sultan against the Company were of British manufacture. Indian saltpetre was also exported to Europe on a very large scale. At the beginning of the French Wars, muskets made by the East India Company factories were used in Great Britain. Later, home arms production expanded very fast, especially after 1804 when the Board of Ordnance established its own office at Birmingham for provision and began production at the Tower of London. Arms exports and related financial subsidies were an important dimension of British wartime diplomacy. In 1813, for instance, Britain exported to Russia, Prussia and Sweden, 218 cannon, 124,000 muskets and 18 million rounds of ball cartridge. A huge total of armaments was also supplied by British and Indian factories to southern European and Asian regimes over these years. Indeed, the export of the British arms surplus between 1804 and 1824 played a critical part in arming the forces of the state at an international level and ensuring its victory over internal dissidents, peasant rebels and armed plunderers.

The expansion of the Royal Navy as an imperial fleet, and the reconstruction of its command and logistical structure has received much more attention from historians. In a sense the Navy represented the first true multinational manufacturing corporation: the earlier East and West Indian Companies had farmed out most of their construction and production work. On a global scale the navy was a great arm of 'ecological imperialism'. Smaller islands in the West Indies, St Helena and Ascension Island, had already been denuded of their timber, like the forests of southern England. During the French and Napoleonic Wars the process achieved global proportions. Within the space of a few years massive inroads were made into the teak forests of the western Ghats of India and coastal Burma; Australian hardwoods had disappeared by 1820 and exports of pine spars from Canada and the United States expanded at a startling rate. The estimated annual consumption of oak alone in 1809 was supposed to be 400,000 tons for the Royal Navy, 115,000 tons for the East India Company service and two and a half million tons for merchant shipping, much of it used for military service (*QR*: 8, 1812, 47). Royal Navy shipyards in Britain, the West Indies, Malta (after 1802), Bombay and Calcutta grew rapidly. Malta became a magnet for the Greek and Jewish merchants of the whole Mediterranean region. To Bombay came increasing numbers of Parsi shipwrights, the fathers and grandfathers of the famous Parsi compradors and notables of the Victorian era, the most successful case of cultural assimilation by the British in Asia. Again, the political and economic implications of these injections of cash and political energy by a direct arm of the imperial state should not be underestimated. Loyalty was often purchased across the barrel of a naval gun.

If the Navy was the most developed arm of the British empire, the police were the least developed compared with agencies of control and surveillance in most European states. Ideological antipathy to police as an aspect of 'French tyranny' fuelled more pragmatic antagonism of English local magistrates to the interference of watchdogs of the central state in their affairs. Pitt's London and West Police Bill of 1785 was dropped in the face of opposition and Francis Burton's Police Bill of 1792 merely created a system of more efficient and higher calibre justices. Pitt's régime did, however, change the mentality of the agencies of internal control. Use of local militias, the Aliens Act and harassment of 'seditionists' by a greatly expanded public spying system enthused Bow Street Runners, justices and constables with a sense of mission (Ehrman 1983: 137). In Ireland, as we have seen, the gradual escalation of peasant and sectarian violence after 1783 prompted the creation in 1787 of the first true police force in the United Kingdom (McDowell 1979: 62). This had become the only alternative to the growth of vigilante organisations under control of Protestant magnates. The Irish Constabulary was not properly organised until the 1820s, and even then only 850 of its 2,700 members were Catholics. Policemen leaned to the Ascendancy, intervening in folk practices such as poaching salmon fry and running illicit distilleries. The colonial state was now able to intervene in local conflicts.

In India the British inherited various forms of urban and rural police from the Mughals. Jurisdictions overlapped, the range of public intervention in customary or moral law was questionable and there was much coercion and violence. In the 1780s, however, the major colonial settlements began to see attempts to create more efficient and accountable services. Interestingly, the beginnings of 'moral panic' about the criminality and depravity of the lower classes in England found echoes in India. Social tension during the wars against Mysore and the French popularised the notion that the city of Madras was 'swarming with spies and informers of both the Asiatic and European powers'. Sir William Jones, the great orientalist, then sessions judge, remarked on the constant tumult of affrays and robberies in the rapidly expanding city of

Calcutta. The target of these guardians of the peace was not so much the 'corrupt' native but the supposedly decadent, treacherous and usually Catholic half-caste communities which were coming under increasing pressure at this time from the growing British populations. The Boards of Police in both Calcutta and Madras was one aspect of the attempt by expatriates to gain control of 'their' cities and to distance themselves from Indians and from the European and Eurasian riff-raff of the bazaars. Wellesley's wars added the jacobinical menace to the Catholic and Muslim ones. Much stricter control of the major settlements was accompanied by early attempts to create a rural police force to aid in the collection of government revenue and maintain the security of property. Once again, it was in the areas where customary, decentralised systems of control and arbitration had once been strong, but were now buckling under the pressure of alien rule and economic change, that the imperial state was forced first to extend its purview. This was as true of Ireland as of India.

CHAPTER FIVE
Imperial Britain: Personnel and Ideas

On the surface, British politics between 1783 and 1815 remained personal and factional. The issues of Catholic emancipation and the conduct of the Peninsular War were rallying cries, and something like a permanent opposition and a forceful 'public opinion' outside Parliament had emerged. In general, affiliation was still determined by family connection, friendship and the distribution of jobs, and this in spite of politicians' obeisance to the ideas of economical reform. Pitt and his successsors were, however, able to call upon a much wider range of expertise than earlier ministries and, perhaps in response to the intellectual and administrative élan of the French republic and empire, policy at home and abroad achieved much greater ideological clarity.

THE IMPERIAL ELITE AND GENTRY RESURGENCE

Politicians were now unusually well connected among the secular and ecclesiastical intelligentsia. The influence of Adam Smith was extended through the medium of improvers such as Sinclair and Arthur Young. Wilberforce, Hannah Moore, Grant, Shore and other Evangelicals were close to Pitt himself. This relationship bloomed during the campaign against the slave trade and it extended to other issues including Irish and colonial government. Pitt was also connected with Anglican moral reformers in the hierarchy, notably Beilby Porteus, Bishop of London, and with reforming heads of Oxford and Cambridge colleges. Dundas's coterie, which included Scots intellectuals and imperial administrators such as

Wellesley and Macartney, ramified into the early Colonial Office under Bathurst. The collective mentality of this governing circle was Anglican and anti-Jacobin. It was fired with a sharper sense of British national and imperial mission. It represented a conservative philosophical cabal, as influential as that of Milner, Curzon and Baring a century later, during another period of 'new imperialism'. In the earlier eighteenth century only the Elder Pitt's war ministry had been anything like this, and even then had lacked its cohesion and long-term influence.

The war ministries were able to draw upon a much wider pool of talent in their attempts to create a national military and imperial effort. The growing commercial middle class provided some military men and state servants: Sir Thomas Munro, Governor of Madras, son of a ruined American tobacco trader from Glasgow, was an outstanding example. There were new state servants from even poorer backgrounds. Lachlan Macquarie from the Isle of Mull, a tenant farmer's son, though related to the local lairds, rose to become Governor of New South Wales (1810–21) after an East India Company military career. He brought many of his relatives into East India service and into government posts in Australia (Ritchie 1986). However, it was the more substantial gentry, and in particular gentry from outlying regions of the United Kingdom, which was most forward in filling the many new positions in state and colonial service. Paradoxically, the one state in Europe where the notion of an 'aristocratic reaction' in the late eighteenth century seems to have some basis was Britain (Cannadine: forthcoming). Gentlemen took a new interest in local government, regained control over Parliamentary electorates and became more active again in local voluntary bodies. Political interests which grew out of efforts at economic improvement partly explain this. Sudden changes of economic fortune, the product of fast but unbalanced economic change, also pushed younger sons into military or state service (the indebted Elgins were a good example of this). Indeed, the long period of war evoked a response from a class which was traditionally concerned with warfare and domination, recreating in Great Britain and Ireland a *noblesse d'épée* of the sort which had not been seen since the seventeenth century. For this period at least, Joseph Schumpeter's notion of imperialism, as an atavistic reaction of gentlemen rather than a hobby of merchant adventurers seems to have something to recommend it.

The argument is more convincing if individual cases are considered. Members of the greater aristocracy were represented in colonial service and the new army. The Beauforts, one of the first half dozen families of the realm, provided South Africa with its most famous early governor, Lord Charles Somerset, and six other representatives. The Moiras, leading Irish peers, brought family members into the Irish, British and ultimately Indian services as their influence expanded after 1780. Both families were very close to the Crown, and in particular to the Prince Regent after 1806. Among the Whig aristocracy, the Cavendish-Bentincks provided Lord William, Governor of Madras and later Governor-General of India. Sir Charles A. Fitzroy, eldest son of Sir Charles Fitzroy and grandson of the Duke of Grafton, was Military Secretary to Beaufort on the Cape and Governor of the Leeward Islands. He married the daughter of the Duke of Richmond, Lady Sarah Lennox. At the same time, members of the lesser gentry from the Scottish Borders and Ireland found their way into very prominent positions either through the patronage of the great magnates or through independent merit. Notable here were the Elliots (Lord Minto) the Edmonstones, Elphinstones and Maitlands of south-eastern Scotland, Lothian and the Borders. From Ireland came the Wellesleys, the Macartneys, Castlereaghs and Fitzmaurices. And the more distant English provinces had also thrown up families which became entrenched in military and colonial service: the Clives of Shropshire had a head start, but were later joined by Cornwallises and Norths.

The strong representation of Scottish and Anglo-Irish gentry was mainly Dundas's doing. Dundas was connected with Moira, while Lady Ann Lindsay was married to Lord Macartney, so the whole group formed a loose kinship unit which brought in young men from among their humbler connections. In the perfervid atmosphere of wartime London, the relationships tended to reinforce themselves. So Lady Anne Wellesley, sister of Wellington, married the Hon Henry Fitzroy, and their daughter, Georgina, married Henry Somerset, the future Duke of Beaufort (very much an open élite this). Lady Anne Wellesley later married John Napier, father of Sir Charles Napier of the Greek Islands and later conqueror of Sindh. In time, the Peninsular campaign created a network or relationships and an esprit de corps which carried the military, diplomatic and colonial services into the Victorian Age. Two governors-general of India and three governors of the Cape were among the most prominent graduates of Wellington's great open-air public school on the River Tagus.

Broader social changes were also working here. Partly it was a matter of access. Even a declining gentry family could raise sufficient credit for the necessary investment for purchasing an opening in East India Company service or for a commission. Only wealthy or well-connected merchant families could do the same. Also, if the Scottish Enlightenment had provided a moral centre for the lesser Scottish gentry in the mid-eighteenth century, imperial service both in Europe and outside began to play this rôle towards its end, becoming a focus of specifically Scottish national pride. The appointments pages of the Edinburgh *Blackwood's Magazine* became an inventory of the expansion of the British empire; so many families of Scottish descent had thronged to fill the thousand or more highly paid jobs which were created in the Indian and colonial service after 1790. The Scottish and Irish groups maintained their cohesion in the colonial setting. The Madras Scottish Society, for instance, had its annual meetings where Scottish issues were aired. At one such, the enclosure and depopulation of the Highlands was denounced (Anon., Binny 1969: 28). Money from colonial ventures was returned home to establish schools with an orientation towards state and colonial service, such as the Forfar Madras College. The creation of an empire with a powerful Scottish or 'North British' character became a self-sustaining myth and provided an avenue for the socially mobile. Scottish 'agrarian patriotism', educational ideas, botany and statistics came, in turn, to have a formative rôle in the construction of the colonies.

THE CHURCH MILITANT, RACE AND LAW

The last chapter considered the changes in institutions within the British élite which gave form to the Second British Empire. Even if there was no 'Regency Révolution in Government' there was a considerable extension of the rôle of the state and its arms of coercion, and this was particularly true of the peripheries of the 'British Empire in Europe'. However, there was a much sharper discontinuity between the 'first' and 'second' empires in the realm of ideas and attitudes. Racial superiority was now more firmly inscribed in institutions. This was a change which predated by some years the full impact of evangelical and utilitarian ideas in the 1820s and 1830s, or of the Indian Mutiny of 1857, which many historians have seen as turning points in the emergence of British racism. Two other elements were also important. First, there was a growth of evangelical ideas within the established churches (Anglican, Church of Ireland and Scottish Presbyterian). Secondly, agrarian patriots who had once been hostile to empire took their message abroad. The dominant ideological character of this Second British Empire was aristocratic, autocratic and agrarianist. By contrast, free trade and early 'liberal' ideas were much more characteristic of what might be called the 'Third' Empire which emerged in 1830s and after.

These currents of ideas did not, of course, sweep all before them. Nor were actors on the political stage uniformly affected by them. Many evangelicals were suspicious of colonial conquest; a few even felt that the institution of slavery could be made morally acceptable. On the other hand, there were imperial proconsuls such as Mountstuart Elphinstone who remained pure eighteenth-century deists; or royalists like Thomas Maitland who were sceptics and 'pagans'. Rather, what happened was that public discourse was powerfully influenced by the more strident rhetoric of well-organised proponents of the new 'moral majoritarianism' (Hilton 1988). Again, the prescriptions of evangelical thinkers for Britain and for her dependencies might differ considerably. People whose commitment to an individualistic moral rearmament in English society was closely connected with their advocacy of free trade and a distrust of paternalism, could be found arguing that in the colonies, or even in Ireland, 'the state of society' warranted benevolent British intervention in the market and indigenous customs. Thus divisions between 'liberal Tories' and 'high Tories', between dissenting evangelicals and conservative Anglicans, which bulked large in England, often dissolved in the colonial context. To this extent, colonial projects helped reinforce a national consensus at home.

There was a myth propagated by liberal historians of empire that religion played only a small rôle in the British imperialism which was a pragmatic construction of hardy entrepreneurs and agnostic statesmen. By contrast, religious zeal was characterisitic of the Iberians and French overseas. Though direct missionary activity or forced conversion was rare indeed among the British, the spirit of the revived empire of the Napoleonic Wars was throughly infused with a kind of Anglican providentialism which acted more or less subtly on policy. This helps to explain that though Crown and Company preached religious neutrality, indigenous people, non-Protestants and non-Anglicans almost everywhere feared religious assimilation. Their reactions ranged from Catholic nationalism in Ireland through Calvinist separatism in southern

Africa to the fear of 'frankish' or unclean influences which inspired the Vellore Mutiny of the Madras army in 1806.

The view that British overseas dominion was the creation of an Anglican Providence had often been voiced before, even in the Bengal of the 1770s when the secular values of the Enlightenment seemed dominant. The classical fear that empire necessarily corrupted civic virtue through luxury and decadence was already on the wane by the 1770s (Marshall 1981). Following the growth of Methodism and the trauma of the French Revolution, the link between evangelical Protestantism, nationalism and empire was forged more strongly. There was a change of philosophical perspective. Some Old Dissenters and Rational Dissenters (such as Unitarians) had drifted from allegiance to the British Crown during the American War and had denounced patriotism. Anglican radicals such as Wyvill had preached the cause of the Americans and reform.

After 1790, Unitarianism rapidly declined. Anglicans, Baptists and Presbyterians all vigorously attacked 'unpatriotic' dissenters such as Richard Price. Whereas the religious form of philosophic individualism had tended to downgrade 'the affections', including affection towards nation, the younger generation drew upon the philosopher Hartley who argued that 'the constitution of the human mind requires family affections and patriotism as necessary preconditions of general benevolence'. Writers such as Wilberforce or full-blooded Anglicans such as Burke and Coleridge seemed to suggest that religion was integrally patriotic. For Coleridge, indeed, national and social discipline seemed more important for the religious life than individual struggle, and 'national unity is secured by the Church'. The importance of private, philosophical judgement was never completely rejected, but moral seriousness, godliness and patriotism seemed ever more closely aligned (Stafford 1982: 385).

This was largely a reaction to the growth of Methodism, which was only later intensified by fear of French Jacobinism. For many among the gentry and wealthier merchant class, Methodism was a 'state within a state'. It was a sect which propagated itself by the manipulation of family ties of affection, and one which might undermine both the established Church and the Constitution. This was because loyalty to country was essentially an extension of affection to family. From this perspective, Wesley had become almost a 'Romish Saint', while Methodists were now 'a distinct people in the Empire, having their peculiar laws and manners, a hierarchy, a costume, even a physiognomy of their own' (*QR*: 4, 1810, 480). So a new Anglican patriotism had to be called into being because the legitimacy of the Church and the definition of nation as a religious community was being contested in England for the first time since the end of the Catholic challenge of the Pretenders in 1745.

When the Methodists formally seceded from the Church of England (1795) and spawned yet more advanced religious opinions, concern about them grew. Their success in attracting lower middle-class and labouring people, particularly in regions distant from London, was also a source of suspicion for a ruling class increasingly worried about popular unrest. The Methodists' outwardly conservative political stance did not fully allay such fears. Yet the first reaction from within the ruling class, the evangelical movement, was almost as suspect as the Methodists in the eyes of many Anglicans. Of course, Wilberforce's attempts to establish a public godliness and sobriety, trumpeted in his *A practical view of the prevailing religious system of professed Christians in the higher and middle classes of the country contrasted with real Christianity* (1798), ran parallel to the emerging orthodox Anglican movement which associated ungodly living with political radicalism. Like them, Wilberforce stressed the 'corruption of human nature' as contrasted with the Enlightenment philosophers, and he bewailed the spread of vice especially among the middle classes of the cities (Wilberforce 1798: 385). Like them, he also lauded 'the tendency of religion, and especially of Christianity to promote the well-being of political communities' (ibid.: 35). The problem was that the attitude of Wilberforce and the Anglican evangelicals to the Church hierarchy was ambiguous. Some Anglicans saw among them a dangerous sect, another implicit challenge to the authority of priest and bishop. What was needed, therefore, was a militant revival within the Anglican communion, but one directed by bishops who were to be the leading edge of an imperial moral rearmament. For this type of Anglican, reform of the lower classes and the moral salvation of the colonies were closely equated. They represented a break with the eighteenth-century tradition of decentralised lay Anglicanism which had seen the wider empire as little more than a bin-end of ecclesiastical patronage.

A key figure in the revitalisation movement within the Anglican establishment was Beilby Porteus, a native of New England, who was Bishop of London from 1786 to 1811. Porteus's support for the relief of the political disabilities of Dissenters and Roman Catholics brought him near to the position of Pitt, Wellesley and Dundas, who favoured a policy of imperial 'assimilation'. Not all Methodists or Anglican evangelicals were as tolerant of Catholicism. Porteus and his acolytes also favoured a moral revival within English society. He opposed Sunday political debating societies which sprang up in the 1780s and was struck by 'the increasing profligacy of the times' (Hodgson 1821: i, 92). He was also active in the 'Society for Enforcing the King's Proclamation against Immorality and Profaneness'. Later some of his friends helped promote the movement for a national educational system espousing Anglican values (the National Society for Promoting the Education of the Poor in the Principles of the Anglican Church).

The emphasis in all these bodies was less on individual redemption than on social control. London must be the crucible of change because this was where the 'emissaries of infidelity were most actively occupied in their work of mischief'. Moral change would come about not through sects and holy cabals but through the reorganisation and centralisation of the Church itself. Porteus attempted to establish a code for the Church in his *Charge to the Clergy* (1794). He also tried to regain control over the appointment of East India Company chaplains because of 'the importance of religion in our eastern settlements' (Hodgson 1821: i, 146–7). As a man of colonial origins himself, he worked hard in the cause of the abolition of the slave trade and the cautious evangelisation of the West Indian slaves. The method was to be one of godly demonstration by a revived Anglican hierarchy in the Caribbean over which the Bishop of London was to have much greater influence. The Church, which had so far confined itself to benevolent inactivity and distant encouragement of Moravian and other continental Protestant missionaries, was now to be more active. The civilisation and conversion of the 'negroes in the British West Indian Islands' should begin with the Church's own trust estates. Enlightened planters instructed by the king through the Colonial Office would then initiate a scheme for the promotion of Christianity among their own slaves. The newly-founded Anglican Church Missionary Society would work cautiously and slowly in the areas of British influence.

The tone of Porteus's activities was typical of the establishment version of the new Church militant. Like more radical Anglican evangelicals of the Wilberforce connection and the luminaries of the dissenting London Missionary Societies (founded 1795), Porteus believed that the 'providential' destiny of the British nation had been amply proved by the events of the French Wars. As his intellectual successor, Claudius Buchanan, Chaplain to the East India Company, put it, 'Great Britain unquestionably holds the place now which Rome formerly held, in regard to the power and means of promoting Christian knowledge.' Why else indeed should providence have saved Great Britain from the 'general wreck of nations'? (Buchanan 1813: 11)

Yet zeal was restrained by prudence. The great aim was to strengthen the Christian witness of British citizens, particularly those abroad, along with slaves and servants directly in their charge. A secondary aim was to convert to Protestantism, Catholics, Syrian and eastern Orthodox Christians or any of those who could be held to have already been exposed to God's Word but in a perverted form. The direct evangelisation of free, heathen peoples was another matter. Many establishment evangelicals believed that education and enlightenment must precede evangelisation and that Christian demonstrations of godliness were more appropriate than the direct assaults on the souls and affections of heathens approved by more radical evangelicals. Buchanan's *Colonial Ecclesiastical Establishments* summed up these views. The aim was to 'extend the national Church'. There should be 'bishops in each of Great Britain's principal provinces'; the universities should become active in language and translation, and Anglican literary establishments should be founded in all of the main sectors of the globe. The location of these missions is of interest. The reclamation of the planters and their charges in the West Indies was of prime concern. A slow spread of evangelical thought had begun among Anglicans connected with the West Indies following James Ramsey's 'An Essay on the Treatment of African Slaves in the British Sugar Islands' (1786). This argued that Christianity could prevent 'insurrections and murders' and undermine the bases of African superstitions among the slaves. Buchanan added that 'Mulattos' were to be saved 'because of their English descent'. The Anglican establishment was slow to promote societies for more widespread conversion, but the pressure of abolitionist opinion and periodic slave revolts had begun to force movement by the early 1820s. In Africa, Christian witness should be continued among the inhabitants of Sierra Leone. This colony had been founded for trade. It was also designed to evangelise the Dark Continent and remove from the streets of London the thousands of 'negro beggars' who had been released into them by Lord Mansfield's judgement of 1776, freeing slaves in England. Commerce, religion and domestic social control marched hand in hand.

In Europe and the East, particular attention was to be paid to Malta and the eastern Mediterranean because here the decay of the Romish Church was very clear; also to the ancient Christian Churches and to the Jews (often a target of Christian interest during periods of providentialist revivalism). In India, Anglo-Indians and the servants of East India Company officials were ripe for proper conversion; but so also were the oriental English themselves, only recently turning away from the dangers of 'brahminisation'. Buchanan argued that it was particularly important to cement the bonds with the Anglo-Indian, since if the United States had been Anglican it would not have revolted against the Crown (Buchanan 1813: 112). Thus Buchanan's ecclesiastical establishments were to be the frontier posts of a Christian empire.

This was the understanding of the rôle of Anglicanism in empire which came closest to that of the political élite. As we have seen, Wellesley's Fort William College and the East India Company's Haileybury were designed to release the oriental Briton from the danger of corruption by the 'depravity of the people of India'. This was to be done through the inculcation of Christian sobriety and Indian languages, for the latter would obviate dependence on native informants and factotums. There should certainly be an Anglican hierarchy and an Anglican cathedral in India as Lord Valentia, a close friend of Wellesley, noted. Yet its aim was not direct conversion. Instead, 'the splendour of episcopal worship should be maintained in the highest degree our Church allows' and this would awe and impress the 'natives ... accustomed to ceremonial pomp' (Valentia 1809: i, 245). Thus conversion would come through grateful emulation rather than zealous evangelisation which might provoke tumult and opposition (here Valentia's vision of ecclestiastical pomp closely mirrored Wellesley's new secular grandeur). Buchanan's prescription was even clearer: 'An Archbishop is wanted for India – a sacred and exalted figure. We want something *royal* [my emphasis] in a spiritual and temporal sense for the abject subjects of this great eastern empire' (cited in Thompson and Garratt 1934: 247).

For this reason, early Anglican efforts in the East concentrated on work among existing Christian communities and nominal Christians. In southern and south-western India, attempts were made to reconvert Catholic Indian Christians perverted and 'led astray' not only by Popery but also Hindu superstition. This culminated in the efforts of John Munro, Resident and later financial officer of the Kingdom of Travancore, to seduce the ancient community of St Thomas Christians from their Monophysite or 'Jacobite' allegiance into the Anglican fold, a project which involved the Resident's personal intervention in Church matters (Bayly: forthcoming). These efforts went alongside those of the more radical evangelicals such as Charles Grant of the India Board of Control who influenced the Company to send out godly chaplains, encouraged the building of churches and tried to set a new pious standard of behaviour for the once wild Company servants. In Ceylon meanwhile, nominal Christians (those who had been 'converted' by the Dutch Company in order to qualify for public office) were all provided with copies of the works of Bishop Porteus with the blessing of the first governors of the new Crown colony (Hodgson 1821: i, 281).

Much has been written on the influences of Wilberforce and the more advanced Anglican evangelicals or of Dissenters on the moral and educational history of the British empire in the early nineteenth century. What we have called here the establishment evangelicals have emerged less clearly. Yet their influence on the future tone of British imperialism was quite critical. They had helped convert Anglicanism from the lay conformity of mid-century into a national and imperial faith, but one which was directed particularly to British nationals and their immediate legal descendants by birth (people of mixed race) or by law (slaves). Empire and national church were henceforth closely connected but in a much more ambiguous way than was the case with the French Catholic churches or the Portuguese Padroado (Crown patronage).

One reason that men of this strain of thought were opposed to direct evangelisation along the lines long practised by the imperial powers of France and southern Europe was a philosophical one. Man could only come to Christ through the exercise of an awakened reason; St Paul preached to the Greeks and Romans, not directly to the Barbarians. This was the line of thought which also held sway in the Calvinist Church of Scotland until the early years of the nineteeth century. Another more powerful reason was political. There was a deep distrust of miscegenation and the dangers of 'unrestrained colonisation' which was held to increase the likelihood of the mixing of the races. Buchanan thought that uncontrolled colonisation had caused the American Revolution. Lord Valentia spent a large part of his *Travels* denouncing the East Indian half-caste: 'in every country where this intermediate cast has been permitted to rise, it has ultimately tended to the ruin of that country'; the latest and most horrific example of this was the 'mulatto' and slave revolts of the island of Saint Domingue. But there were others who disagreed. A writer in the *Quarterly Review* refuted the argument, claiming that the Portuguese had infinitely benefited from the emergence of people of mixed race in Brazil. In India such a class would be English in inclination but well adapted to the climate and with deep roots in indigenous society. In either case, the establishment view was that 'the Church of India [should] be truly the bulwark of the state' (*QR*: 2, 1809, 98–9; Valentia 1809: i, 241–3).

Despite differences over 'colonisation' and the merits of direct or indirect evangelisation of indigenous peoples, the patriotic and nationalist tone of missionary work outside the fold of the establishment Anglicans was just as striking. In one sense, indeed, the dissenting churches, the Church of Scotland and the non-episcopalian evangelicals became 'nationalised' through their activities in the colonial mission field, dispelling the stigma of radicalism which had arisen from their work among the lower classes in Britain. The efforts of Wilberforce, Grant and their circle significantly increased public pressure for intervention by Westminster against the colonial assemblies of the West Indian islands which persistently sought to frustrate attempts to evangelise the slaves on the ground that this would increase rather than diminish the danger of slave revolts. Unrelenting public scrutiny of efforts to suppress the slave trade in West Africa and to monitor the treatment of slaves in the Cape Colony set the agenda for Lord Bathurst's expanding bureaucracy in the Colonial Office. At the same time, Methodist missions to the South Seas appear to have borrowed their organisational skills from the Royal Navy and the East India Company (*QR*: 3, 1809, 25). Subscriptions were channelled into central holding organisation, and the importance of settling the Polynesians to 'useful trades' was emphasised, missionary ships set sail, amidst psalm singing, under a missionary flag showing 'three doves argent in a purple field bearing olive branches in their bills'. Methodists and radical Anglicans also took their 'protestant' crusade to Ireland in the early years of the nineteenth century. They abandoned an earlier circumspection and directly attacked the 'Romish superstition' on the grounds that it held the Irish peasant in thrall and encouraged popular disaffection against the Crown (Bowen 1971).

The connection between cultural assimilation within the United Kingdom and evangelism as an imperial project is equally clear in Scotland. Scottish Protestants had been sending missions to Gaelic Catholics since the beginning of the eighteenth century. Towards its end the influence of English Methodists and evangelicals prompted a new wave of activity. Great Scottish ladies such as Lady Maxwell, Lady Glenarchy and the Countess of Leven promoted Sunday

Schools and the Edinburgh Tract Society in the 1770s and 1780s (Mathieson 1916: 51). Later, John Alexander Haldane, captain in the East India Company's marine, joined Simeon, a Cambridge divine, and toured through Fife and the Highlands in 1796 distributing tracts; in the following year they visited the west of Scotland founding Sunday Schools. After 1797 the effort gathered momentum with the distribution of 27,000 tracts in the Orkneys (ibid.: 63–4).

Several prominent people in these movements had east or west India connections, although at this time the dominant Moderates of the Church of Scotland had little time for Asian missions. William Carey, a Baptist and one of Bengal's most important missionaries, was denied help in 1797 (he began work instead in 1800 under the aegis of Danish missionaries in Serampore, Bengal). However, an interesting indication of the growing national and imperial consensus was the later rapprochement between the once-radical Bengal missionaries and the Wellesley circle. In 1799 Carey had dropped the 'teachings of the French' for 'things of greater consequence' (Potts 1967: 171). This paved the way for Carey and his comperes to become involved with language teaching at Wellesley's new Fort William College. Meanwhile, the ideology of the Church of Scotland was itself changing. Many moderate churchmen had argued in an enlightenment philosophical tradition that secular learning and 'civilisation' must precede conversion. After 1815, however, the growth of pietism and the conviction of Britain's providential mission broke the dam (Mathieson 1916: 272). The French Revolution had eroded faith in Natural Philosophy, and Scottish churchmen like their English counterparts began to emphasise Faith. Nor did they wish to lose out in the explosion of evangelical activity (Hetherington 1843: 227–8). A great tide of missionary experience and zeal was unleashed in the East, notably in Dr Duff's Indian mission. It was now urged that the Hindu soul could make a quantum leap to Grace through an intuitive grasp of the meaning of the Gospel. Church of Scotland missionaries were equally important on the Cape of Good Hope. Their leaning towards Calvinism made it easier for them to adjust to the inheritance of the Dutch Reformed Church. Yet their settlements among runaway slaves and Hottentots played an important part in constructing a network of specifically British mission stations outside the control of the Cape Dutch farmers, and at times that of the colonial authorities themselves.

Protestant missionary activity, then, was an important aspect of the creation of a British nationalism. Attempts at cultural and religious assimilation were intended not only to hold out salvation but also to create a pious and united Protestant empire through the distribution of tracts or the founding of schools. The stimulus to these changes in Europe and outside was in large measure fear of rapid social change. Lower-class sedition, the 'rise and progress of popular disaffection', inspired attempts to reform the morals of the London populace, just as Anglican schools in rural Ireland and Presbyterian Bible centres in the Highlands were an answer to the problem of the Celtic Catholic peasantry. Even in overseas settlements, evangelising and the strengthening of the forces of law and order were often directed not so much towards indigenous peoples as towards disciplining the European and Eurasian or Eurafrican underclasses which were developing in the major imperial centres. The inhabitants of Madras, for instance, had decided to found a Protestant Orphanage to reclaim the illegitimate children of European military 'who are thought to number many thousands' well before large-scale missionary activity got under way in the Company's territories. The colonial establishment feared that such people might otherwise become agents of sedition for the European Catholic or Indian powers. Similar movements were afoot before the turn of the century in British Cape Town and the Caribbean islands.

The ripples created by these activities spread far, and the signals received by non-Christians and non-Protestants seemed at odds with the official proclamations of religious neutrality. British judges and collectors in India and Ceylon, for instance, insisted on the swearing of oaths on scriptures or Ganges water, invoking the will of 'Almighty God' in their courts. Churches were sometimes built with drafted labour. Insidious efforts were made to root out 'corruption' in temples and pagodas (Appadurai 1981). Such ideologies were alien to Asians, for money had always passed between worshipper and officiant in the course of ritual and endowment. More, these colonial initiatives occurred at a time when purification movements among Muslims and state-sponsored cults among Hindus and Buddhists had fostered greater sensitivity to the relationship between power and worship.

The result was the deepening of mistrust and a growing belief that British rule and Christian power were one and the same, a fear that had some justification, despite the secular protestations of Company neutrality. Well before the Christian 'Age of Reform' of the 1830s, when missionaries entered India and Ceylon more freely, Nazarene values were insidiously influencing the doctrines of empire in both East and West. In the past, many historians held that the failure of *formal* conversion in Asia proved that missionary activity was irrelevant to social history. This position seems less convincing now. Even popular religious movements seem to have responded to the Christian challenge, becoming more concerned with text and authority and organising themselves for direct proselytisation. Almost from its inception this empire, then, was a force in the deeper historical experience of non-European peoples, not simply an incubus of its élites.

RACIAL HIERARCHY AND BENEVOLENCE

The pressure for assimilation through religious emulation was matched by the need to categorise, rank or exclude certain social groups which could not easily be made 'loyal Protestant servants of His Majesty'. The sharpening of nationalism and evangelicalism was paralleled by a sharpening of racial attitudes. Popular attitudes themselves are of course notoriously difficult to capture, but what seems important is that notions of racial hierarchy were increasingly embodied in institutions and codes. This was not simply a result of ideological and administrative changes in Europe. Indeed, the formation of classes in indigenous societies remained the critical condition for the maintenance of racial and occupational hierarchies in Britain's colonial possessions. All the same, changing attitudes in metropolitan society were formative influences and should not be discounted.

One of the difficulties of measuring racial attitudes is their longevity. In the mid-eighteenth century, quasi-biological theories, theories of climatic difference, and theories that mankind developed through different historical stages were all prevalent to different degrees both among the populace and the élites (Williams and Marshall 1980). Any ideological crutch from the Fall of Man to the kinship of negro and ape was used to justify the brutality of the slave trade. In Asia it was the age of enlightenment when Warren Hastings or Sir William Jones saw in India's ancient civilisation the lineaments of Arcadia served by Brahmins 'truly elevated above priest-craft', whose sages Valmiki, Vyasa and Kalidasa were the equal of Plato and Pindar. Hinduism for him should rejoice in the philosophy of *karma* which embodied the possibility of eternal moral improvement rather than the 'horrid Christian notion of punishment without end'. But it would be naive to believe that racialism was expunged from the conduct of daily life by the principles of virtue. A little later we find Jones for the first time having to buy his 'daily rice' following the collapse of the interest on his Company bonds. Approaching an Indian moneylender, he records: 'I was forced to borrow of a *black man* . . . it was like touching a snake or a South American eel' (Jones 1970: ii, 561). This pejorative use of the term 'black man' in the later eighteenth-century Orient seems to be most often associated with disadvantageous financial dealings between Europeans and indigenous moneylenders. Court room perjury was a 'universal characteristic of black men' or 'the character of the native merchant is . . . completely Jewish' and 'that low cunning, stratagem and deceit which characterises the money transactions of persons of narrow intellects, applies almost without exception to this class of the Hindu native servants' (Tennant 1804: i, 86).

It is probable that wary accommodation interrupted with outbreaks of savage racial hatred had long been characteristic of the relations between Englishmen and traders from southern Europe or Asia. What began to change in the last twenty years of the eighteenth century was that the notion of 'native depravity' became generalised to all Indians, and that the concept became a feature of public debate at the centre of the British state. This was achieved through a series of dramatic events and coups de propaganda in which the trial of Warren Hastings, the morass of the 'Nawab of Arcot's Debts', and the legend of Tipu the 'Mahomedan Tyrant' were the most important. Vague trends of opinion were brought into sharp focus by changes in the ideologies of the state and the mentality of ruling groups both in England and in India.

In the earlier part of the eighteenth century, 'luxury' and empire were thought to be corrupting, but the continuing importance of India to the stability of the British financial world and the honour of British élites ensured that even the disasters of 1779–83 did not dim the importance of the Indian empire. How could the disasters be explained? This task was easier if it could be shown that quite apart from the implacable hostility of Hindu and Muslim 'tyrants', British national character in India was being undermined by the wiles of the native servants of government and the private Hindu commercial factotums (dubashes and banians) used by Europeans in their private capacity. British commerce in India had surged forward on the crest of the dynamic commercial economy in commodities and political rights which had burst the bounds of the Mughal empire. But who was to control the empire, Asia's indigenous capitalists and landlords or Britain's 'gentlemanly capitalists', increasingly more gentlemen than capitalists?

So now there were campaigns against the 'hydra of dubashism' and the corruption of the banians. Hastings and his coadjutors had been corrupted by the 'big money' of the East India Company, but also by the 'petty cash' of the Indian commercial classes. In India, Cornwallis moved heavily against European revenue officers involved in Indian trade and tried to create a wall of regulations to separate the Indian and European worlds. He was deeply suspicious of the 'constitution of Asiatick monarchies'. The consolidation of the powers of British district collectors and the separation of powers between the judicial and revenue branch under his reforms of 1793 was partly designed to remove the influence of Indians over the organs of government. In a pragmatic, untheoretical way it was being stated that the social environment and superstitions of Indians made them irremediably corrupt. Interestingly, this injunction was also extended to persons of mixed race who had been of critical importance to all European empires in India. After 1793 Eurasians were also excluded from political and military office under the Company for two generations. Indian influences had inevitably tainted them. Because many of the Eurasians were of Portuguese origin they compounded the superstition of Catholicism with the depravity of their Indian origins. In this way, 'blood' came to define suitability for civil office and political power.

A clearer racial hierarchy was emerging, with Europeans, Eurasians and various groups of Indians ranked according to their public virtue. Something like this had long existed in the Caribbean, renowned for its minute gradations of quadroons, octroons, etc. But the racial hierarchy of the sugar islands had emerged out of the needs of the creole élites; in the Orient it was now being generated by the state. When the British conquered Ceylon after 1796 (and also during their brief sojourn in Java, 1810–16) they exported these new sensibilities to the conquered territories. The 'Dutch burghers' of Colombo and other Ceylonese cities were similarly excluded from office despite the fact that they had been the key group in both Portuguese and Dutch administrations (McGilvray 1982). The new racial exclusiveness was enhanced by concern for the loyalty of the Dutch descendants and contempt for the Catholic confession of the Portuguese Eurasians.

This political discrimination on matters of race had local origins in the societies of Asia, and for that matter of the

Caribbean and southern Africa. Yet it also gained considerable strength from aspects of British thought and political economy. The notion of corruption brought about through the operations of money and virtue had become an ideology of the reforming 'court' as well as the 'country' during Pitt's ministries. 'Economical reform' also sought to distance office in Britain from money and heredity. The idea of an uncorrupt and virtuous civil service was coming into being at the very same time as money-making and commerce became increasingly despised by the gentry, finding new energy in the aristocratic reaction. Wellesley's well-publicised contempt for the 'cheesemongers of Leadenhall Street [the Directors of the East India Company]' was a mirror of the many pamphlets and books which denounced manufacturers and traders as inferior to gentlemen. England's 'gentlemanly capitalism' profited from business through the emerging banking and financial structure; but it increasingly sought to keep business and production itself at arm's length. Haileybury College and Wellesley's Fort William College were designed to produce a total environment for young civil servants to educate them in virtue and isolate them from 'the climate and the vices of the people of India' and that people's 'peculiar depravity'. The development of oriental language skills was particularly important here. The rediscovery of classical Indian languages and translation of modern texts was initiated by the savants of the Enlightenment, but its 'practical' purpose was soon emphasised. To the men of Wellesley's generation, young civil servants could only be released from dependence on Indians by command of their language. In a revealing passage Wellesley, only two weeks in India, wrote about Thomas Oakes, member of the Madras Board of Revenue. He was a clever man, but 'he is entirely ignorant of the languages and therefore must be in the hands of a durbash [sic]'. Significantly also, 'his character in point of integrity is not without blemish' (Ingram 1970: 171). These themes echoed educational ideas in contemporary England which foreshadowed the norms of Victorian moral education. In the same way, the revived public schools in Britain, the new Royal Military College and, to a lesser extent, the reformed colleges of Oxford and Cambridge were designed to educate the young in an Anglican, aristocratic model of state service isolated from the lures of money, sinecure and hereditary office.

If these state-sponsored institutions were new, the philosophical principles which they taught were firmly rooted in the eighteenth century, though more clearly worked out and 'captured' by the new imperial Court Party. A word constantly in use in moral and racial discourse was 'independency'. Collectors, judges or members of the new Treasury could only be honest if they had 'moral' and financial 'independency'. What distinguished the Briton from the Irish, the Italian or the Bengali was moral independency enshrined in their laws, constitution, and Protestant religion. The notion of independency as a prerequisite of civic virtue has strong roots in eighteenth-century political discourse and particularly in the Scottish Enlightenment. Scottish moral philosophers pioneered the study of what they called 'moral culture' in which the virtue of moral autonomy in the individual was lauded both as the basis of political liberty and of economic success (Phillipson 1974). From Andrew Fletcher at the turn of the eighteenth century, through to Adam Ferguson, the lack of these virtues was seen to result in taxation, bloated government and poverty. The ethical basis of later notions of liberty and prosperity assured through free trade unshackled by monopoly or arbitrary government is particularly clear in Adam Smith's *Theory of Moral Sentiments* (1759) which provides much of the sociological and philosophical underpinnings of the *Wealth of Nations*. Here the notion of 'self-command', the avoidance of extremes – luxury, licentiousness and debt – is elevated to be the ideal pattern of life. In this way we avoid 'the corruption of our moral sentiments' and the 'worship of the rich and powerful'. By mid-century, Socrates had been replaced in the works of philosophers such as Dugald Stewart by Cicero and Seneca; the virtuous Scottish public worthy was being replaced by the virtuous political expert, and some of those experts were to be found working for the East India Company and in the new colonies.

Such ideas of moral independency and the need to foster it lay near the centre of modern British moral and political sensibilities. They informed Adam Smith and the whole free trade school which saw the enlightenment transaction of free individuals as the guarantee of both virtue and prosperity. This set of ideas is also central to the arguments of the anti-slavery and anti-slave trade movement. Slavery corrupts the moral sentiments of the human soul since it creates baseness among both masters and slaves. Slaves must be freed in order to cultivate their own moral sentiments and understand Christian religious life (Anstey 1975). In turn, economy would benefit since the work of freemen was always better than slaves and the capital wasted in the 'money lottery' of the sugar and slave trades would be invested in serving the consumption and production of an increasingly prosperous and contented body of free peasants and labourers. The dominant *historical* interpretation of the differences between human societies remained that of the Scottish Enlightenment: the idea that society moves through 'stages' of development from nomadism to high civilisation through the application of 'industry'. This was not really dethroned until the early Victorian Biblical revival. But what is interesting is how it was increasingly assumed that a Christian empire could intervene and speed up this development through stages. Thus Pitt in his 1792 speech on the ending of the slave trade argued that the Roman empire had intervened to conquer and ultimately christianise Britain, 'once a slave-market'. Hence empire could 'break down the natural incapacity of the Britons'. The theories of 'moral sentiments' and human development through stages were thus easily uncoupled from their individualist and historical underpinnings, to be taken up and employed as the dominant public discourse of a new Christian imperialism.

It is sobering to consider that this notion of 'moral independency' was crucial to the development of British racial stereotypes and racial exclusiveness during the same period. Racial attitudes again lay near the heart of the late eighteenth-century transformation of enlightenment values into the rhetoric of the new imperial 'Court'. Catholics, half-castes and Hindus (later Turks and Egyptians) were degenerate because 'superstition' and 'Muhammadan tyranny' had corrupted both their moral sentiments and their political constitutions. Ideas such as this became common currency in the second half of the eighteenth century as enlightenment admiration for oriental civilisation was extinguished. The Rev. William Tennant, a visitor to India and other colonies in the 1780s, expounded many of these ideas in his *Indian Recreations. Consisting chiefly of Strictures on the Domestic and Rural Economy of the Mahomedans and Hindoos* (1804). For Tennant the Hindus had some virtues. Hinduism breeds abstinence and frugality, which are good; again, Hindus are generally less vicious than Muhammadans because of their early marriages and, as he astonishingly observed, their numbers of wives 'offers them an opportunity of gratifying or extinguishing their passions as soon as they arise'. On the other hand, Hindu festivals spoil much of the good work 'as they tend to dissipate the minds of indolent people and withdraw them from those labours from which they derive their support' (Tennant 1804: i, 102). Exactly the same arguments were, of course, being used of the working classes in Britain. However, Hindu caste at this period is condemned not mainly because of its inegalitarian features, its tendency to act against the greatest good of the greatest number, or even as an impediment to Christianity (as in the 1820s and 1830s), but because it impedes the principle of 'emulation of betters' which is the foundation of moral and economic progress. Virtue and industry in Hindu society can offer 'no additional rank' (ibid.: 105); so the false division of labour based on caste pre-empts any virtuous division of labour based on the free play of industrious sentiments. In the hands of other and later writers the racial denunciation became more shrill. For superstition had led this 'mild and patient' people to commit every day 'the most atrocious crimes without compassion and remorse', infanticide, ritual murder and widow-burning.

This rule-of-thumb assessment of the extent to which a race's moral sentiments had been corrupted by its institutions provided a crude tool with which to inscribe and enforce racial hierarchies. European nations could be squeezed easily into the moral grid. The Portuguese had become effeminate through miscegenation and Catholic superstition. The French, already corrupted by Catholicism, had become further depraved by tyranny and police. Paradoxically, tyranny had made them a 'light and docile population'. Paradoxically again, the ecclesiastical tyranny of the Spanish Inquisition had 'encouraged the search for licentious books', and had consequently (?) led to depopulation. The Dutch, once the flagship of Protestant freedoms, had chosen the path of monopoly and dependence (Marshall 1987). Monopoly had destroyed industriousness, making them 'lazy revengeful and cruel', while Dutch settler and farming communites overseas had been brutalised by the institution of slavery. Cape Hottentots and Malays, for instance, had been made 'fanatical' by the barbarity of Dutch punishments (Percival 1806: 72–93). When the British conquered French territory after 1793, they demolished the liberty trees and held Anglican services. When they took Dutch settlements they publicly burned the wheel and other instruments of torture which continued to be used under Dutch Roman Law, and they did this in the name of 'benevolence'. So pervasive and programmatic became these racial assessments that they merged one with another. The Irish were oriental; Sanskrit, once the oriental sister of Latin and Greek, became an amalgam of 'hottentotish and barbarous words' (*QR*: 9, 1809, 57); Frenchmen became 'Marathas', and Brahmins 'Aztecs' (ibid.: 3, 1809, 217).

These principles were quickly applied to new areas of British political interest such as the Middle East. 'Muhammadan tyranny' and the 'enthusiasm of priests' (as in the Catholic Irish case) had led to domestic licence and indolence. What was true of Muslim India was equally true of the 'corrupt and decadent Turk' as observed by J. L. Burckhardt, whose *Notes on the Bedouins and the Wahabys* (based on observations made *c.* 1800–16) anticipates many clichés of British Arabism through to the present century. Those Arabs the farthest removed from the corruption of the Turk and his money were the best. Those like the Howeytat who were important in the trade from Cairo to Mecca and Medina were less 'honourable' (Burkhardt 1831: i, 366–7).

Egalitarian tribal societies raised some problems in contemporary British thinking about race. Many took the eighteenth-century view, propounded by Montesquieu, that 'the wild arabs were a race of roaming thieves' (Richardson 1777: 125–8). But both romanticism and the hatred of centralised 'tyrannies' which had emerged out of the Napoleonic struggle counselled a different position. Evidently, the Beduin Arabs had freedom after a fashion. Their 'puritan' disdain for near-worship of the Prophet and Islamic saints demonstrated a moral independency. On the other hand, ideas of the development of society through historical stages put nomadic tribal societies quite low on the hierarchy because of their lack of immovable private property whose possession would inculcate habits of industriousness and economic development. If the British were contemptuous of decadent and effeminate townsmen with their priests, festivals and hierarchies, they were equally worried by nomads and pastoralists. This had been demonstrated on the Highlands of Scotland, Ireland and in late eighteenth-century India where district officers had begun to try to settle and subdue wandering peoples who they regarded as carriers of roguery and dissidence. Amidst this ambiguity developed a new, romantic strain of British thinking about race. Free races, uncorrupted by superstition and dependence and redolent of an age of heroism and innocence, still inhabited parts of the earth. In time they too might turn their natural love of freedom to the pursuit of self-sufficiency through industry.

This strain of romantic adulation of the egalitarian primitive was closely related to the movement to rediscover folk culture which had gathered pace in Europe in the previous fifty years. The saga of Ossian's ballads in Scotland had been part of the transformation of the barbarous and superstitious Gael into the noble Scottish tribesman which reached its apogee in the work of Sir Walter Scott. There are echoes of it in Mountstuart Elphinstone's admiration for the ascetic Pathan of central Afghanistan and in

James Tod's *The Annals and Antiquities of Rajasthan*. Tod wove a neo-Gothic romance out of the ballads and genealogies of the princes of Rajasthan whom he encountered in the first two decades of the nineteenth century. Their virtues of honour, independence and loyalty were contrasted with the effeminacy of priesthood and the corruption of the towns. This romantic stereotyping of races also informed practical action. The need to protect tribal innocence was used to justify the diplomatic and military segregation of areas such as Afghanistan and Rajasthan, or later northern Nigeria and the Sudan under systems of indirect British rule. Areas which had once been major centres of trade and urbanism could thereby be isolated from both indigenous and European capitalism, and the dangerous conflicts to which they might give rise.

The emergence of racial attitudes common in the nineteenth century has sometimes been traced to the impact of utilitarianism and evangelical Christianity, especially in the 1830s (Stokes 1959), or to the arrival of British women abroad after 1860. Empirical, biological racism was certainly a phenomenon of the later nineteenth century. Most of the ideas of race which informed British policies under Victoria have, however, a somewhat earlier pedigree. They were generated out of enlightenment ideas of moral independency and the romanticism which came into vogue after 1780. Both these strains of ideas were appropriated by the aristocratic imperialists of the Regency and reinforced by the triumphalist Anglicanism of the era. Yet while these ideas were used to legitimise and confirm racial hierarchies which were emerging from autonomous social changes in Britain's European, Asian and Caribbean colonies, they were not viewed as static or unchanging. Officials and thinkers of this period also had a clear policy of what would now be called economic and social development. Here two themes stand out. First, the transformation of what we have called 'agrarian patriotism' into an imperial creed and, secondly, the export to the Celtic fringes and overseas of a radical form of the notion of private property and freedom of contract. The roots of these ideas lay once again in the Whig, 'country' tradition, though they were immeasurably refined by the work of Adam Smith, Kames and their contemporaries among the English judges.

AGRARIAN PATRIOTISM AND FREEHOLD

Agrarian patriotism originated as an anti-authoritarian creed of country gentlemen. By the time of Kames it had become a national creed of integration through agrarian improvement, a gentleman's version of 'digging for victory'. The agrarian patriots' view of overseas empire was ambivalent, as we have seen. After 1783 their rhetoric was enlisted to condemn 'distant schemes of colonisation', particularly when this led to the draining away of able-bodied peasant labour and the consequent diminution of the European empire's military manpower and stock of 'industry'. Agrarianist themes nevertheless informed many of the key policies of the new empire. The most striking and best documented example of this was in the influence of ideas of agrarian improvement on Lord Cornwallis's settlement of the Bengal land revenues in 1793, brilliantly described by Ranajit Guha. Both Phillip Francis, Warren Hasting's fierce opponent on the Bengal Council, and Cornwallis received distant echoes of French agrarian philosophy (les physiocrates) through the mediating influences of Thomas Patullo and Alexander Dow. The leading ideas were, however, those of the agrarian improvers. The trade of Bengal and the Company could only be rescued from the decline brought about by English and native misgovernment by the application of capital to land and the bringing under the plough of large areas of waste in north Bengal. This in turn could only be achieved if the local landed aristocracy was given security of tenure and an equitable and predictable rate of land tax. The landed aristocracy was identified, through a massive effort of wishful thinking, with the post-Mughal revenue farming class, and the land tax proved to be neither equitable or predictable. As early as the first decade of the nineteenth century, commentators were complaining that they had saddled Bengal with an 'Irish' system of absentee tyrants rather than an 'English' régime of improvers. But there is no mistaking the influence of the English agrarian ideas on the debate.

One feature of the Cornwallis settlement and others modelled on it in North India was its emphasis on the agency of the large landlord who it was hoped would become a commercial improver. Another, and ultimately more important, strand of agrarianism was the Scottish one. Kames and the Scots agrarianists tended to argue for smaller estates and the very rapid development of a buoyant land market such as they had seen revivify both the Central Lowlands, Caithness and the southern Highlands in the generation after the 1745 revolt. These thinkers and their disciples among the Scottish gentry and Edinburgh lawyers had little time for large holdings and feudal remnants, putting much less faith in deference and emulation as tools of economic improvement; this smacked too much of 'moral dependency'.

This emphasis on a progressive yeoman farming class also found its way into debates in the colonies. The *ryotwari* (literally 'peasantwise') system of land settlement in southern India was designed to create a relationship between the colonial government and the substantial peasant whose fields were (ideally) to be surveyed and assessed individually. The settlements should be temporary and detailed so that government could take account of the improved value of the land and also avoid large concentrations of political power in the hands of recalcitrant magnates. The schemes owed much to the system inherited from Tipu Sultan by the early Scots administrators Alexander Reade and Sir Thomas Munro (Stein forthcoming). However, the emphasis on yeoman economic individualism, the distrust of magnates and romanticism about local virtue was typical of Scottish agrarianism. It was later extended to western India by Mountstuart Elphinstone (scion of a Borders landed family) and had considerable influence on British arrangements in Java and later Malaysia. Abolitionists similarly seemed to favour a peasant-based land system in the Caribbean once the negroes had been emancipated; the reduction of duties on sugar would make it a proper staple food like wheat and it would encourage the propagation of other food crops. Local versions of the 'yeoman solution' even found their way into the Mediterranean during the rule of those redoutable Scots, Sir Thomas Maitland and Sir Charles Napier. During his term on the Greek island of Cephalonia during the 1820s, Napier set himself firmly against the Russian-leaning aristocracy and tried to foster a commercial peasantry. He later elaborated this into a general theory. In his *Colonization* (1835), he argues that the best way to prevent the horrors of famine in England and Ireland was 'to break up large estates into small ones and create a yeomanry' (p. 29).

In the years between 1783 and 1830, agrarian patriotism had undergone another important transformation which is evident in Napier's works. The export of people – emigration – which had been hotly opposed by the writers of the 1780s was now favoured, even officially sanctioned. The relative success with which the British provided recruits for the French and Napoleonic Wars, while keeping up a very high level of agricultural and industrial production, banished fears of a bleeding away of Britain's manpower. On the contrary, the fear was now of agrarian revolt consequent on parcellisation of land or of industrial unrest resulting from

157

unemployment. This came to the fore in the 1790s and even more during the slump after 1815. The dire consequences of the natural tendency of people to reproduce had been emphasised by Thomas Malthus and other political economists of the 'Anglican' school. These theoretical objections having been dissipated, both ministers and private labour speculators began to develop mass emigration from the Western Highlands, southern Ireland and to a lesser extent from the English counties. Groups of Scottish settlers were planted with the aid of Lord Bathurst's Colonial Office in the St Lawrence valley and southern Africa to make these territories safe for the empire; the Passenger Acts eased emigration to a more benevolent United States; Napier himself was involved in the first plans to settle sturdy farmers (as opposed to convicts) in Australia. Meanwhile Scots and Irish Catholics swarmed over the world from South America to the South Sea Islands (Cage 1985). In these empty lands there was much less to fear from miscegenation and political dissidence. New, tactfully governed colonies in which the institutions of Church and state had been carefully implanted would encourage commerce, and 'besides, it is glorious to people a new continent and spread the language and renown of England in distant regions' (Napier 1835: 29).

While there had been differences among agrarian imperialists about the virtue of direct colonisation and the relative merits of large as opposed to small landed holdings, they all agreed on the great importance of freehold in land. Unfettered ownership and personal property holding would best foster moral independency and economic progress. The end of restraints on trade and labour relations were desirable for the same reason. For there was always a basic harmony between public and private interests. The rise of the notion of 'freedom of contract' in English (and Scottish) law occurred precisely at the period when the transformation of empire was taking place. The second volume of Blackstone's *Commentaries* on English Law (1760) was a text for the assault on feudal privileges and restraints on testation. This generation also saw a more determined attack on surviving common rights and joint forms of property, notably 'run-rig' tenures in Scotland and caedl in Ireland. Bentham's *Defence of Usury* signalled the climax of the movement against medieval conceptions of moral economy, just price and usury. Contract should be unfettered and trade unrestrained by the operation of guilds and schemes of apprenticeship (Atiyah 1979).

These ideas influenced the new colonial policies. The desire to create private, alienable property in land was a powerful impetus to the Indian land-revenue settlements. Common rights in waste land were quite widely demolished and under the *ryotwari* settlement in south India wastes were assessed as a component of the land revenue, and provisions were made for dividing it up. These views led colonial officials to try to sell off government lands wherever these had continued to exist. The Dutch East India Company had often retained title to land and had settled farmers on it as share-cropping tenants. Both in Ceylon and on the Cape of Good Hope arrangements were gradually made to put these lands on to the market. As in Ireland and Scotland, so in India, Ceylon, the Cape and Upper Canada, the rights of nomads and peasants to wood, hunting and grazing were eroded by the combined action of courts and administrative fiat.

Yet the revolution of freedom of contract, like the drift of public opinion towards free trade, was limited during this period not only by practical constraints but also by ideological objections. Some ancient customs and rights were preserved, particularly when they promoted the cohesion of landed aristocracies. So, for instance, primogeniture was deemed a good thing in parts of western Scotland and it was also urged upon Rajput landholding families in north India. In both cases the motive was to prevent undue subdivision of land and the undermining of political authority. Similarly, state control over labour was preserved for two generations into the nineteenth century in most parts of the empire. Slavery was 'an unconscionable time a-dying' in both the Orient and the West Indies; in several areas it even experienced a revival after 1815. Caste identities in India and Ceylon and tribal identities in Africa were shored up to provide labour for private and public projects which directly benefited the state. To some degree this was a matter of pragmatism. Governments under pressure were prepared to use any resource to survive. Moreover, theorists such as Adam Smith and Bentham generally agreed that the optimum conditions of free trade and freedom of contract might not be possible to implement during time of national emergency and international war.

Yet the 'conservative' position was also supported by some theoretical arguments. Liberties and rights were often justified because they derived from an 'ancient constitution' appropriate to the Scots or, for that matter, the Indians and the Sinhalese. The romanticism of a James Tod or Walter Scott now flowing freely into the neo-Gothic revival strengthened this reluctance to tamper with custom and established institutions. Even apologists for the continuing existence of slave-ownership in the Caribbean pointed not only to the value of the sugar economy, but like Bryan Edwards to the glorious history of these colonies as a bulwark of English Protestantism and the liberties of Englishmen in a hostile environment. Slavery as a social system survived more than thirty years beyond the formal abolition of the slave trade. Above all, the East India Company itself survived the assaults of free traders and the enemies of corrupt institutions until 1834. Only then did it lose its monopoly of the valuable China Trade; and its government of India even beyond that date was based on an oppressive tribute system and a monopoly of opium production. Once again, there were theoretical justifications beyond the simple inertia of an old corporation. Sir John Shore and many others argued that the Company should continue to exist mainly because it was still too dangerous for liberty in Britain to hand over the directors' huge patronage in jobs to London politicians.

The ideological inheritance of Britain's new imperial age contained important internal contradictions. Yet the dominant tone was agrarianist and aristocratic. Disposable property in land and agrarian improvement were virtues because they would reveal a natural hierarchy, not because they would unlock the industry of the 'middling sort' as rent theorists and utilitarians of the next generation were to believe. Free-trade ideas were spreading; they were employed in support of empire and sometimes complemented the case of the 'agrarian' patriots. But they were not yet the centre of economical thinking among imperial statesmen. In the case of the English Corn Laws, for instance, or the Ceylonese cinnamon monopoly, the need for stable civil society overrode the demands of laissez faire.

CONCLUSION

During the French Revolutionary and Napoleonic Wars, British statesmen were aware that they were creating a new empire both in Europe and beyond it. Their model – both positive and negative – was the Roman empire, but they gazed uneasily at their French enemy across the Channel. Some thought the British should follow the Romans in a wise policy of the assimilation of élites, leaving the mass of the populace secure in their own religion and laws, be they Scottish, Hindu or Dutch. Others demanded a 'Roman' policy of the Age of Constantine, a Christian evangelical empire of assimilation by administrative patronage. For them the battle of the Milvian Bridge, which would usher in the millenium, had been Britain's abolition of the slave trade in 1807, at a time of great danger. It was only a matter of years before the 'millions of our fellow creatures consigned to the mercies of Brahma [sic Wilberforce]' (Furneaux 1974: 120) would follow into the light.

The shadow of the French empire was also long. By 1795, practically everything French was denounced. But there was a quiet emulation in private and public style. Sphinx-footed chairs and imperial symbols spread through the land. Public buildings became grander where they could throw off the restraints of the Military Engineers' style of architecture. Regent's Street was imposed upon London's mass of Kentish small towns. The Grand Gesture of Benevolence became a feature of imperial ritual previously run by the cheesemongers. Cornwallis's public reception of Tipu Sultan's children as hostages in 1793; Minto's public burning of the symbols of 'Dutch bestiality' on Java; the first investiture of the Order of St Michael and St George in the Brighton Pavilion; all these might have been recorded by Napoleon's painter David, and were recorded by his imitators. Picturesque views of places associated with fallen or rising empires recorded by Captain Cook's artist Thomas Hodges or the Daniells were sold in numerous editions. Soon a new generation of imperial heroes such as Elphinstone and Malcolm flooded the market with reminiscences and apologias. The favoured new styles were those of Tacitus, Livy, Seneca and Caesar; Horace, Plutarch and Ovid receded from the scene. Domestic poets such as Sir Walter Scott and Wordsworth lauded patriotic virtues of independence, 'enterprise' and martial valour. It was bliss to be alive and be a conqueror. Over all this reigned the new imperial Crown supported by an expanded and energetic aristocracy. Hanoverian corruption had been washed away, or so it seemed, by the blood of battle.

During these years the state also developed important new tools for control and intervention in England, but more particularly in Scotland, Ireland and the colonies. A revivified army, a political and financial bureaucracy and a series of boards of control. The state knew more and acted more, whether it was preparing statistics of occupation in Scotland, revenue in India or slave-holding in the new World. The disasters of the American War had produced an interlocking network of parliamentary committees with their own experts; so administrations also had to know more and be better prepared.

Many of the administrative developments and movements of ideas which were central to political debate during these years reached maturity in the 1830s or after. Free-trade pressure, parliamentary reform and the abolition of slavery were merely the most striking examples. However, the Whiggish tendency in historical writing which always searches for the seeds of the future and the rise of liberalism is in danger of missing the most important features of the period. Colonial 'reform' between 1780 and 1830 was autocratic in style, tending to create or confirm social and racial hierarchies through the liberation of private property. Government remained militaristic and monopolistic in practice in spite of the softer protestations of constitutional and political theory. Taken as a whole, the British empire had as much in common with the continental neo-absolutisms which emerged out of the Napoleonic Wars as it did with the liberal nation state of the 1850s into which it did, very slowly and unevenly, transform itself.

At the same time, Great Britain's colonial and European empires remained unfinished and aborted in important respects. Many Britons remained ambivalent about the domestic political consequences of foreign territories. Many refused to perceive empire as a unity, even when imperial policies across the globe bore sharp resemblances to each other (Koebner 1961: 287–9). The large new home bureaucracy and defence forces provoked considerable hostility, particularly after the depression which accompanied the final end to the wars. Pitt's plan of political assimilation and religious emancipation for the Irish Catholic gentry and middle classes remained unfulfilled because of the fierce opposition from the Royal Family and other important interests in England. Deteriorating economic conditions and social conflict ensured that Ireland could never fit into the Union even to the extent that Scotland had done. In British Canada, the Caribbean and southern Africa, even the new Colonial Office was unable to resolve local political and economic conflicts in a manner which would revivify their economies and please the creole élites. The Indian empire and its Asian extensions proved even less tractable. Java was abandoned in 1816; Ceylon scarcely paid. On the sub-continent itself the expansion of formal British rule simply compounded the huge financial problem of getting India to pay for its own defence and administration. As early as 1828 even Sir Charles Metcalfe, a man of the heroic Wellesley generation, was gloomily remarking on the incidence of anti-British revolt, the dubious loyalty of the army and the forthcoming bankruptcy of the government of India: 'a very little mismanagement will cause our rapid expulsion' (Philips 1977: i, 311). The new empire was born with the genetic faults which would bury it. The next chapter considers the shifting sands of international crisis on which it was built.

CHAPTER SIX
The World Crisis, 1780–1820

The 'general wreck of nations' which followed the defeat of the monarchies of Europe by the armies of revolutionary France was accompanied by an unprecedented wave of revolts, popular disturbances and messianic movements. These ranged from the revolutionary actions of reforming cabals determined to sweep away feudal privileges or the constraints of old constitutions to symptoms of general panic, disorganised and largely undirected: 'the great fears' of Georges Lefèbvre. The passage of revolutionary armies and the diffusion of pamphlets and agents ensured that these movements and the reactions to them had an international dimension unprecedented in European history. Out of the general dissolution were created new types of political discourse and definitions of the individual, new political alignments and new types of state.

This chapter does not seek to retell this well-known story but to draw out the much wider international context of these convulsions. For the European 'Age of Revolutions' was only one part of a general crisis affecting the Asian and Islamic world and the colonies of European settlement. To be sure, the themes of Liberty, Equality and Fraternity and the ripostes of their Christian, monarchist opponents were exported to the world outside Europe, intensifying conflict among Europeans overseas and between Europeans and Asians and Africans. In colonies as far distant from Paris as Kingston, Jamaica, Cape Town and Calcutta, governors imprisoned or exiled opponents on the grounds of 'jacobinism'. The extreme brutality characteristic of the Maroon wars in Jamaica or the early British government of Trinidad reflected a deep fear and loathing of levelling republicanism which was giving new vigour to slave revolt and half-caste mutiny.

Yet the international scale of these disturbances can also be attributed to the clash of competing ideologies and political forms which were indigenous to the great extra-European societies. Previous bouts of European conflict, notably the Seven Years' War, had spilled into Asia and the Americas, heightening tensions resulting from social and economic conflicts overseas. Not since the Mongol invasions of the thirteenth century, however, had there occurred such a general and critical disruption of economic systems, patterns of kingship and popular mentalities. For the period 1780–1820 was one also when the long-term political conflicts unleashed by the decline of the great hegemonies of the Ottomans, Iran, the Mughals and the monarchies of the Far East and southeast Asia came to a head. Succession struggles over this huge area were intensified by the intervention of Europeans seeking glory, treasure, produce and slaves. There were also deeper social changes taking place which made urban and rural communities throughout Eurasia fertile fields for the emergence of new religious cults and new definitions of communal identity. The decline of the old urban artisan communities in the Islamic world and the rise of new forms of indigenous capitalism ran parallel with, but were not directly caused by, the rapid growth of European agriculture and the beginnings of the industrial revolution in England. The world crisis outside Europe was brought about by changes working within these societies and economies, as much as by the export of European conflict.

One purpose of the chapter is to draw attention to some of the common moral and material conditions which underlay the global conflicts of the Age of Revolution. A second aim is to begin to provide a general account of the changes outside England and outside the ruling groups discussed in the last chapter which moulded the form of Britain's new empire. For popular reaction and economic change at the grass roots were as critical as ideological and military imperatives generated in London in this process of change. Out of the international 'wreck of nations' emerged a revised international order. In this order, old legitimacies–the Papacy, the kingdoms of England and France, the Sublime Porte–emerged revivified. But everywhere they were fortified with new systems of economic and political management and began to promote a much greater degree of state intrusion into society. Some of these states took the form of colonial provinces, the

British Indian or Dutch East Indian empires, for instance. Some, however, were quasi-independent régimes such as Qajar Iran, or Muhammad Ali's Egypt, or the Ottoman empire of the Tanzimat reforms of the 1830s.

All these political economies, whether inside 'Europe' or outside, were influenced by changes at an international level. So from one perspective, the British, Dutch or French Asian and African empires, or the revived Ottoman régime, should be viewed in the context of the neo-absolutist states created in Europe following the Congress of Vienna. And by the same token, 'Europe' itself must now to be understood as the product of these wider, international changes. At the same time, the form of the new states derived from the particularities of individual societies–from clashes over kingship, religion, the control of labour and indigenous capital. National historiographies and the historiographies of different cultures cannot be ignored. Yet they must also be set in their broader context. First, then, the chapter will briefly recapitulate the sequence and types of revolt and heterodox popular movements which occurred during the height of the world crisis and then it will analyse their origins, and discuss the response to them of élites and governments.

DIMENSIONS OF CONFLICT

By far the most exhaustively studied popular movements of these years are the revolts among the peasantry which accompanied the French Revolution and spread to the peasantries and political fringes of many of the enemies of France. Some of these uprisings were self-consciously directed to the reconstitution of older 'moral economies' by abolishing the privileges of landowners and royal tax farmers. Of this type were the revolts in northern and eastern France in 1789–90 or the Irish revolts against the tithes of the hated Protestant clergy and the taxation on hearths which was triggered in 1797 and 1798 by the proximity of invading French forces. Others such as the Vendée rebellions of 1793 or the revolts between 1808 and 1811 of Calabrian and Tirolean peasants against the Napoleonic state were apparently reactionary, a violent closing of ranks by rural society against the invading revolutionary régimes. Yet in both cases these uprisings were directed against an intrusive world outside the peasant society, whether a revived and grasping aristocracy or the agents of a new state and bureaucracy.

Movements such as this had clear parallels in contemporary European colonies of settlement. The British and Dutch East India Companies and the remnants of royalist French government in the colonial world had moved along the same road as the European nobilities and the last pre-revolutionary governments in the last quarter of the eighteenth century by mounting a fiscal attack on peasant farmers. This set the scene for widespread uprisings when central control was weakened by international war and conflict.

The Dutch East India Company encountered increasing resistance from the Boer peasant farmers of the Cape and the partly acculturated Hottentot (Khoikoi) small cultivators in the last twenty years of the eighteenth century. Pressed by the same financial crisis which affected European states, the Company had tried to hold down the prices of commodities it purchased for naval provision from the local community. It also restricted the expansion of arable agriculture in order to avoid conflict with the surrounding black tribesmen and monopolised lucrative offices in the Cape for European Dutch citizens. In the settler communities of the Eastern Cape such as Graaff Reinet, a fierce movement of resistance to the Company and its local officials developed in the 1780s (Cory 1910: i, 39). Between 1778 and 1791 some of these agrarian communities expressed their grievances in the language of reform typical of the contemporary pro-French 'Liberator' party in Holland (du Toit and Giliomee 1983: ch. i). When the British took the Cape in 1795 and again in 1806, they also encountered resistance from the Boer peasant farmers. Though the British slowly relaxed the Dutch Company's monopolistic policies, there were constant conflicts over land rights, the distribution of state land and control of the frontier. These exploded into open revolt in 1795–6 when Graaff Reinet declared itself a 'republic'. Though both Dutch and British officials worked to suppress 'jacobinism', there were many conflicts between the farmers and state over the next two generations. There is no clear link between these events and the Boers' Great Trek out of British territory between 1835 and 1848. Still, the underlying conflict between a bureaucratic administration, concerned with revenue or external trade, and settlers trying to assure their land control against competing black pastoralists persisted through the whole period (Elphick and Giliomee 1983: 203, 351–4).

The East India Companies in south and southeast Asia faced similar problems of control, though in a very different social and economic context. We have already seen that the Dutch Company's rigid policy of monopoly encountered fierce resistance from the trader-peasants of the islands of the archipelago and from the cinnamon pickers of Ceylon. The Dutch Company's policy, like that of the British, was designed to supplement dwindling profits from external trade by control over local production. This was achieved by squeezing more out of peasants through enhanced land revenues or labour services. Before 1800, such policies had aroused resistance movements on the north coast of Java, the Moluccas and northern and western Bengal where once prosperous peasantries battled against the high land revenues or ruthless labour services imposed by the Companies. Yet these were not straightforward clashes between colonial government and peasant. For instance, serious conflict arose in Java between incoming Chinese money-lenders and villagers (Breman 1980: 17). As we have seen, the Chinese had become increasingly important on the north coast of Java under Dutch rule; towards the end of the century they were playing a significant rôle in the economic fabric of the Mataram successor states. Peasant communities fought against the effects of the tax farming monopolies sold to Chinese by both European and indigenous states. Sporadic revolts became more general when Napoleon's lieutenant Daendels began to operate a more ruthless policy of labour requisitioning during the period of the Batavian Republic. Trouble arose again after 1811 when British rule and the imposition of a cash revenue system widened the scale of operations of Chinese entrepreneurs (Carey 1986b: 117–18).

In the New World the violence of creole revolt now passed to the Spanish empire of the south. But even in North America the pace of conflict and rebellion scarcely slowed after 1783. While Canada saw violent clashes over the fruits of westward expansion between farmer and merchant, native American and white or government and trapper, it was in the Caribbean that the fiercest social conflicts occurred. The slave revolts on Saint Domingue which followed the French Revolution, and the emergence of a 'Negro Empire' under Toussaint l'Ouverture and Jean-Jacques Dessalines, was mirrored in many small-scale explosions on the British and Dutch sugar islands which gave rise to a lasting fear of slave revolt on the part of the creole élites. The convulsions on the French islands which resulted from the fall of the monarchy unleashed the ambition of the free 'coloured' population for improved political status. This in turn set the scene for a mass slave upsurge.

The frequency of rebellions and mutinies already appears

to have been increasing towards the end of the eighteenth century independently of the effects of revolution in Europe. The reasons are by no means clear. Many planters blamed Christian propaganda circulated by Moravian, French and, later, English Dissenting preachers. The abolition of the slave trade in 1807 was seen by many slaves as a first step in their own liberation. The social organisation of the slave communities was probably changing also. They were becoming mature as rising prices forced owners to try to conserve their slave populations by deploying medical services among them. More mature slave populations spawned their own leaderships and nurtured their own craving for freedom. While slave revolts earlier in the century had usually been led by very recent arrivals from Africa, in the early years of the nineteenth century the leaders were home-bred slaves. These more rooted slave populations developed more complex relationships with free negroes and people of mixed race, and this toe-hold in civil society encouraged hopes of liberation. It was for this reason that in 1797-8 the whites on Jamaica began military operations against the colonies of runaway slaves and free peasant farmers designated 'the Trelawny Town Maroons' (Braithwaite 1971: 57). The Maroons were dangerously independent and might infect the slaves. The massacre and mayhem of the French islands lay only a few sea-miles away (Bridges 1827: ii, 223).

This rising tide of conflict was not limited to areas of longstanding European settlement. The consequences of the decline of the old hegemonies of the Islamic world also reached their climacteric between 1780 and 1820. Internal tensions were further aggravated by Western invasion. The Ottoman central administration had been sorely weakened by a series of defeats at the hands of Russia in the second half of the eighteenth century. External pressure coincided with the gathering movement of revolt and secession within the empire associated with the rise of powerful magnate *ayans*. In the Christian territories of the Balkans the success of Russia and conflicts between Christian townsmen, peasants and merchants and Ottoman soldiers and tax-gatherers provoked numerous rebellions. The weakness of the Ottoman Porte in the face of Russia, Britain and revolutionary France stirred the embers of Greek nationalism, particularly as it was the Greek traders of the islands who had done very well out of the growth of European trade within the Mediterranean. In 1800, prompted by Russia, the Greeks of the Ionian Islands, liberated from the failing grasp of Venice by Napoleon's invasion, declared themselves the Septinsula Republic. Though the islands quickly fell under British 'protection', they provided an object lesson and a magnet for Greeks under Ottoman dominion in mainland Greece and the Aegean Islands.

In Egypt the relative prosperity of the years of Ali Bey gave way to increasing internal tension and external intervention after 1785. The quarters of Cairo and other cities threw up a series of revolts against mameluke attempts to raise taxation. Conflicts between factions of the beys and also between the beys and Ottoman authority (which attempted to reassert itself in 1792) encouraged rebellion among the semi-settled Beduin. Finally, the Napoleonic invasion of 1798 – and the British riposte during the following years – set off a series of galvanic eruptions in the fabric of Egyptian society. Opposition to the French was by no means universal, but in 1798 and again in 1800 most of the artisan quarters of Cairo led by influential religious leaders revolted against the intrusion of French military authorities (Raymond 1968). Between 1799 and 1809, by which time Muhammad Ali, the leader of the Albanian faction within the Turkish army, had consolidated himself as ruler, Egypt was wracked by almost continuous conflict and popular uprising. The defeat of the mameluke armies by Napoleon at the Battle of the Pyramids gave rise to a long struggle for succession (Raymond 1973: ii; Al-Sayyid Marsot 1984: ch. 2).

The distraction of both Egypt and her overlord the Ottoman Porte, along with the disruption of trade throughout the whole region, were material factors in the second great 'tribal breakout' associated with the fundamentalist Wahhabi rebellion in the Arabian Peninsula. The Wahhabi capture of Mecca, Medina and Karbala threw the southern half of the Ottoman empire into religious and military frenzy. Finally, between 1806 and 1808, political conflict at the very centre of empire in Istanbul came to a head. A move for political military reform to strengthen the empire against both Europeans and the growing power of provincial armies and notables was temporarily successful, but later defeated by a combination of the old military guilds and *ayans* who feared a revival of the power of the Sultan. Still, the spectre of a successful coup at Istanbul and the growing circulation of ideas of efficient government and self-strengthening which derived from the turmoils in revolutionary Europe irrevocably changed the conduct of politics at the heart of the Porte (Shaw and Shaw 1977: i, 260–77).

Over this period, Iran and the Mughal empire were undergoing their final, convulsive transformations. In these two political cultures the dissolution of both the imperial centres and several of their successor régimes provoked sharp struggles of succession. The main combatants here were on the one hand the military detritus of the old order – 'cossacks', pindari raiders, cavalry soldiers – and on the other, armed peasant and tribal corporations manoeuvring for a stronger position while the towns, trade routes and political authorities which they succoured were in disarray. Movements of religious protest melded with the social conflicts which derived from sharp political and economic changes. Rural sufi movements battled the revanche of orthodox Shiism and the towns in early Qajar Iran. In north India the decline first of the Mughal and then of the Afghan state opened the way for the final consolidation of Sikhism, which drew in peasant landowners from the whole of the old Mughal Punjab and spread outwards into the Muslim lands to the west and the Gangetic valley to the east. Throughout Peninsular India the ultimate struggle between the East India Company and its surrogates and the independent Indian states of Tipu Sultan and the Marathas intensified both religious and ethnic conflicts. When the British were finally successful they presided over a vast tract of country in which competition between social groups and ethnicities had been suppressed but not eliminated. Revolts such as the Poligar Wars (1799–1802) and the mutiny at the southern military station of Vellore (1806) drew together themes of peasant resistance and eschatological religious fervour against the intrusion of Christians and foreigners. Everywhere the competition between European powers and indigenous states revealed fissures in societies which had built up over the long term, but had been released by the climacteric of economic and political pressure between 1780 and 1820.

IDEOLOGIES AND ETHNICITIES

The aim of the last section has been to give a broad view of the range of severe social and political conflicts in the wider world which accompanied the European 'Age of Revolution'. These conflicts and revolts represented more than a simple 'export' of European turbulences and European ideologies overseas. In what did the extra-European 'revolutions' consist? What were the underlying unities in this international 'wreck of nations' beyond the simple expansion of military conflict and economic distress? These are important questions because they bear not only on the nature of the disorders themselves but also on the form of the international social order which was hesitantly reconstructed after 1815.

Generalising about radical social upheaval and conflict flies in the face of the recent concern among social theorists and historians with difference, individuality and special meaning. This concern is itself a reaction against earlier tendencies to reduce complex social movements and ideologies to simple analyses of social or economic structure. While each of these revolts had special features and meanings, it is also true that there were links between them. This was not only because broad economic conjunctures acted on peasant societies in similar ways, but because the sense of confrontation between ideologies was sharpened among ordinary people and not simply among élites. What is striking about the evidence which survives of the mentalities and aspirations of even humble actors in the world crisis of 1780 to 1820 is the extent to which they claimed universalistic aims and inspiration, whether these were couched in terms of revolutionary egalitarianism, Christianity, Islam, Buddhism or other faiths. The Doctrine of the Rights of Man was met by a newly vitalised crusading Protestant Christianity. This clash occurred at the same time as the struggle between revivalist and latitudinarian, between reformer and orthodox, reached new intensity in the Islamic world. In southeast and south Asia, millenarian movements and religious conflict signalled the passing of the old order and the onset of colonialism. With the decline of the former imperial protectors of true religion, the hierarchies and devotees of religious communities searched for new legitimation in appeals to transcendent religious values. Of course, most popular movements also continued to justify themselves with appeals to the rights and obligations of particular societies and often found their support closely limited to specific localities. Still, the broadening of ideological scale and awareness after 1780 seems very clear, both in Europe and outside.

One reason for this change was that global war and intrigue opened up a vast range of new communications between areas previously only dimly aware of each other. It also released across the world large numbers of travelling religious men, political activists, displaced merchants and freelance soldiers who took with them new ideas and styles of political discourse. This happened at all levels from 'high politics' to the village meeting. For instance, while politics and battle along the north African coast had long been conducted (at least formally) in the rhetoric of religious war between Christian and Muslim, this had not been the case to anything like the same extent in India. Now rulers in India were more likely to couch their opposition to British expansion in terms of a universal struggle between Islam and Christian infidelity. Seeking allies outside India and trying to build up a new model Muslim army, Tipu wrote in 1799 to the Ottoman Sultan – where the notion of the Islamic warrior-state had always had some currency – that the 'infidels were a force of evil to all God's creatures ' and that in the country of Bengal and in all other places where their authority has prevailed, 'they set up swine butchers and cause them to sell the flesh of hogs publicly in the streets' *(Papers relative to Tipoo)*. The French Republic responded in kind, seeking to cement an alliance with Tipu employing the rhetoric of Liberty and *levée en masse*. It is not known what donning the Liberty Cap meant to Tipu and his soldiers, but chroniclers leave no doubt that he saw himself as a new man, a populist Islamic hero like the great military sultans of the Islamic frontiers of the past who was opposed both to Mughal effeteness and British tyranny (Kirmani 1834: 147–8). Napoleon himself had made similar appeals to woo the citizens of Cairo in 1798 using French printing presses to propagate a view of himself as liberator of Rome from the Pope, ancient bugbear of the Islamic world (Boustany 1971: 6–7). In the same vein the Sharif of Mecca, in unsteady alliance with the British Indian expeditionary force against the French, would rouse his troops 'under the Prophet's banner from Medina and under God's from Mecca' to liberate Egypt from the foreigner (24 May 1801, IOL: Home Misc. 476).

Yet it was not only the language of international diplomacy which was galvanised by a new fervour. Popular movements and local resistances echoed, perhaps even initiated, the use of universalistic ideological slogans. While the use of the printing press and circulation of letters helped to 'textualise' political conflict among the more literate, older lines of communication were used also. In both Java and south India, puppet shows played a part in mobilising popular resistance to British and Dutch conquests. Javanese awaited the coming of the 'Just King' and sought legitimacy in revolt from agents of the 'Sultan of Rum', the Ottoman emperor (Carey 1986b: 117). Again, before the Vellore Mutiny of the Madras army in 1806, puppeteers were seen giving performances depicting the French and Islamic troops driving the British from India (Chinnian 1982: 15). South Indians now saw their own affairs as part of a more general struggle. Religious teachers fanned across the south linking together the acolytes of Muslim warrior saints with the new cult associated with the martyr Tipu Sultan who had perished defending his capital in 1799.

As in later world war, the movement and eventual demobilisation of soldiers spread ideas, stimulated comparison and sharpened ideological commitment. In European historical writing it is a commonplace that the wars formed a seed bed of popular nationalism, stirring the southern Italians against the Bourbon tyranny, northern Italians against Austrians, or Greeks and Moldavians against Ottomans. Outside Europe the effects of prolonged ideological conflict remains shadowy though much is known about economic and social changes. It was argued in an earlier chapter that the new compact regional kingdoms which emerged out of the decline of the Muslim land empires tended through acts of patronage and in the interest of building political support to stress the religious and racial identity of their domains. Sections of the population with a stake in an overarching order subscribed to this marking out of religious-based ethnicity, though the lines were always blurred by a myriad of cross-cutting affiliations to other 'religions', other perceptions of deity. The climacteric of 1780–1820 appears to have further sharpened this process, creating through deeper social and economic conflict more closely defined ethnicities. Rulers and ruled often fought against each other with different ideological affiliations so that issues of popular sovereignty, liberty or community tended to be phrased more frequently in terms of transcendental ideology. These ideologies were often linked to a sense of an ethnic consciousness. To this extent, in the world outside Europe, prolonged global warfare helped shape identities which are broadly comparable with the 'nationalisms' which form the main staple of European history from 1789 to 1870. What we call 'nationalisms' within Europe and 'communalisms' or 'ethnicities' outside Europe were in fact comparable, and were fashioned to confront similar pressures over a broadly similar period. Gellner (1983b) has argued that ethnicity can be distinguished from nationalism because the former is a predominantly rural phenomenon while the latter is urban. But this distinction does not work well for the formative period at the turn of the nineteenth century. In both 'Asia' and 'Europe', rural élites involved in the market promoted both 'nationalism' and 'ethnicity' in the context of newly-formed regional states. The difference between Europe and Asia, between tradition and modernity, appears illusory.

This view also runs counter to most recent attempts to analyse the origins or antecedents of nationalism, communalism and ethnicity for much of Asia and North Africa. These have usually been conceived of either as ancient cultural 'givens' or as the result of very recent political 'modernisation' and the designs of the late colonial powers. It is important, therefore, to give some examples of how ideologies of resistance and conflict became more general at the same time as they were claimed more firmly for specific ethnic groups or localities.

LIBERTY, EQUALITY, FRATERNITY

Though it was certainly the most striking addition to international discourse and led indirectly to the heightening of tone of most other ideologies, the direct impact of French notions of radical republicanism was limited. To be sure, the struggle between the Patriot and Liberator parties in Holland which was infected with French arguments against the old régime spread to the colonies and determined the Dutch colonial population's relations with the later British authorities. The atheistical underpinnings of French ideology were deeply repulsive to the Boer farmers. Their hatred of royalty, state officials, corruption and monopoly, and the bias of contemporary French thought towards agrarian republicanism, was congenial to the settlers on the eastern Cape and even to a few in Ceylon and Java. The Dutch Reformed Church was after all republican in form and the Church assembly was also the assembly of the local community. The new British rulers quickly alienated the Cape Dutch farming community, and that community's growing ethnic solidarity had many causes. But the melding together of Calvinist and republican themes during the conflicts of the 1790s was an important precondition for the later 'tribalism' of South African politics. British attempts at cultural assimilation were doomed to failure, particularly when urged forward by High Tory and Anglican governors.

At the other end of Africa, French nationalist libertarian ideology was also a powerful catalyst. Napoleon's brief rule in Egypt and the military destruction of the mameluke élite intensified regional Arab feeling which had been fostered by the later beys (Hourani 1962). The French swept away what they thought of as oriental versions of feudal privilege and destroyed the great ruling households. They tried instead to institute an Egyptian Muslim republic based upon the intelligentsia and minor notables of the old order (Boustany

1971: 81). They tried especially to recruit the Coptic managers and literati, the more complaisant of the rural and religious élite – the *sheikhs* – and merchant communities such as the Syrians and north Africans which had prospered through earlier contacts with Mediterranean trade. A remarkable flowering of the rationalistic and legalistic tradition within Arabic writing took place (Gran 1978). At the same time there appears to have been a first stirring of the notion of 'Egypt for the Egyptians', though one limited to certain social and confessional groups. Here the Copts were in the forefront. An Egyptian Delegation to the Powers of Europe had several Coptic members (Elgin to London, Sept. 1801 PRO: FO, 78/33), and the British wishing to understand this powerful force in the Egyptian body politic assembled French reports to the effect that 'without these Copts the Turks would never be able to collect any revenue' (*cf.* Boustany 1971: 59, 74). While it altered the ethnic balance and encouraged an Egyptian ethnicity upon which the régime of Muhammad Ali was later to build, the French invasion also unleashed powerful forces of Islamic and Egyptian reaction. The revolt against the French in the quarters of Cairo in September 1799 took the form of a religious war. A British observer noted how the plane trees which the French had typically planted in order to Gallicise the Egyptian roads had all been uprooted by furious mobs (Walsh 1803: 253). The British, intervening in 1801 and again in 1807, found themselves contronted by equally fierce resistance.

Libertarian and egalitarian ideology was, however, most power-fully annexed to popular resistance in the slave revolts of the Caribbean between 1791 and 1808. The initial spark for the disturbances on Saint Domingue which were to spread shock waves through the Caribbean empires of Britain, France and Spain was the decision by the French national assembly to grant full citizenship rights to persons of mixed race and free negroes in its African and Caribbean colonies. The fierce political struggle which ensued between the old royalist planter élites and the new citizens broke control over the estates and led to a wave of slave revolts. This time, slave rebels fell back not only upon vestiges of African tribal leadership and eclectic religious cults but also upon the rhetoric and symbols of revolutionary France. The 'black emperors' of Haiti were to issue their proclamations and effect their redistributions of white property in the name of Liberty, Equality and Fraternity. Later they established revolutionary courts of justice, revolutionary armies and sought to reproduce much of the political style of the First Empire (James 1938; Blackburn 1988).

CHRISTIAN REVIVALISM AND THE 'WRECK OF NATIONS'

The last chapter showed how social change in Britain and the policies of Pitt's administration and its successors fostered a style of 'providentialist' Christian evangelicalism which became an important component of Britain's new imperialism. The successes and failures of this Christian expansion from the metropolis often had unintended consequences overseas. In an atmosphere of heightened consciousness, local élites and popular movements refashioned their own Christian traditions in ways which could either support or confront the ideological attack of the state. As we have seen, one of the consequences of the rural disturbances in Ireland in the later 1790s was a much more vigorous attempt by Protestant evangelists to mount a crusade against Catholicism in Ireland (Bowen 1971). Since 'Popery' was now seen as an enemy of the King's Sacred Majesty and also as an ally of atheism and republicanism, a new more fervid anti-Catholicism emerged both within the rapidly expanding Orange movements and also among sections of the Anglican clergy. This Protestant attack in turn called forth a powerful Catholic response. Catholic millenarianism flowered, and the hierarchy also began to close ranks against the imperial establishment.

The brutal suppression of the rebellion of 1798–9 was followed by the economic hardship of the war years and the severe depression after the peace of 1815. Previously disparate movements of rural radicalism began to converge with hatred of the Protestant faith. The state became more intrusive. British forces grew in numbers and the overwhelmingly Protestant police force (after 1822) began to intervene more and more in the countryside. People increasingly identified the landlord, the Crown and the Anglican priest as a monolithic threat. However, the Beast's days were numbered. From the early years of the century, peasants and lowly clergy began to prophesy that Protestants were doomed and that God's wrath would soon punish the heretics. Pamphlets to this effect, the so-called 'Pastorini Letters', were widely circulated and provided one of the assumptions on which clandestine rural resistance was organised by the so-called Rockites and other secret societies.

The important point here is that popular movements which arose during the climax of the revolutionary period did not simply respond to the promptings of élite initiatives; they also limited and formed those policies. The doctrine of political assimilation of Catholic gentry and merchants advocated by many of Pitt's followers, and later by Wellesley during his period as lieutenant-governor, foundered not only because the Crown and factions in England impeded emancipation, but also because a broader-based but as yet unorganised peasant nationalism began to emerge. The Catholic hierarchy itself was drawn willy-nilly into re-emphasising Catholic pietism and open political activity before the second decade of the nineteenth century.

In many other parts of the world, clandestine church activity and Christian messianism provided a groundwork for popular resistances against states in crisis: in Calabria and the Iberian Peninsula, Catholic pietism was an influential strand in the fight against Napoleon's republican despotism. In Greece and the Slavic parts of the Ottoman empire, the restiveness of local notables, merchants and townsmen was strengthened by rural Orthodox Christianity. It was this, along with the economic buoyancy of these parts of the Ottoman empire, which made it so much more difficult for Istanbul to reassert its authority over the provinces as it did in the Arab and Turkish lands after 1815.

Yet popular Christianity could also work to the advantage of empires. The 'loyalty' of a large part of the French population of Canada after 1793 was secured by the fear that French republicanism was 'atheistical' and that better a Protestant empire than an atheist one. In the East also, the British were able to take advantage of Christian religious affiliation to secure pockets of support in otherwise hostile populations. The policy of seeking political and religious concessions for the Christian and Jewish populations of the Ottoman empire had already become a British tactic in the Middle East by the early years of the nineteenth century. The British tried to enlist prominent merchants from these communities as their vice- consuls in the towns and ports of the eastern Mediterranean. This gave them access to important commercial and political intelligence, but also allowed British representatives to petition on behalf of influential communities at the Porte. In south Asia again, the creation of 'community' is often portrayed as a product of colonial policies since 1900. However, it was a much more deeply rooted historical process and one which was proceeding particularly rapidly during this period. On the south-west coast of India the evangelical activities of the Church Missionary Society in the first two decades of the nineteenth century encouraged the ancient Syrian Christian community to distance themselves from the rituals and society of high-caste Hindus with whom they had shared worship and customs for many centuries (Bayly forthcoming). The blasts of the evangelical Anglicans against the Syrians' 'heathen and papistical' inheritance obviously played a part. Prominent Christian families also judged it politic to draw nearer to the new source of Christian power in the land now that their former opportunities in the military and commercial service of the local Hindu states were declining.

Things went rather differently in early British Ceylon. Here, eighteenth-century rulers had encouraged a revival of Buddhism. The Dutch, who were entrenched in the coastal provinces around Jaffna, had insisted that their officials in the villages formally professed their Protestant belief. Whole villages were 'baptised' by passing official clergy who sprinkled water on their faces and became 'Government Christians' or 'Christian Buddhists'. Governor North, an orthodox Anglican evangelical, discontinued this practice in the hope that these communities could be converted to Anglicanism by education and example. Most of the Jaffna 'Christians', however, immediately 'relapsed into paganism' or Roman Catholicism (Tennent 1850: 85–6).

Two processes, therefore, were at work. On the one hand, global political and diplomatic struggle encouraged the powers to seek local allies by emphasising religious affiliation. On the other hand, local communities themselves emphasised their broad religious profession in order to secure outside support or to improve internal cohesion in a period of extreme social stress. Community and ethnic affiliations of many sorts were thereby strengthened, often in opposition to one another. An essential precondition for 'national' and 'communal' tensions of the modern world was generated out of the specific historical circumstances of our period.

ISLAM IN CONTEST

These observations are equally true of religious movements among Muslims. During the later seventeenth and early eighteenth centuries a number of contradictory forces had been at work within the Islamic world. First, the Pax Islamica of the Ottomans, Safavids and Mughals had provided the context for a great expansion of communication and common knowledge. Pilgrimage to Mecca, Medina and

Shia Karbala increased, just as the great caravans and sea-voyages brought increased trade from India to the Hejaz, to Cairo and on to North Africa. The later emperors and the rulers of some successor states re-emphasised their orthodox Islamic affiliation out of piety and a desire to strengthen the bases of their legitimacy.

Yet there were also serious challenges to the orthodox Sunni Islam. Some successor states such as Qajar Iran or Awadh in north India were more wholeheartedly Shia, following the practice of their ruling dynasties. This illustrated for Sunnis the rise to power of heretics, and intensified sectarian polemic. Other developments were even worse. Eclectic messianic movements took root again among tribal peoples; in some places, Christians and Hindus increased their power. The result during early eighteenth century was a general turning back to Islamic tradition, the Koran and the Sayings of the Prophet (the Hadiths) in centres of learning such as Medina, Cairo, Delhi and Samarkand. New styles of learning and worship were disseminated sometimes through mosques and teaching schools, sometimes through the mystical Sufi orders which experienced a revival during these years, and some cases were brought more closely under control of the orthodox, textual type of Islamic teacher. Islamic conversions pioneered by townsmen and accepted by tribesmen moved ahead in the peripheral regions of the great Islamic empires where urban society and trade had brought competition, but also the need for a transcendent structure of belief and law. In North Africa (the Sannusia), in Chinese central Asia (the Naqshbandiya), in the Nile Valley (the Salawiya), in Java (the Padri); all these movements marked the internal reformation and external expansion of Islam during these years.

Towards the end of the century, however, the internal conflicts within Islam were brought to a head by the massive onslaught on the central world of an ultra-fundamentalist sect, the Wahhabis of southern Arabia. This coincided with the elimination of a thousand years of Muslim political power by Western expansion at several key centres of Muslim scholarship and belief: in Egypt, in the Balkans, in central Asia, India and Indonesia.

The crisis of the Wahhabi movement sent shock waves through Islam. The tribal warriors, strong in their radical monotheism and textual fundamentalism, not only threatened the temporal rulers of the Islamic world and the recently revived claim of the Sultan to the universal Caliphate. They also rejected some of its fundamental institutions, such as the veneration of 'saints' and sufism. They were deeply hostile to the worldliness which had grown up around the institutions of pilgrimage, the haj. Their sacking of Mecca and Medina and the pillaging of the tomb of the Prophet, following the destruction of the Shia holy places of Karbala had an effect not unlike the loss of Jerusalem and Constantinople on medieval Christendom. According to some the wealth and opulence of the holy cities had enraged the Lord who sent Ibn Saud, the Wahhabi leader, 'like a second Nebuchadnezar' to purge the Temple. These devastating blows from within were overmatched by the threat from outside. Within the space of a decade, two of the greatest centres of Islamic learning, Cairo and Delhi, had been occupied by Christian powers, while the royal centres of Java had been looted by a British army. Istanbul was not occupied by foreign forces but it was weakened and dependent. Some intellectual circles here, as in Cairo, were displaying an unhealthy admiration for Western knowledge and technical expertise. Finally, the secular pillars of Islamic society were weakened. Pious merchants were suffering hardship, the old military nobilities were apparently in decay, the artisan class impoverished and restive, the peasantry prey to messianic and heretical movements which were anathema to the orthodox.

The reaction took several forms. The movements of revival and purification, which had a long history within Islam and which had been galvanised already by the pressures of the eighteenth century, took new vigour. In many areas there was a further revival of the sufi mystical orders, though one which often brought them yet closer to the Islam of mosque and teaching institution. In Egypt, for instance, the notable class (or *sheikhs*) who had close links with the great teaching schools of the al-Azhar mosque, pioneered a sufi revival which was spread to the restive artisan class of the great towns, notably Cairo (Gran 1978). The waves of popular unrest and disquiet could more easily be harnessed to the disciplines of ordered society. In parts of the Ottoman empire the crisis of the state in the first decade of the nineteenth century was accompanied by a revival of sufi institutions patronised by the state, which had the same effect of blunting the impact of heterodoxy. In Iran, popular sufism and more eclectic tribal cults showed great vigour in a context of extreme social disruption. The orthodox Shia jurists of the towns, patronised by the emergent Qajar state, took a leading rôle in the suppression of unorthodox rural sufism and other millenarian movements. In several towns they became virtual rulers of the urban quarters, assimilating local courts to their religious assemblies. It is from this time that the great power of the Shia *mujtahids*, lineal ancestors of today's ayatollahs, derived (Arjomand 1984; Algar 1969). In Iran the political order remained weak, while in Sunni Egypt and other parts of the Ottoman empire the religious teachers and mystics who sought to regain their power over the masses were more closely controlled by the political power.

In India and the Indonesian Archipelago, Islamic religious institutions were subject to the greater strains imposed by the complete victory of Christian military power and the intrusion of the world market. Where they had been strengthened by the eighteenth-century religious revival, around Delhi for instance, orthodox religious leaders took the lead in trying to reimpose order and purify the community (Nizami 1983; Metcalf 1982). In Delhi, scholars and jurists had already gained control over sufi orders through the practice of multiple ordination into them. From these redoubts they were able to influence the people through programmes of education and example. Some leaders considered that the new Christian government was infidel, and hence that religious war against it was canonically justified. Some were prepared to compromise with British rule, serving it as subordinate judges and magistrates.

However, other leaders wholly rejected compromise with the West and with colonial taxation. When such leaders were able to draw support from communities disrupted by war or pressured by intense economic exploitation, popular movements could break through the control of the colonial powers and indigenous ruling groups. On Java, several movements of Islamic messianism exploded between 1795 and 1825, when they climaxed in full-scale religious war and rebellion against the Dutch (Carey 1986b). On Sumatra the so-called Padri movement of 1803–37 drew in villagers seeking a purified religion in a period when changes in international trade were disrupting older patterns of social organisation (Dobbin 1983). In India, declining towns and areas on the fringe of settled agriculture witnessed periodic outbreaks of mahdist millenarianism, when local leaders and charismatic religious figures prophesied the coming of God's rule on the earth, the end of taxation and the extirpation of the infidel.

The southwest coast of India provides an interesting example. Here a Muslim tradition of resistance had been established by conflict over many centuries between the region's Muslim pepper traders (the Moplahs) and their dependent cultivators, on the one hand, and the Christian Portuguese interlopers, on the other. In the eighteenth century that rage had been turned against Hindus as the region's Hindu Nayar chieftains competed for the benefits of the pepper trade with the Muslim merchants. When Tipu Sultan imposed his rule over the coast in 1781, the Moplahs gained the upper hand, appealing to Muslim tradition when securing concessions and patronage from the sultans. The defeat of Tipu by the British in 1793 turned the tables on the Moplahs and unleashed a savage response from the Nayar chieftains whose temples had been destroyed and whose territories had been ravaged. The threat that inter-communal conflict was supposed to pose to the lucrative Bombay pepper trade was a cause of, and a justification for, British intervention in the region. Here, then, many elements of the analysis come together: the intensification of the sense of religious and ethnic identity through actions of the indigenous state and the violence of popular resistance; the role of indigenous petty capitalism; and, ultimately, the intervention by the colonial power to ensure that its commercial interests were not disrupted by social conflict.

All these movements were movements of ordinary people which grew out of specific local circumstances. But all of them fashioned leaders and drew on universalistic Islamic themes. These themes, like those of Providentialist Christianity or of Liberty, Equality and Fraternity, had been given greater currency and coherence by the increase in communication contingent on the world crisis. For instance, it was three pilgrims who saw the Wahhabi sack of Mecca while on pilgrimage who brought the message of purification to the Padris of Sumatra. Again, it was religious stirrings in Arabia which filtered across the Red Sea and sparked off the great expansion of the Salawiya Muslim orders in the southern Sudan. Further east, Sayyid Ahmed of Bareilly who became leader of a purification movement against the Sikhs (and covertly against the British) on the north west frontier of India had recently returned from Mecca and had been trained in the reformist schools of Delhi. Even on the fringes of the Chinese empire where Islamic rebellions against Manchu rule became increasingly frequent after the 1770s, there is evidence to connect their leaders with the wider revival based on Mecca and Medina.

This chapter has argued that the term crisis, often overworked, is applicable on a global scale to the events which took place between about 1780 and 1820. The 'wreck of nations' unleashed an unprecedented wave of popular revolts and protests and with a distinct broadening of ideological and sectarian conflicts. This crisis resulted from the collapse of the old régime in Europe but also from social disruption in Asia, North Africa and the New World which had independent roots. The events in Asia and North Africa were not simply 'local crises' but reflections of deeper changes which were common to large parts of the Islamic world, Hindu India and greater southeast Asia. The emphasis so far has been on ideology and religious tradition because one should not reduce these momentous events to changes in international trade or to social conflicts. All the same, economic conditions provided an essential context within which to understand them. The remainder of the chapter is given over to the economic dimensions of the world crisis. Once again, events in Europe provided a critical element of change, but were not the only salient economic factors. Again, these economic crises outside Europe were not really 'local' events; they were also part of a wider pattern. The next section considers, first, the cumulative pattern of economic decline which appears to have set in around 1780 and then some features of deeper, structural changes in extra-European economies.

ECONOMIC DISRUPTION AND WORLD CRISIS

In south Asia and the Middle East the fifty years after 1780 were a period seriously disrupted by warfare. Natural disasters also intervened to put greater pressures on weakened populations. In north India the great famine of 1783–4 may have killed more than 20 per cent of the population of the great plains. There were also scarcities in the south. Sudden leaps in grain prices elsewhere in the Middle East and western Europe suggest that these years may have seen some type of general global climatic shock. The Indian famine was followed by severe scarcities in Rajasthan in 1791–3, and in north India in 1801–2 and again in 1805. Grain supplies were disrupted by the Anglo-Mysore and Anglo-Maratha wars. But independently of war, the last two decades of the eighteenth century seem to have seen bad or disastrous harvests over much of the sub-continent. While harvests improved after 1803, a new natural scourge appeared with the rapid spread of epidemic disease in the early years of the nineteenth century. Major political change, and especially large-scale conquest, spread disease pools along the routes of armies and navies. For instance, the Mongol invasion or the Partition of Africa in the later nineteenth century had this effect and so did the global wars of our period. Periodic plagues culminated in the spread of epidemic cholera from eastern to western India during the third Maratha War (1815–18). Thereafter cholera made a dramatic leap across the Mediterranean and into southern Europe.

The same sort of sequence seems to have occurred in Egypt and North Africa. In Egypt the demographic decline and economic paralysis of Cairo in the 1720s and 1730s was partly reversed in the 1750s–70s (Raymond 1973: ii, 57). The situation deteriorated again rapidly after 1780. Average decennial corn prices in the capital measured from 1681–90 were 75 in 1761–70, 117 in 1771–80, 291 in 1781–90 and 212 in 1791–8. The years 1792–1800 saw a 'quasi-anarchy' in the province which brought about fighting between the beys, the French and the English but greatly worsened by outbreaks of plague and poor harvests. Scarcities and epidemics also affected large parts of North Africa, damaging Mediterranean trade and bringing to an abrupt halt the booming commercial economy of the island of Malta, under the British Crown since 1800. The downturn in the Middle Eastern and Mediterranean economies had scarcely begun to bottom out when trading conditions were damaged once again by the post-war depression and series of bad harvests which affected western Europe after Waterloo.

Regional economies which had remained quite buoyant for much of the eighteenth century might have weathered the poor natural conditions better if they had not been hit in rapid succession by large-scale military movements and political turbulence. Chapter 2 suggested that throughout much of Eurasia and the Caribbean the ratchet of economic conflict had been screwed up during the eighteenth century. Wars over trade, labour and capital broke out with increasing frequency as the old empires declined and European powers tried to protect their profits by the creation of monopolies and coercion of peasantries. These wars of European mercantilism and Asian or African state-building became more intense, and by the second half of the century they were beginning to reduce production and damage trade. While, for instance, the rule of Ali Pasha had given Egypt a respite from political conflict and a period of economic stability, the intervention of the Porte in 1786 and the ensuing struggle for succession resulted in further disruption of trade and the screwing upwards of land and customs taxes by the contending beys and Ottoman officials. In turn, one of the factors which probably influenced Bonaparte in his decision to invade Egypt was the difficulty of securing adequate grain supplies for the French urban population during the wars. This was a product both of war and of the longer-term failures of French agricultural production. Conflicts and contradictions inside and outside Europe were feeding on each other and reinforcing each other.

India and Iran offer some similar examples. The Georgian Pashalik of Baghdad, the Zand and Qajar successor régimes of Iran and, ultimately, the British were drawn into deeper conflict over the trade of the port of Basra as inter-regional commerce was increasingly disrupted by their own attempts to monopolise and control it. In India, the Marathas and the Sultans of Mysore, despite the 'black tyranny' imputed to them by the British, consistently worked for the economic development of their conquered territories, not least in order to outmatch the resources of their Indian and European enemies. As late as the 1770s, unbiased observers praised these sovereigns for running their lands like rich estates. After the wars of 1779–81, however, the position deteriorated. Tipu Sultan waged an economic war against the Company in Madras and tried to disrupt the trade of its allies on the west coast. A general decline of trade across southern India and outwards to the Middle East and southeast Asia intensified the south Indian conflict. As the British East India Company drew less profit from its trading operations, it was forced to service its operations increasingly by forcing both allies and enemies in India to pay cash tribute to it, or by annexing new territories. The Company's own insatiable demands for money and revenue pushed the Indian states towards more vigorous opposition and paved the way for the great waves of expansion under Wellesley and the Marquess of Hastings (1812–23).

The crescendo of economic warfare was reached when Napoleon and the British began to resort to a world-wide programme of blockade and counter-blockade after the Berlin decrees of 1805. Checkmated in Europe, the British could only carry on their war against the First Empire by seizing and exploiting French colonies and denying to Europe the produce of colonies in the Caribbean and the East. The following decade of economic warfare entailed quite profound changes in international trade and brought wealth or ruin to commercial men, artisans and peasants who had serviced the earlier commodity flows. While the British usually had the upper hand in these naval struggles, they were by no means the only gainers.

In the Mediterranean the conflict between British and French shipping damaged the ports of southern Europe, but encouraged the flowering of a number of middleman states and merchant communities. Greeks, Maltese and Mediterranean Jews benefited greatly, and the restiveness of the Greeks of the Islands and the Aegean coast under Ottoman rule notably increased. The Beys of Algiers and Hamdad Pasha, the strongman of Tunis, captured a large slice of Mediterranean trade and provided grain for the French minister Talleyrand (Valensi 1977b). Mohammad Ali in Egypt, seeking to free himself from British influence now that the French threat had receded, reached an uneasy truce with the Royal Navy after 1808 by supplying its ships with corn for the Peninsular War. Ironically, both these commercial engagements gave the Great Powers commercial leverage in the affairs of the Arab states which they later exploited for political gain.

In general, it was the British who benefited most from the widespread disruption of trade. In the Ottoman empire, they exploited the opportunity caused by the distraction of the French and Russians to increase their sales of manufactured goods within the Sultan's domains. Ottoman textile production had already suffered from the competition of superior Indian textiles. Now political force enabled the British to create a market for their goods in the Ottoman lands which was scarcely less complete than the one they were to secure in India, a formal colony (Inalcik 1987). The continental blockade also gave Britain the chance to strike at the French Caribbean empire and demolish the Dutch East Indian empire, permanently annexing the Cape of Good Hope as a linking point between the two hemispheres. Indian opium, and to a lesser extent British manufactured goods, poured into Java after the conquest of 1805 and though the British returned the islands to the Netherlands in 1815, British Indian opium and later British textile sales were poised to take an increasing share of southeast and east Asian markets.

The population of large parts of the world, then, was faced with a sharp realignment of trade, the collapse of old markets and the intrusion of new ones, at the very time that the demands of the state through taxation and extraordinary requisitions was at its height. This was the context of the widespread social unrest which threatened governments and élites after 1780. Yet cumulative growth of these pressures was only part of a deeper, structural change in the international economy. A critical force in this change was, of course, the English industrial revolution which had begun to marginalise artisan producers in Scotland and Ireland before 1800 and was rapidly restricting the opportunities for growth within the indigenous textile industries of Asia and North Africa by the second decade of the nineteenth century. The abrupt closure of

European markets by Napoleon had acted as a sharp incentive for English manufacturers to redouble their sales to the outside world, notably to North and South America and to Asia. The economic conditions of warfare with high prices and a relative shortage of labour also indirectly encouraged the move towards mechanisation.

However, industrialisation and the associated search abroad for raw cotton or timber was only the leading edge of a global economic shift which also had its origins in the development of capital and production outside Europe. As we have seen, the rapid commercialisation of large parts of the Indo-Islamic world in the seventeenth century had created societies which the great empires and their military nobilities proved unable to control. New classes of gentry, literati and merchants had emerged and these provided the basis for the regional states of the eighteenth century. While European trade and political intervention was already an important influence on these societies, therefore, many significant changes were already in train.

For instance, the decline of the great Islamic administrative–artisan city centres and the long-distance trading routes was already underway in the Ottoman empire, India and Iran well before the Western impact became of paramount importance. This was brought about by the dissolution of the old nobilities and the end of the patronage by the ancient military nobility (*janissaries, odjaks* and *mansabdars*) of their clients among the urban artisans. It also reflected the impact of the great tribal 'breakouts' and the regionalisation of political power. While aristocratic demand was diminishing or abruptly changing its form, ruling élites and merchants were even more concerned to bring artisans under their direct control. Revenue-farmers, the agents of the successor states and, of course, European companies kidnapped and resettled bodies of weavers, reduced them to virtual debt bondage or squeezed out the indigenous middlemen who had allowed them some autonomy in setting prices to buyers. These specialist weaving communities were already vulnerable when they began to face the full impact of Western manufactured goods. First, the European companies ceased their purchases; then British twist and yarn destroyed the by-employment in spinning which had helped maintain the living standards of weavers families; finally, by the 1820s the full-scale invasion of British machine-made goods had begun. Weavers of lower-quality produce, particularly in the countryside, survived, and in some areas even flourished. The quality trade was rapidly undermined and famous artisan cities

– Bursa, Konya, Isfahan, Ahmedabad, Dacca, Murshidabad – changed their form.

Riots and disturbances among urban artisan communities were widely recorded from the Balkans to the Indonesian Archipelago between 1780 and 1820. They took many different forms. Some were inter-communal riots as in Calcutta in 1789 or Surat in 1795 (Subramanian 1984) when Muslim artisans opposed Hindu merchants. Some were messianic movements or outbreaks of popular rage, as for instance those recorded by Sir John Malcolm in the quarters of Iranian cities (Malcolm 1815). Some were strikes against merchants or the political authorities, as in Cairo before and after the French occupation. None was simply a response to economic dislocation, but all were located in this context. This urban and artisan crisis, then, had two aspects. First, it reflected the changes in Asian and Middle Eastern society which had accompanied the decline of the empires, changes which were related to the unbalanced growth of early capitalism within them. Secondly, it reflected the beginnings of the world-wide change in the division of labour associated with industrialisation. These events were the structural parallels to the revolts among north and west country weavers thrown out of work by mechanisation in England or of linen makers in Ireland whose position was rapidly eroded after 1810.

Related structural changes were taking place in agriculture. These also contributed to the unprecedented wave of social conflict. In the British Isles enclosure, mechanisation and the destruction of common rights was at its peak during the agricultural boom of the Napoleonic War period. The extent to which communities and livelihoods had been disrupted only became apparent after the great post-war depression set in in 1816. Tension here took many forms: from the 'Captain Swing' riots of impoverished labourers in the south of England to mass emigration from southern and western Ireland. Here a virtual Malthusian crisis set in as prices fell and individual plots continued to diminish under the pressure of population rise.

Capitalist farming had no such direct impact over much of the Middle East and Asia, but significant changes in the nature of rural society were underway. The last pre-colonial states had already forced up land revenues, brought new products and resources into their taxation régimes. The revenue squeeze on the settled peasantry was intensified as significant areas of production had been lost to successive 'tribal breakouts' or to conflicts between the regional states. Certain types of private property had grown in importance as communal ownership and complex service tenures had proved inconvenient when men needed to know more precisely what their resources would be. The growing demand for revenue in cash had also brought about a widespread penetration of land tax and production régimes by petty rural capitalists; Greeks, Jews, Syrian Christians, Armenians and Copts in the Ottoman empire; Hindu banias, Tamil Muslims in south Asia and Hakka Chinese throughout southeast Asia.

Into this changing situation, the agencies of the European imperial powers intruded themselves. Under pressure of war, Marshall Daendels for the Batavian Republic, Frederick North, Cornwallis, Wellesley and Raffles for the British empire, sought from their subject peasantries a further enhancement of cash revenues or labour services. They also tried to stimulate the production of export cash-crops, cotton, indigo, coffee, spices which now achieved a new importance in the rural economy of Asia and Africa. Agrarian changes introduced by the colonial powers went deeper than this. Wherever possible, individual ownership, forms of private property or administrative law were imposed on more flexible indigenous systems of account, rights and obligations. In many areas, tenacious rural resistance was encountered and it was this as much as the ideological preconceptions of the new imperial rulers which shaped the social relations of the emerging post-war colonial régimes. In Java, for instance, Chinese moneylenders had taken an increasingly active role as revenue-farmers and renters of tolls and monopolies under the sultans of the successor state of Surakarta and to an even greater degree under the rule of Stamford Raffles (1811–16). The pressures generated by Raffles's insistence on cash payment of revenues instead of customary labour services became confounded with detestation of the Chinese outsider. Serious peasant revolts broke out along the north coast and in central Java. It was partly in response to the political dangers which arose from this apparently unrestrained commercialisation that the restored Dutch officials returned after 1816 to eighteenth-century labour services and attempted to isolate the Javanese village from penetration by outside capitalists.

The fight to reassert order and economic control led to a considerable expansion of the state's forces of coercion within rural society. Crude rural para-military forces, often recruited from unemployed free soldiers, were in place in most Indian districts by 1814. At the other end of the empire, the Irish Constabulary, arm of both the state and the Protestant Ascendancy, was finally created in 1822 to confront the increasingly violent struggles of the Catholic peasantry. The search for rural control was not a monopoly of Europeans. In colonial territories the Europeans were supported by the interest in rural order of landlords, moneylenders and the denizens of the reviving towns. Outside the colonies, régimes such as Muhammad Ali's Egypt and Qajar Iran, or the resurgent Ottoman provinces fought to reimpose a similar control over peasant and tribesman.

CONCLUSION

While sharp movements in the international economy underlay much of the social tension which characterised what we have called the world crisis of 1780–1820, shifts in ideologies and popular mentalities seem of even greater importance, and it is to this issue that the chapter finally returns. Beyond rebellion and the introduction of new types of political and religious discourse – Christian, Muslim, Buddhist – one might almost see a critical change in the evolution of civilisations. The destruction or damaging of ancient repositories of learning and political legitimacy, Delhi, Jogjakarta, Isfahan, Cairo and Istanbul, not to speak of Versailles and Rome, marked an abrupt end to many earlier forms of divine kingship and religious authority over much of the world. Political office was widely severed from religious function not only at the highest level but even in small but coherent societies once governed by cycles of ritual and notions of the unity of the king's body and the kingdom.

The effects were most striking on the outer fringes of the world civilisations. The arrival of Captain Cook in Polynesia in the 1770s acted as a religious and social cataclysm; over the next generation, Baptist missionaries, pirates and fishing fleets based on Australia tore apart the cultural fabric of Polynesian society and transformed its understanding of kingship and religion. Equally dramatic events affected societies nearer the centres of world civilisation. The British in Ceylon, for instance, were drawn into ever-sharper conflicts with the interior kingdom as disputes over trade and monopoly inherited from the Dutch, continued to flare up. In 1818 a full-scale war broke out, pitting not just the king and court against the British but also some 800,000 common people. The result was not simply a change of political order but the complete extirpation of the ancient Buddhist culture. Nearly 10 per cent of the population died of disease, famine, warfare or summary British executions; villages were burned; the central symbols of the kingdom, including the famous relic the Tooth of the Buddha, were destroyed; the old ritual link between court and village was entirely destroyed, to be replaced simply by the pragmatic relationship of taxpayer and ruler. Buddhism, once the organisation of society expressed in the form of cult, became no more than a popular religion. It went far beyond the atrocity publicised by radical opponents of the new British empire, who saw it as the destruction of a popular resistance comparable to the extermination of Calabrian independence by the Bonapartists (Davy 1969: 233–47).

The homogenisation of civilisation, the replacement of gifting by taxation as the central act of power, the dominance of bureaucracy and the market were not, of course, abrupt blows struck by the West against the Orient. Much of the practice and ideology of indigenous kingdoms and of an Islamic world still expanding pointed in the same direction. Nevertheless, the turn of the nineteenth century saw an epochal quickening of these trends. That quickening responded both to the expansion of European strife and to the crisis of earlier polities outside Europe. The pace of such developments differed greatly from region to region. In some places 'order' and trade had been restored before 1800; in others the fight-back of the state, the landlord and the merchant against nomad, tribesman and free peasant was still uncertain in the 1830s and 1840s. Yet the trend was already clear.

CHAPTER SEVEN

Proconsular Despotisms: the British Empire, c. 1800–40

The new British empire of the first decades of the nineteenth century complemented features of a revivified conservative régime at home. British society in the first third of the nineteenth century was still ruled by parties representing landed wealth. The power of landowner and squire had, if anything, increased in the counties where territorial magnates confirmed their grip over constituencies and the office of JP. The mercantile interest was generally prepared, as before, to follow the leadership of the landowners, to aspire to their style of life and to pursue the interests of trade under the protection of the state. Lord Liverpool (prime minister, 1812–27 was not an *ancien régime* figure such as Metternich and Guizot (Gash 1984). He was a reforming conservative presiding over an enlarged state. This state still represented a highly restricted political nation which confirmed rather than created ministries through Parliament. There was some liberalisation of trade and the protectionist Corn Laws, but the main thrust of policy was an increase in state regulation with an eye to cutting costs and avoiding conflict. The removal of the remaining disqualifications which prevented Dissenting Protestants holding public office (1812) did not herald an age of emancipation. It was instead an attempt to placate a powerful and conservative section of society. Catholic emancipation was blocked, while one important purpose of the Irish Union and the closer assimilation of Scotland was, from one point of view, conservative. It continued to provide for ministers a large block of disciplined supporters among MPs, who could make up for the loss of parliamentary cannon fodder as 'economical reform' limited the scope for patronage.

Castlereagh's foreign policy can also be described by the term constructive conservatism. While opposing French aims in

Spain and Portugal, he worked closely with the Holy Alliance in other parts of southern Europe and rarely supported nationalist movements except where they were evidently going to succeed. Even Canning (foreign secretary, 1822–7), sometimes hailed as a supporter of liberalism and nationalism, thought the Greeks a 'rascally set' and hoped to maintain a tamed Ottoman empire as a block to Russian and Austrian influence in the Mediterranean. If Canning's reluctant support of the rebellious Spanish American colonies was influenced in part by the mercantile lobby, a much more powerful incentive was to restore social stability under the creole élites and avoid the kind of slave revolt which broke out in Demerara in 1823 and might infect the whole Caribbean. Though Canning was less addicted to a 'regular state of things . . . [and] hierarchical discipline' than Wellington had become, both men pursued a cautious policy, and even the little essays in practical liberalism were, as Metternich pointed out, entirely overshadowed by opposition to Irish nationalism and the long rearguard action against Catholic emancipation (Temperley 1966: 357).

THE PROCONSULAR REGIMES

The colonial régimes of the early nineteenth century were broadly compatible with this society. Rather than being a despotic appendage to a liberal, free-trading industrial state waiting breathlessly for domestic and colonial reform, they mirrored and reinforced it in important respects. Despite the emergence of a more intrusive and centralising Colonial Office (and the growth of the rôle of the home secretary in Irish policy) this empire was only loosely controlled from the centre. The new Colonial Office, for all its incipient Benthamite principles, was politically weak, understaffed and obsessed with the problem of slavery or, more precisely, with the question of how to make more acceptable at home one particular legal form of unfreedom in the colonies. Colonial governors and their deputies had a very free rein on most other issues. Up to 1815 or even 1825, they could cite exigencies of war as an excuse for a personal and often despotic style of rule. War against the French or against indigenous opponents of British expansion, Maratha, Burmese, Sinhalese, Malay or Xhosa, could justify much. The prevailing ethos of loyalism, royalism and aristocratic military virtue provided them with charisma, dash and a ready supply of gentlemen, often younger sons of landowners, prepared to operate as their clients in return for substantial salaries. Fear and loathing of republicanism and disdain for the non-white, non-Anglo-Saxon, or non-Protestant, reinforced by the fashionable aristocratic evangelicalism, helped inform their mentality.

In some colonies the proconsuls inherited the machinery of Dutch or *ancien régime* French despotism or, as in the Mediterranean, were subtly influenced by the miasma of the Holy Alliance. In others they revised and perpetuated the tools of the new Asian and African despotisms which had emerged at the end of the eighteenth century. Economics again tended to reinforce the character of empire as a series of loosely linked aristocratic fiefdoms. During the wars and the depression which followed them, the paramount concern of the Treasury (as it was to be so often later) was to limit the cost of the colonies. Where governors could raise their funds locally they were encouraged to do so, even if this meant shoring up monopolies and systems of taxation which were anathema to the noisy but still often ineffectual apostles of free trade and laissez faire.

Colonial government therefore had much in common with the aims and attitudes of the régimes of the new conservatism in Great Britain. The social and political system which held sway between the death of Pitt and the Great Reform Bill was not simply a last gasp of an ancient monarchical order. It represented instead the creation of new tools of control and the reinvention of an aristocratic landed tradition. The early nineteenth-century empire was an outgrowth of this 'Court' philosophy and practice transformed and generalised to an international scale by the world crisis of the turn of the nineteenth century and by the ideological clarity to which it gave rise.

Although these revivified colonial régimes rooted themselves in starkly differing societies, they had common features and comparable results. In general the new viceroys abolished or eroded the powers of existing representative institutions and tried to create an official class separated from the lures of commerce or entanglement with 'native' life. The new official class benefited, however, from massive salaries and sometimes from patronage in Crown lands. The existing loose racial hierarchies were purged of direct and irresponsible violence against slaves (wherever possible), but defined more subtly through law; indigenous peoples (even white non-Protestants) were excluded from office. Indigenous and settler landlords were rewarded as far as possible through the creation of untrammelled property rights to the detriment of common rights and shifting tenures, but large concentrations of power were avoided when these were not in the hands of officials. A 'yeoman' solution was particularly favoured where the Scottish school of 'moral independency' held sway. Some moves to free trade were put in train, but monopolies were often maintained on pragmatic grounds and forms of coercion of labour apart from abject slavery were vigorously employed. Finally, a subtle anglicisation and, where possible, anglicanisation was in the air. Direct proselytisation by missionaries (especially those of lower class) was frowned upon, but the English gentlemen and Scottish public servants tried to inoculate these societies with Church and the supremacy of law.

IRELAND AND THE MEDITERRANEAN

Naturally, it was in Ireland that the viceregal style of government came under greatest pressure from the tendency to centralise in Westminster. Yet the lieutenant-governor, or viceroy, under the Crown still retained considerable powers. Until 1815 he held the position of commander-in-chief, and with the growth of British military and para-military forces in the country between 1816 and 1825, lieutenant-governors were often able to influence the day-to-day deployment of the coercive power of the state. Until the 1830s the Irish chief-secretary in London also helped to shield the lieutenant-governor from interference by the British home secretary. Several of these still-independent viceroys of the early nineteenth century attempted to use their authority to cut back the pretensions of the magnates of the Protestant Ascendancy and to coax the Catholic gentry and merchant classes into the imperial project. Wellesley-Pole openly espoused the cause of Catholic emancipation after 1812; his brother Richard Wellesley married a Catholic and tried to extend his patronage powers in order to honour Catholics and exclude extremist Protestant Orangemen from office (Brynn 1978: 51, 84). Trinity College Dublin was quietly encouraged in its rôle as an 'imperial academy' and the officially sponsored St Patrick's Day celebrations and rituals of the Order of St Patrick were a conscious attempt to nurture a conservative Irish patriotism within the empire similar to that which was already paying dividends in Scotland and Wales (Hill 1984).

In Ireland these policies were doomed to failure even before

Britain's Second Empire began to disintegrate in the 1830s. Orangeism, spiced with the livid anti-Catholic rhetoric which had emerged during the disturbances of 1798–9, was already well entrenched. A vigorous Protestant evangelical crusade frightened Catholic clergymen into alliance with Daniel O'Connell and the first generation of conservative Catholic nationalists. It also gave popular millenarian Catholicism a new lease of life. Moreover, the state was too closely tied to the landlord offensive against peasant farmers to act as an arbiter between Catholic and Protestant. The expanding Irish police force tended to intervene more and more in local custom, while judges supported the principles of fee simple against peasant communal tenures. Worse, the economic conditions after the end of the Napoleonic War encouraged landlords to turn back once again to pasturage, ruthlessly uprooting the rights of arable peasant farmers whenever they could. In the land wars of the 1830s and 1840s the British establishment was to find itself supporting the 'law and order' of the landlords against the Catholic peasantry. The imperial state found itself more impotent to transcend its dependence on the creole élite than it was in the Caribbean or Canada.

Viceregal despotism had a more successful career in areas newly conquered during the wars. In the Mediterranean the British had before them the admirable example of the paternalistic régimes of the Noble Order of the Knights of St John in Malta, the Kingdom of the Two Sicilies (during their brief rule in that island) and the Signoria of the Serene Republic of St Mark on the Greek Islands. They lived up well to these grand precedents and had ceded almost nothing in the way of local representation or constitutional assemblies before mid-century. Their aim was to create a sheltered haven for British trade, fend off the claims of Russia and to promote a 'modern' landowning class more tractable than the old feudal barons, but adequate to control the peasantry. To one degree or another, they also attempted to anglicise though not to anglicanise the ruling groups of the islands. Liberalism was no part of their project.

In Malta the British had the great advantage that they had been invited in by the notables of the island in 1799 as Napoleon's power in the Mediterranean weakened. They resisted the recreation of the old Consilio Popolare or assembly of the islands. This had existed (though in an eclipsed form) under the Knights, but at one time had held limited legislative powers and included commoner representatives of the villages. Tension over failing trade and high taxation resulted in a popular movement in favour of the recreation of a popular legislative body between 1806 and 1810. The campaign was led by a great noble, the Marchese Testaferrata, and an English radical publicist called William Eton (Laferla 1938: i, 80–1). In 1812 a Commission under the Great Seal was sent to Malta to investigate these grievances and to enquire into the island's civil and judicial affairs. It consisted of the British Chargé-d'affaires at Palermo, a Chief Justice of the Caribbean island of Dominica and the Governor himself. Not surprisingly it reported that the people of Malta were 'singularly unfitted to enjoy any portion of political power', and that any move along these lines would be attended by 'the greatest danger and ruinous consequences' (ibid: 82), an apparent reference to the possibility of Russian influence or the reappearance of covert republican enthusiasm.

In both Malta and the Ionian Islands the form of the colonial despotism was most robustly illustrated during the rule of 'King Tom' Maitland, Governor of Malta and Lord High Commissioner of Ionia. Maitland, a one-time radical, had become a great royalist following his experience as Governor of Saint Domingue in 1797 and a subsequent period as Governor of Ceylon. This Lowlands Scots gentleman was no theorist of empire, but he fell back increasingly on the argument of 'the King's service' to justify what were seen as unpopular or arbitrary decisions (Lord 1935). Ultimately, he thought 'definite power, however extensive, is a lesser evil in any state, than power alike uncontrolled and undefined' (ibid.: 201). The Ionian Islands inherited a number of institutions of self-government from Byzantium and the Venetians, but the power of the nobles had grown as the Signoria had declined in the late eighteenth century. Their autonomy was perpetuated during the period of the French occupation. A group of nobles, influenced by Orthodox affiliations and led by John Capodistrias, once a councillor of the Russian empire and a major landowner, supported Russia against British influence. The nobles also resented the attempts of British governors to abrogate their feudal privileges in matters of justice and to centralise power on themselves. In 1817, Maitland formalised the *de facto* autocracy of wartime in a constitution for the islands which he claimed would prevent the Ionians from 'running wild'. It consisted in the complete domination of a subservient Legislative Assembly by a Primary Council of acquiescent nominees from among the great notables: 'Maitland's magnificoes' (Lord 1935: 196). These men, like their compères in Malta, were bound to the governor by patronage and the distribution of honours such as the newly invented Order of St Michael and St George. The new 'constitution', a facade for a British autocracy, was ratified in the Throne Room of the Brighton Pavilion in December 1818.

In both Malta and the Ionian Islands, notables and landowners considered safe were given more influence over administrative and judicial measures in the villages. In Malta, for instance, village leaders lost the office of 'luogotenento', and were replaced by grandees styled 'lieutenant-governors'. The British element in the administration was expanded. As was the case throughout the colonial world after 1793, indigenous peoples were excluded from all but the lowliest offices of state. Since Ionians and Maltese could not aspire to the more important jobs, as they had done under the Venetians, Russians and Knights respectively, the number of British officials swelled rapidly. In judicial matters, native-born people were even more rigorously debarred. This policy reflected a widespread view, voiced by one of the more moderate officials, Charles Napier, that 'the Ionians are the greatest liars in the World'. Joseph Hume, the London radical, denounced the unfettered proconsular patronage that this created; local politicians noted with alarm the flood of 'well-born young gentlemen, whose sole duty seems to be to loll on our verandas'. Yet the system was continued largely unchanged until the British evacuated the Ionian Islands in 1863. On Malta, despite the addition of an elected local advisory council in 1835 and a new constitution in 1849, government remained autocratic and a monopoly of British officials until 1887. It is interesting to note, in fact, that the premier 'liberal' power, the contemporary protector of the Greek revolt against the 'bloody Turk', operated a more exclusive and despotic policy in the Mediterranean than its neighbours, the neo-absolutist régimes of Austria and Russia.

British cultural policy in the Mediterranean also yields examples which illuminate more general imperial themes. On Malta and Gozo the British sought and ultimately came to an agreement with the Vatican which excluded the influence of the Kingdom of Sicily over ecclesiastical presentations but unequivocally affirmed the Catholic status of the islands. This reflected the drawing together of the Vatican and the British government as common enemies of French republicanism after 1800, an entente which was symbolised by the Papal acquisition of a painting by Lawrence of King William IV. The British for their part hoped to use the influence of the Vatican against Irish liberal priests and to neutralise the activities of Irish members in the House of Commons, who were quick to pick up any evidence of the harassment of Catholic subjects throughout the colonial world (Bezzina 1985: 90). On the Ionian Islands, British officials were similarly circumspect in their dealings with the Orthodox hierarchy.

Though they were very cautious in matters of religion, this did not prevent successive governors using anglicisation as a tool of political control. In the case of Malta, this policy coincided closely with that of Bathurst, the Colonial Secretary, who urged the policy of replacing Italian with English as 'identifying their affections and interests with the British connection'. Proceedings in the Supreme Court were in English as were government proclamations; an English public school was founded and English was added to the curriculum of the university and higher schools. This policy was responsible for the continuing vestiges of English influence in Corfu and Zante, such as cricket and ginger beer.

Promotion of the English language and English institutions were not the only cultural strategies employed by the colonialists. Equally important, the British fostered subordinate forms of nationalism within the empire. There was a series of attempts to encourage indigenous peoples to rediscover their own language, literature and customs but within the broad framework of loyalty to the imperial Crown and a notion of natural aristocracy. This policy was seen at its most successful in the case of Scotland with the invention by Walter Scott and his generation of a Scottish mythology of national identity under the Crown. As we have seen, Richard Wellesley and other early nineteenth-century viceroys of Ireland were perhaps groping towards something similar in their patronage of Irish culture and the revamping of the rituals of the Order of St Patrick. In the Mediterranean the parallel was with the 'establishment' Philhellenism promoted in particular by Frederick North, another former governor of Ceylon finding his way to pasture on the islands. In many respects, North and his confrères followed the tradition set by Byron at Missolonghi. North affected ancient Greek dress, wearing a kiton, often carrying a lyre and wearing a laurel wreath on his 'mad, bald pate', as Napier put it (Pratt 1978: 110). More practically, he set up a Hellenic University on Corfu which was intended to act as a magnet for Greek youth from throughout the Ottoman empire and the Mediterranean. The university did, in fact, preside over a minor renaissance of Greek literature and acted as a significant political centre until the new King Otto of Greece landed on the mainland at Nauplion in 1832. Maitland was suspicious of the university in spite of his own fabrication of the Order of St Michael and St George, and he managed to have it blocked until 1823. All the same, North's schemes should be regarded as imperial projects. He undoubtedly hoped for the creation of an independent Greater Greece, but it was to be one which looked to her British protector above all and replaced the Ottoman empire as guardian of the British interests in the eastern Mediterranean. Both the realpolitik and the romanticism was to recur periodically in the minds of British statesmen through Gladstone to Lloyd George.

Finally, the Mediterranean islands – a small laboratory inhabited by white races – throw light on the early nineteenth-century empire more broadly if one looks at the relationship between state and economy. While most officials, even during the wars, paid lip service to the ideals of free trade and laissez faire, mercantilism was a long time dying and was hedged around with practical protection and even some philosophical justifications. In the Maltese islands the old monopolistic institution of the Knights, the Universita, which sold state-purchased provisions of grain, cattle, macaroni and oil to the populace at greatly inflated prices, continued down to 1822, when the grain trade was freed (Laferla 1938: i, 107). On the Ionian Islands, the state monopoly of the currant and wine crop also persisted well into the 1820s. One reason for this was the desire of the British government both during and after the war to have colonies pay for themselves. Another was the large and inflated salary bill which resulted from the determination to bring in British officials in preference to local people. In 1820, nearly 50 per cent of government revenue and expenditure went on civil salaries in the Ionian Islands – a much higher percentage than under the Venetians (*cf*. Napier 1833: 21). In Gozo (Malta), British loans, military and naval expenditure brought into the island only about 30 per cent of what the Knights had brought in, but again, official salaries were high (Bezzina 1985: ch. 2). In a period of relative agricultural depression and at a time when Mediterranean exports were doing rather poorly in the British and international markets, local sources of revenue were of critical importance.

This generally restrictive, even monopolistic practice was also seen in commercial policy. Malta, of course, had grown as an entrepôt for southern European trade when the continental blockade was in operation. The protectionist urge continued into the 1830s and 1840s. Maitland particularly had 'three principles . . . to give preference to British manufactured and colonial goods; second, to encourage the export of Maltese produce and thirdly, to encourage the use of Malta as an entrepot' (Lord 1935: 162). Though the position was not easy to maintain, he and following governors worked surreptitiously to exclude French, Spanish and Portuguese shipping and goods from the islands, as well as to bring free Maltese and Greek shipping under British control and protection. The age of free trade dawned very late in the Mediterranean as it did over much of the rest of the colonial empire.

SOUTHERN AFRICA

Many of the principles and policies which were typical of the colonial state in the Mediterranean were pursued in other colonies of white settlement. We see the same sort of paradox in southern Africa. The advent of the supposedly liberal state on the Cape was accompanied by the establishment of official despotism; the first moves against slavery and the 'barbarity' of the Boers were to result in the imposition of a more subtle, yet more pervasive social hierarchy (Elphick and Giliomee 1983). A colonial power supposedly little concerned with its 'mission civilisatrice' encouraged assimilation and covertly discriminated even against white Protestants who were not Anglo-Saxon. Again, this might be seen as the victory of brutal pragmatism over liberal idealism; except that almost all theoretical statements by individuals in power emphasised the need to monopolise office for racial and ideological reasons. The Dutch statist inheritance was important but especially because it fitted well with the aristocratic triumphalism of late Georgian British society.

Several early governors and senior civil servants on the Cape had Indian experience, notably Lord Macartney and Sir John Cradock. The tone of their administrations and the nature of their concerns was reminiscent of that of Cornwallis's India. The military element was strong. In 1810 there were 6,500 British troops on the Cape, more than at Gibraltar or Malta, in addition to the large para-military force of Dutch and their Hottentot servants which were at the disposal of rural officers known as field-cornets. Even though the first British administration (1796–1803) worked on the assumption that the colony would be handed back to the Dutch, they acted more purposefully than the Dutch Company had done against both white and black dissidence. The settlers of Graaff Reinet in the eastern Cape who harboured notions of republican independence were swiftly brought to book, and 'jacobinism' was suppressed. Xhosa incursions against the Cape colony were vigorously repulsed and under General Dundas a policy of divide and rule by treaty was worked out. Beginning with Macartney, the British also put into effect a public policy of paternalistic 'benevolence' towards the indigenous people, people of mixed race and the large slave population which was of African, Indian and Malay origin. The instruments of torture employed by the Dutch against slaves were publicly destroyed (as happened in Ceylon and Java). In 1807 the slave trade was abolished and attempts were made to mitigate the severity of treatment of slaves by their Boer masters.

To the British, the sociology of Cape society was quite simple. The Dutch Company's monopoly had been so rigid and corrupt that trade had been interdicted. The Dutch 'peasants' once energetic had become lazy, 'even when gain was evidently the ultimate reward, the indolence of these degenerate colonists prevailed even over their avarice'. The institution of slavery and the ready availability of Hottentot (Khoikoi) servants had corrupted their moral independency with the result that agriculture was poor and the country sparsely populated. Oppression by the peasants had in turn corrupted the domestic economy of the Khoikoi who, when not being abused by their masters, spent much of their time sleeping. 'Hence arises that indifference to marriage and the propagation of children for which this race of people is distinguished' (Percival 1806: 81ff.). Sentiments such as these which echo so closely what contemporary Englishmen were saying about the Irish, the Indians or the 'free people' of colour in the West Indies were amenable to similar treatment. The British government was 'to carry civilisation, opulence and industry into every quarter of the globe'. In particular, the British should seek the support of the 'Hottentot' against their creole oppressors. A corps of 500 'Hottentots' was raised to help the British against both Dutch and Xhosa. An assumption was made that the indigenous people's 'industry may be excited . . . by equitable treatment barbarously withheld from them by the Dutch'.

Such ideas lay behind the so-called Hottentot Code promulgated in 1809 by the Governor, Lord Caledon, which was intended to bring the Khoikoi population within the scope of British law. The code aimed to stop the expanding Boer farmers reducing new groups of Khoikoi to slavery and to mitigate the harsh treatment handed out by masters to servants. Khoikoi were to be able to leave service if they wished and also had direct access to the law. At the same time, the Caledon Code proclaimed that the Khoikoi had civic obligations 'in the same manner as all inhabitants'. These obligations, however, 'simply spelled out the servile and subordinate position of the

Khoikoi in the colonial order' (du Toit and Giliomee 1983: 95). Later regulations were framed to give them full civic rights, but in practice an informal hierarchy of legal and social status had come into being in place of the loose and unregulated situation under the Dutch Company. The British were mindful of similar principles when they came to tackle the issue of slavery, and the results were equally conservative. The importation of slaves was banned in 1807; controls were gradually introduced over the punishment of slaves by masters and the institution itself was finally abolished in 1832. But labour was scarce on the Cape so that many extra-legal forms of coercion and control had developed to ensure a continuing flow of manpower.

The evangelical Christianity of the Anglican establishment and the Church of Scotland played a rôle in the formation of this British order on the Cape, well before non-conformist influences became stronger in the later 1820s. Since the Khoikoi and slaves were already formal Christians or dependents of Europeans, there was none of the reluctance to proselytise evident among officers in Asia. Caledon in particular was keen to employ mission agencies whether Dutch or British in the settlement of the expanding frontier. He wrote to Castlereagh about the efforts of the Moravians: 'By the exertions of the missionaries, the wandering natives are formed into . . . societies and taught by labour to supply their wants, whilst the Hottentot soldier, formerly without a feeling of religion knows the nature of an oath and appreciates its value' (PRO: CO 48/2, 4 Feb. 1808). There was no vigorous attempt to impose Anglicanism on the Dutch population, and Church of Scotland missionaries from a related Calvinist background played a prominent part in British religious efforts. Still, the introduction of Anglican services, English language, laws and schools created a subtle apex to the social hierarchy of southern Africa from which the Dutch were, or felt themselves to be, excluded. This perception of exclusion was of some importance in stimulating the slow development of separatist feeling among the Boers of the interior.

Alongside 'benevolence' and Christianity, the British hoped to infuse the Cape with the benefits of law and private property. English legal forms were only slowly introduced, but the operation of the law in general was considerably expanded by the creation of a system of circuit courts in the interior in 1811. Judges and administrators discouraged forms of property other than absolute and alienable private property. The system under which Dutch farmers had leased land from the Company (the loan farm system) was gradually allowed to fall out of use (Duly 1968). Waste land and pasture was assessed and divided and communal forms of tenure discouraged, even when these changes conflicted with the farming practices of Dutch and African.

If Macartney, Caledon and Cradock seem to hail from the tradition of Cornwallis, the more aggressive paternalism of Lord Charles Somerset (Governor, 1814–32) has echoes of the Wellesleys. Somerset was a Beaufort who had spent time at the Prince Regent's 'Court at Brighton' and used his Plantagenet blood as a political weapon. On the Cape, Somerset developed a yet more autocratic style of government, serving as Governor, Commander-in-Chief of the Castle, Vice-Admiral, Commander of the Forces and Judge of the Court of Appeal. He worked through a few trusted Dutch and British officials and delegated much power to his son, Colonel Henry Somerset. The old 'burgher senate' was entirely a nominated body, but the colonists had begun to agitate for direct legislative representation. Somerset approved of the expansion of British settlement in southern Africa but resented the independence of the generation of pioneers which reached the Cape in the 1820s and was deeply hostile to their demands for increasing control over local affairs and a freer hand with the Xhosa. While Somerset was clearly hostile to slavery, he was suspicious and resentful of the growing intervention in African affairs of the evangelical Clapham Sect and the London Missionary Society. This strain of humanitarian thought was gaining more influence in the Colonial Office and Parliament. A major victory for it was the establishment of a Commission of Enquiry for the Cape and other territories, set up in 1822 to collect evidence on slavery and colonial government. The scene was set for a series of bitter controversies with emerging British settler opinion which brought the autocratic nature of Somerset's régime into the open. In May 1822, for instance, stung by public criticism, Somerset banned public meetings by the Cape colonists and went on to attack the press. This was likened to the imposition of the contemporary 'Gagging Acts' on the British press by conservative ministers.

Political controversy acquired a cutting edge in the course of a bitter personal conflict between Somerset and his main critic, Sir Rufane Donkin, an old Indian hand and querulous Whig. Yet beneath the issues of personality and administrative style, the deeper conflicts related to the control of this expanding settler society. Somerset, like his contemporaries in the Mediterranean or Canada, wanted a complaisant British and Anglican yeoman farmer class in the Cape, which would expand the production of corn and wine and balance the colony's precarious budget. His aim was to create a cordon sanitaire around the Xhosa, to pen them into the lands beyond the Fish River and to limit commercial relations between the settler economy and the Africans; Lord Charles 'interdicted all intercourse with the Caffrees [Xhosa]' (PRO: CO 48/75). Above all he wanted to avoid making of the land speculators who headed the parties of new settlers 'Dukes of Bedford' (Millar 1965: 180) who would reduce Africans to servitude and embroil government in more costly wars in their defence. The settlers, on the other hand, fought against government control and wanted a free hand in the Xhosa lands. Donkin as Acting-Governor in Somerset's absence had surreptitiously encouraged the British settlers of Bathurst and Albany to expand into the rich no-man's-land between them and 'Kaffrania' or the Xhosa territory.

CANADA, AUSTRALIA AND THE CARIBBEAN

Government at the Cape was an example of the classic dilemma of an early imperial state trying to control the expansion of 'settler capitalism'. It bears comparison with the problems facing contemporary British governors in western Canada where the fur and logging economy was racing forward into Indian lands; and was to have later parallels in Australia and New Zealand. It is only one of a series of issues common to different parts of the early nineteenth-century empire. Religious conformity was another. By comparison with the Cape where the Dutch Reformed Church was seen as a tetchy ally in settlement, or the Mediterranean and Ireland where Anglican evangelisation was limited by fear of Catholic reponse, Canada saw a much more vigorous holding operation by English episcopalians during these years. The Church had been endowed with lands by the Constitution Act of 1791 and considerable funds continued to pour in from England until the 1820s. SPG missionaries taught in new schools which had been established after 1790 in the eastern provinces. They also found a base in institutions such as the King's College of Nova Scotia, chartered in 1802 and the empire's first university, or King's College of New Brunswick which received its charter in 1829. The more vigorous face of Anglicanism here reflected an imminent danger from the secular United States. It was also an extension of the establishment's conquest of the Scottish Highlands in the previous generation, for the communities particularly targeted for 'conversion' were Catholic Highlanders such as those of Antigonish. The British tried to build up a hereditary landlord and office-holding class to maintain this Anglican settlement. The policy was supported by rising land prices and the soaring value of timber resources which were maintained at an artificially high rate by the huge tariffs levied on Baltic and other non-British produce, even after the end of the war. On the other hand, the attempts of governors to limit free constitutions were less successful in these older colonies where a degree of local representation had been built into their very foundations. Sir James Craig as Governor suspended the assembly of Lower Canada in 1807, but he and his colleagues were faced by a growing and restive middle class of Francophone and Anglophone lawyers and merchants.

The early history of New South Wales (which had a population of 8,235 in 1820) provides another example of imperial despotism in miniature. The population of freed felons and non-felons was growing rapidly, representing 41 per cent of the total by 1821. Some freed felons had been allotted lands and many officers and subalterns of the New South Wales Corps, the military unit intended to protect and control the penal system, had also become landowners and land speculators. A booming commercial economy had developed but one critically dependent on control of the grain market and manipulation of Treasury Bills for the means to pay for expensive imports by a few wealthy entrepreneurs. A new 'settler frontier' was beginning to develop, fortified with a rumbustious Australasian version of the 'rights of freeborn Englishmen', and the Scots and Irish variants of this creed. The Colonial Office began to worry and in 1805 sent in Captain William Bligh as Governor. Bligh, as is well known, was a man bred in the best tradition of royalist authoritarianism but he seems not to have had the luck of Maitland or Somerset. Within three years, Bligh's new 'tyranny' had led to a mutiny by the New South Wales Corps; once again he found himself imprisoned by his underlings.

The Colonial Office responded vigorously, alarmed by the precedent of the naval mutiny at Spithead and the Nore in 1796 and the pervasive atmosphere of republican libertarianism. Lachlan Macquarie, the farmer's son from Mull, was sent out to quell the mutiny. He disbanded the NSW Corps and created his own despotism through his complete control of all state offices. In Macquarie's 'lairdship' there was nothing other than 'my reign', 'my government' and 'my laws'. His policy also had a positive side. He abandoned state tenures and tried to create an Australasian 'yeomanry'. He expanded trade with the Pacific Islands, and surreptitiously with India. He rigorously controlled grain prices through the government Commissariat, built Anglican churches and schools. Macquarie, in fact, unleashed the policy which had guaranteed the assimilation of the Highlands of Scotland a generation earlier. His rule reflected not so much a long-term plan evolved in London as a vigorous response to mutiny on the 'settler frontier' (Ritchie 1986).

Finally, the new autocratic policies were amply demonstrated in the Caribbean. In the old colonies of settlement the Colonial Office tried hesitantly to impose its authority over recalcitrant assemblies concerned to fight off measures for the amelioration of the slaves, and in particular the influence of Christian missionaries. Governors had little room for manœuvre. Some like Lord Manchester on Jamaica were successful because they 'creolised', taking the part of the planters but allowing the home government to win a point or two from time to time. Others like Nugent, also Governor of Jamaica, tried to cut back settler pretensions, but with little success. On islands conquered from the French, Dutch or Spanish, however, there was no question of allowing the establishment of a full 'British constitution' (Murray 1965); these were to be Crown colonies governed by commissions of instruction. During the height of the Caribbean War when slave revolts had broken out in many of the French islands, the British seized Trinidad, partly to provide themselves with a useful trading post for South America but more immediately for defensive purposes. Under General Picton a ruthless (but 'impartial') despotism was established on the island. The old organs of Spanish royal government were maintained while the authorities continued to hand out bestial punishment to slaves and free blacks, influenced by a hard core of refugee planters from the French islands who were terrified by the prospect of 'jacobinism' and slave revolt (Brereton 1981: 34–7; Manning, 1933, Ch. XI).

In time the situation on Trinidad became too embarrassing to a home government committed to 'benevolence', and Picton was shorn of some of his powers. But despite agitation for a British constitution on the part of new settlers in Trinidad and colonial assemblies elsewhere, several interests combined to perpetuate and refine the Spanish system. Chief executives such as George Smith (1808–11) guarded their autocratic powers on the grounds that any concession to local self-government would play into the hands of the slave-owners: 'If you mean to ruin the colony, you will give us a British constitution'. This stand was supported by Lords Bathurst and Hawkesbury in England who viewed free colonial assemblies with the greatest of suspicion, but also by the abolitionist lobby, notably James Stephen, who would rather have an autocracy under the Crown than rule by planters. In a timely development, free blacks and coloureds on the island petitioned against an assembly and this gave the Colonial Office grounds for vetoing it. Unfettered executive power continued to rule the conquered islands, but the planters and officials both took care to slap down the free blacks and coloureds whose position, like that of the Khoikoi, actually deteriorated over the next generation (Brereton 1981: 44). On many islands, therefore, the values of the *ancien régime* were reinforced by those of humanitarian paternalism. In slave society, it was held, government needed to arbitrate, and also to uphold the racial basis of society, so that 'English liberties' had to be curtailed along with those of the natives.

It will be clear that the political arrangements and policies operated in all these colonies were not simply examples of British pragmatism or 'muddling through'. Though never planned from the centre, they were enforced by similar military despotisms, informed by similar autocratic ideals, and directed against widespread and interlinked manifestations of social crisis.

THE 'REGENCY EMPIRE IN THE EAST': INDIA, INDONESIA AND CEYLON

One condition which had allowed this loose proconsular empire with its Anglican, royalist, military and paternalistic character to flourish had been the impotence of detail of Bathurst's Colonial Office. In the East, the British despotism was shielded even more effectively by the continuation of the Company's monopoly over the China trade until 1834 and the Court of Directors' control over patronage in appointments. Even after 1813, moves against the Company's powers raised fears that ministers were seeking to annex to themselves a vast new area of patronage and they proceeded with great circumspection until the pressure from the free-trade lobby grew overwhelming in the later 1820s. The result was that the style of personal and paternalistic despotism established by Wellesley was perpetuated in the Indian provinces until mid-century. Wellesley and Wellington both, of course, made a careful theoretical distinction between civil and military rule. In practice, the two spheres overlapped. Several of Wellesley's young acolytes who helped determine the character of the new empire, notably Malcolm, Metcalfe and Munro, were military officers by origin. The cutbacks in civil expenditure which resulted from the Company's growing indebtedness in the 1820s led also to an increase in the precentage of residencies at the courts of Indian rulers held by military officers. In many ways India was still a military empire.

The triumph of the principle of *ryotwari* or 'yeoman-based' settlement of the land revenue after 1813 emphasised the paternalistic character of government. If the state was to draw tax more or less directly from peasant leaders, it would need to know more about the constitution of the villages and the character of the fields. Cornwallis had been influenced by the 'English' school of agrarian patriotism which looked to the landlord as agent of agrarian improvement. Though Wellesley himself still favoured landlord or *zamindari* settlements, his subordinates in the south and west of India were more in the 'Scottish' agrarian tradition – devotees of alienable private property and the colonisation of waste, yet suspicious of 'dukes of Bedford' like their contemporaries in the Mediterranean and the Cape. They inherited a revenue structure which had been flattened and simplified by the last indigenous régimes. These had already sought to break through the levels of magnate and revenue-farmer to reach the peasant. Pragmatism and theory pointed in the same direction.

These young officers also saw in a purified and revived form of the Indian village council or *panchayat* a guarantee of the moral independency of the yeomen in whom they put so much trust. Indian society for them was to be an aggregation of improving peasant farmers freed from all magnate influence, yet guided by the beneficent despotism of a small body of British officers. Where, as in Rajasthan, a true Indian aristocracy existed, rather than the corrupt progeny of Muslim tyranny and Hindu tax farmers, it should be preserved, and embellished like the more enlightened magnates of the Highlands of Scotland. In either case the regeneration of Hindustan was not to be carried out by missionaries or British settlers but by the revival of the spirit of the ancient 'Hindoo constitution' in village and in court. The British should therefore remain patrons of temples of Indian arts and learning and a sense of dependent Indian ethnicity should be fostered through the rediscovery of classical literature as similar sub-imperial ethnicities were already being invented in Scotland or Greece. The doyen of this generation, Sir Thomas Munro, had relatively little to say about free trade or India's place in the international economy (Stein forthcoming).

If the British imperial tradition which had been developed in Scotland and Ireland was exported in modified form to the Cape, the Mediterranean and North America, the British Indian imperial tradition had its own realms of conquest in Ceylon, Malaya, Burma and Java. Apart from Burma (annexed 1824–6), these territories were Crown colonies. But their administrative and financial arrangements were deeply influenced by Indian precedents. Stamford Raffles and James Crawfurd did not, of course, work in a vacuum. They were constrained by the form of the eighteenth-century Javanese state. The vigorous policies of expansion and control implemented by Marshall Daendels (1807–11), Napoleon's Batavian proxy in the archipelago, also provided them with a model of aggressive European action. Still, some of the new assertiveness of British power witnessed in Wellesley's India rubbed off on them. Indonesian rulers were roughly pushed aside whereas previously they had been allowed, even on the north coast, a residual honour and royal status. The destruction of the royal palace of Jogja in 1812 and the looting of its library was a calculated act of 'desacralisation' only slightly less brutal than the destruction of the Kingdom of Kandy some six years later. Raffles's disdain for native authority was also seen in his treatment of the minor Javanese nobility or 'regents'. Whereas Dutch Company conservatives had been favourable to the regents, men who had been influenced by supposedly 'liberal' ideas such as Van Hogendorp regarded them as 'idle men . . . [who] only endeavour to squeeze out as much as possible for their own subsistence'. This was also Raffles's view; he 'wished to liberate the peasantry by setting aside all the harmful influences of the Mahometan government, and by bringing it into contact with the mass of the native population'. But this was no 'liberalism'. Raffles was an 'authoritarian in his outlook', a 'virtual Napoleonic philosopher' (Bastin 1957: xx). Only in cases where there was no option but to compromise with the authority of the native chiefs, as in western Sumatra where Raffles was governor from 1816-22, was he prepared to leave the chiefs to retain direct control over labour or production (Bastin 1957: 135). Raffles and his agents were no more 'liberals' than Munro and the apostles of *ryotwari* in India. Despite their concern for private property and brief attempt to introduce a money-based revenue system into Java, they maintained a rationalised form of the Dutch monopolies and many forms of labour coercion, at the same time they sought to extend paternalist European agency throughout the countryside.

Finally, early British government in Ceylon reflects yet another amalgamation of elements which we have seen elsewhere in the colonial world. On the face of it this was a 'liberal' régime. Some of the restrictions on trade and immigration maintained by the Dutch Company in its final, sclerotic phase were lifted. There was consequently 'a great influx of people of all descriptions', but mainly of the Tamil Hindu, Muslim and Christian merchant communities of the coast south of Madras. The British set out to cure the abuses of the Dutch which they judged had 'exasperated the natural ferocity' of some of their Sinhalese subjects but had equally excited the laziness, timidity and avarice of others, mainly Tamil. The holding of public office was no longer dependent on Protestant Christian confession, and the new government tried to mend fences with the Catholic Church and with the Buddhist priesthood based on the yet-independent inland capital of Kandy.

On the other hand, early British colonial policy tended to reinforce racial hierarchy. Dutch law with some English additions was gradually set down and finally brought together in the Malabar Code of 1832 (PRO CO: 54/123). The courts and administrators perceived caste as the fundamental unit of Ceylonese society but by codifying and operating 'caste custom' tended to sharpen distinctions and to further institutionalise the power of headmen. An informal hierarchy also emerged among Europeans, with the British at the top, the Dutch burghers below, followed by the Portuguese Asians or Topases. These last were 'the worst race of people in India', mongrels of Dutch women corrupted by the climate so that 'any blackfellow who can procure a hat and shoes with a vest and breeches, and who has acquired some little smattering of the Catholic religion, [can] aspire to the title of a Portuguese' (Percival 1803: 104). The legal and statistical measures of early colonial rule in India tended to separate out and make more 'real' caste units which had been more fluid and more theoretical under indigenous régimes. The expansion of cash-cropping also subordinated tribal and marginal people, making of them 'low castes'. This pattern, however, was much more clear cut in Ceylon since the state's revenue depended directly on the existence of a low caste of bonded serfs.

As important as legal status in redefining caste society on the island had been the system of forced labour, or exemptions from such labour in return for cash, which had lain at the heart of the Dutch system. The critical point of this had been to maintain the division of labour which forced the Chalias to pick the all-important cinnamon crop and other castes to provide the Company's export staples. The Dutch system on the north coast had been a hybrid of slavery and forced labour alongside a commercial economy which already exhibited a well-developed land and produce market. From the earliest days of British occupation there was a strong body of opinion which urged retention and reinforcement of the Dutch system. The rebellion which broke out in the northern provinces in 1797 was attributed to tinkering with the *status quo* and the invasion by south Indian Tamils which followed the British occupation. All the same, Governor North attempted to end this system. He began to substitute cash wages for labour services among the Chalias cinnamon pickers. More dangerous even, he resumed rent-free lands gifted to village headmen and instituted a cash salary for them.

But as in Java this change quickly ran into trouble and was met by the Ceylonese population with desertion, arson and strikes. Within three years Maitland had reversed it again and reimposed a variety of the Dutch monopoly and the Dutch forced labour system. This was, of course, a pragmatic reaction to the collapse of Crown income, and a recognition that the government of the island would have to be funded out of any secure source of it. If this meant perpetuating the cinnamon monopoly and coercive labour, then, so be it. But the revival of labour services also ran with the temper of many of the new rulers. The paternalist philosophy underlying the new imperialism found expression in one of Maitland's few known theoretical statements, a plain man's rendering of the Scottish historian Robertson's theory of the stages of human development. He argued that Ceylon was not ready for free trade and a free labour market, it was as if 'one of the ancient barons had pulled out of his pocket Adam Smith, and said: I will apply to you vassals principles that you do not understand and will not properly apply to your circumstances for another 500 years' (Lord 1935: 81–2). Here then was one nostrum of the Scottish Enlightenment being used against another in the interests of benevolent paternalism. Much else that the Governor did was in a similar vein. He opposed direct evangelisation of Hindus and Buddhists and was castigated by Wilberforce in person as a 'pagan'. At the same time he tried to limit and control the influx of Tamil commercial people into the island, and to circumvent 'black intelligence' and the chicanery of indigenous servants with British virtue, retaining 'total control over patronage'.

Little change occurred in this mercantilist despotism until the 1840s, when European plantation agriculture began to develop. The formal abolition of some labour services after the destruction of the Kandyan Kingdom in 1818 had little effect. Chalias continued to pick cinnamon, the great staple of the island which rendered a profit on the London market of about £100,000 per annum compared with the measly £20,000 from land revenue. Labour services were still exacted especially by Sir Edward Barnes (governor, 1822–7) who extended the royal forced labour system in order to build roads and canals. The Colebrooke Commission of Enquiry of 1832 castigated the autocratic powers of the governors and asserted that 'the claims which have been enforced by the government to the labour of the native inhabitants have also been very unfavourable to agricultural industry and improvement'. A combination of fierce indigenous resistance to the imposition of cash revenue alongside the government's need for financial stability had frustrated moves towards a free market in land and labour. But more than this, a large body of opinion within the Crown service in Ceylon hankered for an unfettered autocracy, and they found it easy to live with labour services.

In all the new colonies, colonial policy and its execution were moulded by the particular histories of each separate society or region. Forms of landholding and definitions of kingship in non-white societies, ancient assemblies and intricate hierarchies of freemen and slaves in colonies of white settlement, blunted or captured the energy of the proconsuls and their deputies. All the same, there were striking parallels in the form and impact of colonial régimes. In part this derived from the universal fear of internal and external subversion of the social order raised by 'jacobinism' and widespread peasant or slave resistance. Fear of this sort galvanised the aristocratic and paternalistic attitudes of men brought up in England or Scotland in the previous generation. Economic dilemmas which arose when imperial régimes attempted to control the early stages of integration into the world market of new regions, or the outward expansion of the frontier of settler capitalism, also gave rise to similar policies and similar outcomes.

Yet there was one further general condition which linked the political system in England with the form of colonial government. That was the expansion of empire as a form of patronage in office. Despite the controls introduced in the 1780s, Pitt's political supremacy saw an unprecedented growth in the financial patronage of central government as war contracts multiplied and the problems of government at war grew in complexity. Rubinstein has demonstrated that as many as 25 per cent of persons receiving more than £150,000 but less than £500,000 (the national élite beneath the richest magnates) were drawn from the ranks of office-holders, including clerics, lawyers, judges, bureaucrats and placemen in the early nineteenth century. This lay behind the charge laid by radicals that the profligate use of government patronage in office had survived economical reform and indeed that the 'French Wars and the Pitt system had materially increased the scale of the Old Corruption' (Rubinstein 1983: 63). Patronage deriving from Britain's European and extra-European empires were succulent fruits in this cornucopia. Dundas's massive Scottish patronage was a constant source of comment; Ireland provided plenty of offices such as Purse Bearer to the Chancellor of Ireland (worth £500 per annum), and a new range of military positions as the permanent garrisons expanded after 1799.

Some of the richest pickings arose in territories newly conquered during war where executive government was less constrained by local assemblies. The East India Company, of course, provided a considerable indirect subsidy to Britain's élite. Again, a 'Demerara Planter' petitioning for 'a British Constitution' in the conquered Dutch, Spanish and French islands denounced the 'rank Jobs [corrupt office-holders] which crowd and stalk among us under the guise of fit persons to rule'. The perquisites of colonial office-holding were even more valuable when as in Canada they were indirectly tied to the use of Crown lands. Denouncing the 1791 settlement, G.A. Young wrote that 'under Mr. Pitt's Bill, the mimic sovereigns of Canada enjoyed in a mediate state, some of the prerogatives of royalty' (Young 1839: 50). A scrutiny of the twenty-seven members of the Legislative Council of Upper Canada revealed huge salaries pertaining to justices, speakers of the various bodies, official auctioneers, Commissioners of the Jesuit Estates and officials of the Indian Department. Here executive patronage reinforced the embattled social hierarchy which the framers of the 1791 Bill had sought, perversely, to create in a situation of land-plenty.

It is very difficult to compute the total value and number of offices added by the wartime conquests. Taking the Indian service, the military and the Crown colonies, as many as 10,000 new positions carrying salaries and perquisites of more than £500 per annum may have come into existence. This compares, for instance, with the 30,000 doctors and 20,000 clergymen on roughly similar incomes practising in England about 1845. The support thereby given to the metropolitan upper middle and landed classes was certainly not critical, but it was highly significant. Above all, the new patronage helped to foster the view that empire was valuable, even when a strict accounting of the opportunity cost of the colonies for British society as a whole might have shown that exactly the opposite was true. Office and perquisites helped to sustain an empire once acquired in an atmosphere of panic and providential messianism. It also provides an explanation, less exalted than that provided by anti-slavery sentiment, for the concern of ministers to gain some kind of grip on events in the colonies. The quite sudden influx of metropolitan 'jobs' finally helps explain the emergence in varied colonies remote from each other of similar policies and similar types of colonial discourse.

CHAPTER EIGHT

Colonial Society in the Early Nineteenth Century

The last three chapters have explored the creation of Britain's new empire after 1783. Chapter 4 showed how many of the institutions of that empire and the ideas that infused it can be traced back to changes in the metropolis which arose from the pressures generated by war and domestic social tension. The next chapter indicated how world-wide conflict and the decline of trade and systems of labour control hastened the re-establishment not only of colonial provinces but of indigenous extra-European states. Chapter 6 in turn demonstrated how local conditions and metropolitan influences both acted to mould the policies of the imperial despotisms of the early nineteenth century. In this chapter we consider the wider social changes that took place in the colonies during Britain's new imperial age and the parallel evolutions of Asian and African states which subsisted alongside them. Finally, the chapter considers the slow dissolution during the 1830s and after of what some contemporaries called 'Pitt's system'.

LAND, LABOUR AND TRADE

What useful generalisations can be made about the relationship between colonial state and society in the period 1790–1830? Above all, as we have seen, colonial administrations were concerned to retain or enhance control over land and labour. Superficially, this concern clashed with the judicial and administrative philosophy of contemporary Britain which was imbued with ideas of freedom of contract, freedom of trade and free title to land. In fact, the regulation of civil society in the colonies was intended to create the conditions for 'civilisation' by constructing modern landed élites and industrious peasantries through the exercise of state power. Once civil society had been constructed it would be possible for the state to recede from intervention. These administrative programmes also responded directly to colonial conditions. They sought to create a framework for the management of disputes in order to avoid the conflicts over labour, land and resources between the imperial state, creole élites and indigenous peoples which had hastened the expansion of eighteenth-century empire but had also brought it near to extinction. In this project the interests of the colonial authorities often went hand in hand with those of the indigenous landed classes and the commercial interests which had weathered the eighteenth century. Eighteenth-century landed magnates and yeomen became the linchpins of empire. Where they did not, the outcome was uncertain. Faced with outright military opposition the colonial power often resorted to coercion as, for instance, against the poligar chieftains of southern India or intransigent farmers and planters in the colonies of settlement. In other places the authorities were forced to compromise. Everywhere, though, there was contest as the British Crown laid down its markers and fought its corner. Early nineteenth-century colonial rule was not weak, so much as differential in its impact. The study of empire, even of British society, remains essential for an understanding of those societies which were touched by imperial power.

Many of the devices for enhancing control over labour were quite indirect, or only dimly recognised as such by the men who created them. Ironically also, they were often derived from the political arsenals of the kings and magnates of the eighteenth century, those 'Muhammadan tyrants' and other despots whom the British had so fiercely denounced. For instance, the heavy and rigidly collected land tax which was imposed by a financially straitened East India Company on its peasantries had the effect of tying countrymen to the land and restricting movement. Since peasants were subject to a high revenue which had to be paid in cash, they had to borrow from moneylenders and magnates and this in turn forced them to cultivate more valuable crops for the market. The assessment of waste lands which was a feature introduced to western and southern India by the new *ryotwari* land settlements, also had the effect of encouraging petty arable farming at the expense of grazing. Measures curtailing the movement of the nomadic cattle-keepers and grain traders who had ranged across the face of the sub-continent in the eighteenth century were designed to 'limit the spirit of emigrating', as one official put it.

Early governors of the Cape colony had similar interests in creating a settled peasantry out of the mobile and fluid society of Hottentot (Khoikoi). In the more distant future, when the dangerous expansionism of the Afrikaner farmers had been checked, they hoped to settle Bushmen and Xhosa through a policy of 'Christianity and humanity'. The Africans were to be congregated around mission stations and taught the domestic arts and arable cultivation. Similar projects were being developed world-wide, among the Aborigines of New South Wales, the Polynesians being domesticated by the London Missionary Society or among the Amerindians stranded by the retreating beaver frontier in North America. Such methods, in which colonial officials tacitly conspired with indigenous landlords, raised productivity, but also created new types of poverty. Settled and disciplined populations were less able to insure themselves against the effects of disease or bad seasons by moving to take possession of alternative resources, or by changing their styles of life.

In pursuit of this aim, most colonial administrations tried to create simplified forms of alienable private property for colonial élites. This would encourage them to expand cultivation and settle their dependent peasantries. In time, Crown lands were sold off in Ceylon and Canada; on the Cape the Dutch loan farm schemes were generally abandoned in favour of selling farms directly to the settlers (Duly 1968). During the régime of Sir John Cradock, strenuous efforts were made to create land titles for white settlers where formerly there had been simply a widespread system of squatting. In India a new form of private property in land was created by amalgamating the right to profit from the collection of land revenue and forms of direct proprietorial right which had been separate under the Mughals. Here the old battles of the big rural magnate against shifting or communal forms of tenure tended to be settled in favour of the former by the intervention of British revenue courts or armed columns. For often only a slight shift in the balance of coercive power in local society enabled colonial officials to put into practice those dialogues of development which had originated in eighteenth-century England or Scotland. The outcome was rarely what was expected. An official bemoaned the fact that in Bengal the Company's revenue arrangements had tried to create an 'English' paternalist gentry when all they ended up with was an 'Irish' absentee one. Yet the will and the ability to change society was already there.

These colonial projects aimed at encouraging the cultivation of cash crops as much as providing a tame labour force. There was a considerable expansion of intra-imperial trade in basic agricultural products in the first three decades of the nineteenth century, particularly between the end of the Napoleonic War slump in 1817 and the onset of a major cyclical depression in trade in the late 1820s. British administrations encouraged the expansion of the raw cotton trade from Malta and the currant trade from the Greek Islands. By 1810 the Cape colony accounted for some 30 per cent of British domestic wine consumption, and foodstuffs were being exported to Mauritius (conquered in 1810) and St Helena. Cape horses were exported to India, while in the sub-continent itself there had been a rapid expansion of the acreage under cotton and indigo. The economic links thus created were fragile and volatile; but this is not to say that they were superficial. New dependencies created new types of vulnerability, new types of poverty and wealth; prices at an international level were more closely integrated. For instance, the takings from peddlars crossing the bridge of boats in the north Indian city of Agra in 1828 were closely determined by the outcome of the cotton crop in the distant Chinese province of Kwantung to where the local cotton crop was exported. Maltese cotton growers were quickly pushed out of business in the 1820s by the rise of cotton production in Muhammad Ali's Egypt (Bezzina 1985: 58).

The production of these commodities was closely related to the financial problems of the colonial governments and the operations of the economic war against France. Indian exports of opium and cotton to China were the only valuable part of the Company's trade monopoly and helped to keep it afloat financially. Much of the huge volume of Indian indigo sold on the London market was technically unprofitable, but it was a means by which planters and officials could return their salaries and profits to England. Similarly, cinnamon production in Ceylon or wine production on the Cape were stimulated by the financial needs of local government and the artificial conditions of world war and its immediate aftermath. These were 'administrative trades' in the sense that they arose from political imperatives rather than the workings of a free market and that they formed part of local projects of labour control and settlement within the colonies.

SOCIAL INVOLUTION AND THE RECONSTRUCTION OF BONDAGE

Just as indirect forms of labour control were operated through administrative means and by encouraging European settlement, so many direct forms of labour coercion survived the assaults of the anti-slavery lobby until well into the century. In Ceylon and parts of south India, the state retained bodies of bonded labourers on spice and other plantations until after 1832. In the Western hemisphere, slavery in the formal, legal sense had a vigorous and successful history until nearly two generations after the abolition of the slave trade itself in 1807. Various checks on planter power had been pushed through by the Colonial Office in the teeth of opposition of the colonial assemblies, particularly those of Jamaica, Barbados and St Kitts. Slaves were allowed to attend church on Sundays, floggings were controlled and masters were held to account for the death of slaves. But while reformers hoped that this marked the beginning of the demise of slavery, colonial officials saw it more in the light of regulating servitude and avoiding the dangerous and destructive slave revolts which had taken place after 1792. Zachary Macaulay and other abolitionists were bewailing as late as 1823 that the ending of the trade had made no appreciable difference to the incidence of colonial slavery as an institution.

Even after emancipation in 1832, slaves in the Caribbean islands and Mauritius were required to enter into five-year indenture contracts. After 1838 the poor quality of many of the farms allotted to or occupied by freed slaves forced them to reproduce their bondage on their estates, even though they were now legally 'free'. In South Africa the abolition of Pass Laws designed to restrict labour movement (1828) and slavery itself (1834) had relatively little effect. Ex-slaves and poor Khoikoi were too indigent to operate with confidence on the labour market, and soon became debt bondsmen on the lands of the Dutch farmers. The system of segregating Africans adopted by Somerset and also by many of his critics tended to create new pools of exploitable labour for white farmers. Finally, the expansion of the trade in indentured labour from India to Mauritius and the Caribbean after 1832 simply created a 'new system of slavery' rather than aiding in the transition from servitude to a free labour market (Tinker 1974).

The abiding concern among historians with the rhetoric of anti-slavery and the growth of humanitarianism has obscured the power of the contemporary justification of the continuation of a purged and reformed slave system. Slavery and the perpetuation of the West Indies monopoly over sugar production for the British market was essential, it was said, to preserve the vast amounts of capital invested in the islands. A Christian bond between slave and master was an essential ingredient in the further civilising of the dependent negro population. In the same way, monopoly, protectionism and labour services had their theoretical proponents as vigorous as the contemporary fight in defence of the English Corn Laws.

The social and racial hierarchy approved by the governing élites of the early nineteenth century was different in important respects from that of the mid-eighteenth century. Slaves and people of colour were brought within the law, whether this was English, Anglo-Roman Dutch or Anglo-Hindu law. Yet in many ways closer administration and the creation of legal 'texts' actually made the racial hierarchy more complete and more rigid. It was the more rigorous and exclusive forms of Brahminism which were adopted by the British as 'Hindoo custom' in India and Ceylon; caste meanwhile became more a concrete social phenomenon, less an ideal theory of social ranking as it had been under indigenous régimes. In the same way, the unofficial racial hierarchy of race and Bible constructed by the Dutch settlers in Ceylon was rendered more subtle but more pervasive by early British colonialism in southern Africa. The Hottentot code, pass laws and missionary regulation of Khoikoi, Xhosa and Bushman created almost caste-like gradations of status within the society of the Cape.

Different as were the forms of production in the Caribbean, similar processes of social involution could be seen at work here also. Ironically, the ending of the slave trade had the effect of curtailing the movement of slaves into free society. The rising value of slaves on the market and the inclination of the white owners acted against manumission. And in conditions of depression in the plantation sector during the 1820s, few black slaves could buy their own freedom (Smith 1965: 101). The limited changes in the status of free blacks and coloureds introduced by the autocratic governors and other metropolitan influences had subtly increased the gradations of rank within non-white society. White society had also changed. One observer noted that in the 1780s 'the only distinction of ranks consisted in white, coloured and negro persons' and blacksmiths could be found at the white balls. But now 'there is a sufficient number of secondary rank among the white people to form a society among themselves', and one which mirrored the social order of the motherland (Carmichael 1833: I, 18). The influence of Methodism and revived Anglicanism along with the closer communications with London had encouraged this involution of social rank. As ownership of the plantations became less profitable, slave ownership and social rank became values in themselves, so that the effect of 'reform' and metropolitan influence was to reinforce the caste-like nature of the colonial society, not to undermine it.

NEW FIELDS FOR INDIGENOUS CAPITAL

As the previous chapter showed, the new British administration was vigorous, formative, philosophical and absolutist in temper. In many ways this contrasted with the loose and unregulated colonial government of the earlier eighteenth century. However, it would be wrong to assume that colonial government was omnipotent. Where it succeeded in creating a new order it was generally where powerful interests within indigenous society came to its aid, providing capital, expertise and a narrow, practical legitimacy. It was, in fact, precisely in these years 1780 to 1820 that was established the dominance of many of the key administrative and commercial groups which were to underpin the workings of empire up to the 1850s, and were in some cases to provide the élites of the independent states of Asia and Africa into the twentieth century.

The expansion of the British in Asia and the Mediterranean in particular was accompanied by an equally vigorous expansion of merchants, hucksters and clerical people who had been constrained within the bounds of the smaller indigenous states. Early nineteenth-century society was, on the face of it, the heyday of the indigenous capitalist within the empire; thereafter, embattled and more conservative colonial administrations began to worry about the corrosive effects of Indian, Chinese or Armenian capital on the social order of their rural societies. This is not to say that the British empire opened up an unfettered 'age of enterprise' for native capital. On the contrary, the depredations of the colonial power often forced capital out of previous trade routes or artisan manufactures into these new byways. It seems likely, for instance, that the capital which had once been employed in the weaving industry of western India found its way into Indian Ocean trade and petty agricultural finance within the sub-continent precisely because 'deindustrialisation' was proceeding so fast (Chandavarkar forthcoming: ch. i). Again, the decline of the Chinese junk trade to southeast Asia helped push Chinese capital into petty trade, moneylending and usury in Malaya and Indonesia. All the same, the diaspora of the indigenous merchant communities was striking.

223

The British armies invading India along with the Company servants and free merchants following on their tails had been financed and serviced by members of the great Hindu and Jain banking families. Such men easily made the transition from being the guarantors of land revenue and men of business for indigenous rulers to factotums for the British. Gujarati, Marwari and high-caste Bengali traders in the north, Chettis and Tamil Muslims in the south, took commissary contracts for the British, moved their treasuries about through their sophisticated system of credit notes and took a leading part in the development of new export trades in cotton, indigo and opium in alliance with the British houses of agency. By the 1820s some members of this commercial élite, notably the Parsis of Bombay and the Hindu gentry of Calcutta, had assimilated to the norms of the new empire, founding schools, newspapers and reform societies alongside their more traditional practice of patronising temples and bathing places on the holy rivers. The regulated hierarchical form of society emerging in colonial port towns such as Calcutta, Madras and Bombay (all places with populations of over 200,000 by 1800) suited their pretensions to high-caste status and respectability. Here, colonial racial hierarchy attracted and facilitated some tendencies within indigenous Hindu society.

Inferior members of these commercial communities played a prominent part in the colonisation of the sub-continent's internal frontier too. The protection of British arms allowed them to invade tribal lands in search of raw materials and to penetrate areas previously too hazardous for them. They financed the debts of the expanding petty commodity sector, taking part in the process which has been called 'peasantisation'. They underwrote the colonial land revenue while colonial courts supported their claims as creditors to the peasantry.

British conquests outside India also allowed these communities to consolidate their position which they had already established during the rule of the Dutch and indigenous states. Hindu and Muslim Tamil merchants flooded into Ceylon after 1896. Indeed, it was their invasion of offices and territories previously considered the preserve of Ceylonese Buddhists which helped spark off the rebellion of 1797 and later conflicts with the King of Kandy (Davy 1969: 238, 242). Indian merchants and financiers also established themselves along the country's west coast soon after the annexation of northern Burma. In southeast Asia, however, it was Chinese entrepreneurs who filled this rôle. The Chinese had already established a precarious bridgehead on Java during the days of the Dutch Company. During Raffles's administration they strengthened this position. As British Indian opium was pushed into Java after 1810 in an attempt to bail out the finances of the Bengal government, it was Chinese businessmen who distributed it in the interior. When Raffles demanded cash revenue in lieu of labour services, it was the Chinese who lent money or took the farm of government monopolies and perquisites.

After the Peace of Paris in 1815, the British handed back Java and Sumatra to the Dutch. This was part of a diplomatic initiative to guarantee the independence and financial viability of the newly-restored Netherlands monarchy. But the Dutch were unable to re-establish the rigid monopoly which had fragmented the trade of the archipelago in the previous century. British commerce in opium, Indian products and later in manufactured cloths had already established itself firmly in east Asia. Working from Penang (Prince of Wales Island), the British and their Chinese and Indian proteges dominated the west coast of Malaya. In 1819 the search for a more convenient port for the China trade led Raffles to the island of Singapore, previously a minor entrepôt in the Riau–Johore sultanate. By 1825, Singapore already boasted a population of 20,000 and had established itself firmly as a rival both to Batavia and Penang.

The mix of early merchant communities in the city reflected the expansion of eighteenth-century Asian merchant communities under the British aegis. On Telok Aiyer Street, the oldest street in Singapore, are located a Chinese temple, an Indian Muslim mosque and a Hindu temple, all of which were built before 1835. The Hindu temple had been established by a Tamil merchant of Porto Novo south of Madras who actually accompanied Raffles on his first voyage to Singapore. The mosque was an offshoot of the famous Muslim Shrine of Shahul Hamid of Nagore, the Muslim saint, particularly venerated by the sea-going Tamil Muslims of the Madras coast who traded Ceylonese tobacco through the port of Nagore to Acheh in Sumatra and to Penang. The Chinese temple, established somewhat later, represented the first toe-hold on the island of the community that was soon to dominate it, and much of the commercial world of southeast Asia – the Straits Chinese. Literate, forceful and accustomed to pooling their resources for the education and training of young men, the Straits Chinese soon developed a unique culture which blended elements of Western education with Chinese ancestral piety.

Elsewhere in the empire, other entrepreneurial communities expanded their operations under the British flag. Indian merchants and Muscat Arabs multiplied trade in the Persian Gulf and Red Sea. Greeks, from Ionia, Crete and Hydra, linked the ports of the Ottoman empire with western Europe. Safadic Jews and British 'Italian' merchants from Livorno congregated on Malta during the wars. In southern Africa and the Western hemisphere a great diaspora of Scottish merchants and emigres from the east coast and the Central Lowlands moved to Cape Town, Buenos Aires and Toronto, especially during the trade depression after 1815.

While the activities of merchant groups, both indigenous and British, underpinned much imperial activity and imperial trade, the attitude of the state to their expansion was already ambivalent. Administrators were concerned that the penetration of merchant capital into rural society would undermine village communities and exacerbate costly frontier wars. In important respects, colonial governments became more elaborate and interventionist in order to police the conflicts which arose from the further expansion of petty capitalism, both European and indigenous. In India, the Company continued to exclude private European merchants from the ownership of land, despite some relaxation of this policy in the 1830s. They feared that the interests of commerce might conflict with the easy extraction of the land revenue, which remained government's overriding concern. In some official quarters the stereotype of the grasping Indian 'bania' (grocer) had been elaborated long before it became an article of faith with Victorian colonial officials. In Canada and southern Africa, officials worked hard to limit the impact of European trade and landholding on the native populations, creating unofficial reservations which tended to firm up the boundaries of tribe and to fuel resentment among the settlers. The ambivalence of the colonial state towards the expansion of indigenous commerce and settler capitalism was one reason why social and economic tensions had already become severe enough to shake its foundations by the 1830s.

THE NEW STATES ALONGSIDE THE BRITISH COLONIAL WORLD

In support of their revived empire, the British deployed a formidable naval hegemony. The fleets of her main European rivals of the eighteenth century – the French, Spanish, Portuguese, Dutch and Danes – were crippled. Her own tonnage in warships and merchantmen greatly increased between 1800 and 1815 and the expansion of trade after 1818 increased the fleet still further. Informed by the heroic efforts of the eighteenth-century surveyors and motivated by a new zeal against 'piracy' and the slave trade, British squadrons controlled virtually every major sea route. Trading empires such as those of the Muscat Arabs, the Beys of Tunis or the Bugis of the Indonesian Archipelago, which had prospered in times of war, wilted during the peace. Enforcing their own interpretation of the law of the sea, the British went on to demolish those smaller sea-borne states which survived and had the temerity to try and enforce exclusion zones. The Wahhabi port chiefs of the Persian Gulf were disciplined in 1808 and the Arabs of what was to become the Trucial Coast were subjected to several punitive expeditions over the following fifteen years. The British cooperated with the Americans to bring to heel the 'Barbary Pirates' of Algiers. Asian and African shipping which had remained important on the sea routes until the 1780s was almost everywhere reduced to a second-rate status as junks, sampans, 'native craft'. The volumes conveyed in non-British and non-European ships were still vast, but the British excluded them from many of the most important areas of world trade.

More important than economies of scale made possible by the big European ships was political power. The Continental Blockade and then the campaign against slavery allowed the British to register and control the trade of their 'native' competitors. Diplomatic pressures forced régimes to acquiesce in the erosion of their own monopolies and tariff barriers while the British maintained theirs. Even humanitarian measures such as the Lascar Acts of 1818–24 or the Passenger Acts intended to prevent the abuse of seamen and passengers had the effect of diminishing the main advantages of Asian and African shippers – cheap labour. The London insurance market systematically discriminated in favour of European shipping which it considered more seaworthy.

British success is partly accounted for by the fact that outside of England and Lowland Scotland, it acted as a neo-absolutist state similar to those of continental Europe and could call upon régimes which it seemingly opposed on ideological grounds to help impose favourable international norms. In the Mediterranean the British claimed the support of 'the Congress of Vienna'; this really meant Russia, which attempted to undermine the British position wherever possible, but stood with her against 'piracy' and the Ottomans. The British withdrawal from Sicily in 1815 allowed ministers to develop a close relationship with another 'despotic régime', the Kingdom of the Two Sicilies. Liberalism and nationalism were kept at arm's length and monopoly was condoned provided it did not choke off trade and force prices too high. British policy was particularly ambivalent when it came to the question of support for Greeks in rebellion against Turkey or Italian carbonari fighting against Naples. Again, the British shored up and benefited from the Dutch empire in southeast Asia, a dual-faced system like their own: absolutist and monopolistic in the outside world, an oligarchy tempered with liberalism in Europe. The slave-owning planter society of the southern United States and the Latin American creole states fitted well into this pattern.

Yet the new dispensation of the early nineteenth century was not brought about simply by the imposition of Britain and its allies on a static extra-European world through the use of colonial power and naval dominance. It was also formed by the maturing of processes of social and political change which had been occurring throughout the eighteenth century, and it rested in particular on the final consolidation of regional states and élites which had emerged out of the earlier empires. Many of the regional kingdoms which had struggled to be born in the mid-eighteenth century had been severely damaged or even destroyed by the world crisis at its end. Conditions were now more propitious for political consolidation as European peace was complemented by a revival of world trade and the firming of colonial boundaries in the world outside Europe. The 'para-colonial' states managed to perfect some of the techniques of political and economic control which had eluded their eighteenth-century forbears. Free cavalry, 'pirates' and nomadic tribesmen began to be penned in once again. The rulers built up monopolies and export trades which made it possible for them to begin constructing new model armies in earnest. Some gained a greater degree of control over the produce of the land by sweeping away earlier land-controlling groups (as in Egypt or the Punjab, for instance). Others sought to foster stable landlord communities with less complex property rights, as did their contemporaries among European colonial governors. The fitful revival of trade promoted urban growth once again, but it also exposed them to demands from the British for the lowering of internal tariff barriers.

These states included the following: in the East, the Thailand of Rama I (1782–1809); the Chinese coastal provinces of the later

Ching and late Tokugawa Japan displayed this dual identity, responding to external pressures but formed by state-building from within. In south Asia there were Ranjit Singh's Punjab (from 1799) or the Sindh of the Talpur Emirs (from the 1780s) or partially-independent Awadh and Hyderabad. In Iran the Qajar régime rolled back the frontiers of nomadism and held the Russians at bay. In the Mediterranean the Kingdom of the Two Sicilies or the Beylicate of Tunis as they emerged from the trials of the Napoleonic Wars followed the same pattern.

The best examples lie in the Ottoman empire. For Egypt, the Pashalik of Baghdad and even the Sublime Porte itself showed considerable powers of recuperation and internal dynamism in the early nineteenth century, however much Europeans sought to portray them as enfeebled despotisms. The Ottomans and their servants performed creditably against the Western powers during the wars. They had adapted to European infantry and ordnance training through long exposure in the Balkans, but they also showed a capacity for military and political innovation. Wars between the European powers gave the Ottomans and Egyptians a breathing space. In 1792 the private secretary of Sultan Selim III penned this prayer, 'May God cause the upheaval in France to spread like syphilis to the enemies of the Empire, hurl them into prolonged conflict with one another, and thus accomplish beneficial results to the Empire, amen' (Lewis 1961: 65). His prayer was answered. By 1783 the French had already become apprehensive of the southward thrust of Russia which had recently conquered a large Muslim population in the Crimea. So the French government vigorously supported programmes of Ottoman military and political reform. After 1793 the sultans continued to seek French aid. The French, who now feared British predominance in the area, responded with a series of military and technological missions, culminating in the visit to Istanbul of Napoleon's General Sebastiani in 1806–7. These embassies and the opening up of new missions to the west ensured that foreign ideas and scientific or military knowledge continued to spread in Turkey, despite the triumph of Ottoman reactionaries and their Janissary supporters in 1807. They ensured that reforming ideas did not die during the long period of hiatus before the new Sultan Mahmud II was able to purge the Janissaries, reorganise the army and centralise the administration following his coup against the forces of reaction in 1827.

The delicate military and naval balance in the Near East clearly helped maintain Ottoman independence. In India, by comparison,

British commercial supremacy had been translated before 1763 into a military and naval hegemony which made it impossible for Indian rulers to receive sustained support from any other European power. Knowledge of new European techniques also filtered into the Ottoman empire more easily through the Balkans or Greece; India was more distant and its rulers were only well supplied with powerful European or Ottoman-style cannon in the latter half of the eighteenth century. More important, the society, culture and economy of the Ottoman lands already provided a firmer soil on which to construct reformed states and new armies. Istanbul and the person of the sultan provided a symbolic and economic focus for the Turkish, northern Arab and eastern Balkan lands. Here proto-industrialisation had strengthened rather than weakened the sinews of empire. Turkish Osmanli patriotism was reinforced with the inheritance of a cosmopolitan empire, supplied with vigorous new recruits both Circassian and Sudanese.

The sultan's own household and the households of the 'loyal' provincial *ayans* continued to provide an avenue to power and influence so that Mahmud II was able to select reforming officers from it during his conflicts with the conservatives. The state also benefited from the universal system of Muslim education. The *ulama* were among the most conservative elements but the elementary education system attached to the great mosques was flexible enough to provide a flow of recruits for the new technological and diplomatic schools established by the reformers (Shaw and Shaw 1977: II, 47). By comparison, Delhi had never established itself as a single primate city for a whole region like Istanbul, and magnates sought their political future in regional centres such as Lahore, Murshidabad and Hyderabad. Nor, in spite of Aurangzeb's efforts, had the Indian theologians (*ulama*) ever been as strongly associated with the throne as a source of skills and a strong support to royal legitimacy. Indian sufism had been amorphous and localised while Turkish sufism had been strongly centralised providing a chain of command which could be manipulated by astute sultans (though sometimes also by their enemies).

Unlike the Mughals, the Ottomans and their regional magnates had a clear sense of territoriality which seems to have sprung in part from their position on the front-line of Islam for so long and partly from governors' ability to control the lush growth of the commercial economy. By contrast, the Hindu *bania* had been culturally far more distant from his Mughal rulers. This military and political cohesion ensured that the battle honours with the European powers were shared. Jezzar Ahmed stopped Napoleon dead at Acre; the Porte played an important rôle in his Egyptian defeat. Later in 1807, a British attack on Alexandria was beaten off by Muhammad Ali of Egypt, newly in the ascendant. Throughout, the rulers of Baghdad were able to keep the British at arm's length. Successive governors tempered their importunate demands for entrance into the Iraqi market, and in 1823 the British Resident was sent packing. Some of these successes helped support the fabric of Ottoman rule. Though Muhammad Ali later grew restless under the suzerainty of the sultans, and though the Greeks were encouraged by commercial success during the wars and by the influence of Orthodox Russia to push for independence, most regional magnates (*ayans*) and governors remained loyal to Istanbul.

What is striking is that the new regional rulers and many *ayans* in the southern parts of the Ottoman empire were able to carry out policies which were markedly similar to those of their contemporaries among British colonial governors. Benefiting from the power vacuum which was left in Lower Egypt when the mamelukes had been destroyed by Napoleon at the Battle of the Nile, Muhammad Ali, leader of the Albanian troops of the Ottoman empire, seized power and began to consolidate his control over the economy. Selling grain to the British during the Peninsular War and sparking off an expansion of raw cotton cultivation in the Delta, he provided himself with a fiscal base for dynastic consolidation. His son Ibrahim disciplined the Beduin of Sinai and the Syrian desert and brought them as taxpayers into the state's system. The expansion of the arable after the tribal breakouts of the previous century was clear in Egypt by the 1820s and was beginning to spread to eastern Syria and the northern Euphrates valley and the Aleppo region by the following decade (Lewis 1987: 38–45).

Muhammad Ali encouraged Egyptian officials at the lower levels of his new bureaucracy and forged strong links with the village notable class, the *sheikhs*, who had consolidated their influence during the commercial growth of the eighteenth century. State monopoly, the fostering of a stable petty landed class and a sense of regional and territorial identity: these were the policies of Muhammad Ali and Jezzar Ahmed or Sulaiman II of Baghdad as much as Sir Thomas Munro or Mountstuart Elphinstone, governors of Madras and Bombay.

Now clearly, the resurgence and subsequent economic viability of what might be called these 'para-colonial' states arose in part from the development of trade to Europe, or European-dominated trade. For instance, military operations in Europe stimulated North African wheat producers' exports to France and Italy. Later the British purchased Egyptian grain on a large scale. After the wars the rebound of European consumption stimulated exports of raw materials from the 'independent' Eurasian states as it did from colonies. The cotton trade from Qajar Iran to Russia increased (Issawi 1971: 105–9); Egypt, Palestine and the Basra region redoubled their own production for southern Europe and a variety of commodities, from Greek and Turkish currants to Mocca coffee, began to appear increasingly on the British market (Owen 1981). All this helped provinces and kingdoms reconstruct their economies after the trade wars of 1780–1815. Yet these states also relied to a very great extent on internal economic buoyancy. Indeed, the success of the régimes in recruiting élites and rural leaderships to their support must be attributed very largely to the internal social stability they were beginning to recover.

Thus in Egypt, Muhammad Ali drew on sources of internal strength which had been damaged but not eliminated by the conflicts of the previous generation. As Russia became a power in the northern Christian lands of the empire, the Ottoman slave trade turned more and more to the Sudan. The 5,000 slaves annually imported into Egypt by the 1790s was balanced by a growing trade in Egyptian linens, coral, Venetian glass and muskets. Agricultural settlement in Upper Egypt and Nubia, often pioneered by sufi teachers who established colonies among local tribesmen, also expanded the base of the settled, urban economy. A second massive source of strength was Egypt's rôle in the international Islamic pilgrimage to Mecca and Medina, the haj. In the 1790s the commerce associated with the haj was estimated to 'keep in circulation not less than £3 million per annum' (PRO FO: 24, Alexandria to London, 21 June 1789). This stands comparison with contemporary British trade with Bengal. Egypt also acted as an entrepôt and sourcing point for a further £300,000 worth of trade to Syria and Fez and Morocco. Early nineteenth-century reports make it clear that the bulk of Egypt's grain and even some of its cotton was sold not to Europe but to Smyrna and Istanbul, which suggest that demand from *within* the Ottoman empire still remained considerable.

In the circumstances, it is not surprising that a critical phase in Muhammad Ali's consolidation of power was his expedition in 1812–16 against the Wahhabis who had taken the holy places at the turn of the century. In a stroke, the Pasha repaired his relations with the Ottomans, offered protection to one of his most important sources of wealth and stood forth as the champion of orthodox Sunni legitimacy against the purist zealots of Najd. The credit he was able to build up among the leading learned men among the learned of the al-Azhar mosque stood him in good stead with their cousins and followers among the village *sheikhs*. More subtly, by making peace with the divided beys in 1800–9 and asserting his independence of the Ottoman Porte, he capitalised on the 'popularity of the mamelukes' and took a stage further the policy of his predecessor Ali Bey who had already been prevailed upon to declare his 'independence' of the Porte during the previous century.

Since the time of Muhammad Ali's predecessor and model, Ali Bey, the British also had sought more open commerce with Egypt, and an outlet for their Indian goods. At first they were frustrated by the desire of the Ottoman Sultan to maintain his monopoly; later the French invasion and the subsequent conflicts damaged commerce. After 1807, however, the two sides gradually slipped into a policy of wary coexistence which allowed the British to secure the supplies they needed, but preserved the ruler's monopoly and so his fiscal base. This situation persisted until Palmerston as Foreign Secretary forced a reduction of tariffs throughout the Ottoman empire in 1838 and paved the way for more direct European intervention. In July 1811, Misset, the British Consul at Alexandria, denounced Muhammad Ali's corn monopoly in a letter to Castlereagh but cautioned threatening his 'arbitrary powers' on the grounds that 'we want corn for our armies in the Mediterranean and the Peninsula' (PRO FO: 142/1 part 2, 21 July 1811). By 1812, however, Misset was worrying over the danger that Muhammad Ali might fail in his attempt to destroy the Wahhabis and that a revival of 'anarchy' would damage the 'amicable intercourse' which had prevailed recently.

Hereafter, it was only when Muhammad Ali resorted to outward expansion that the British headed him off. In 1826 the Egyptian force fighting alongside the Ottomans against the Greek independence movement was destroyed at Navarino. Later, Muhammad Ali was warned against intervening in the western Mediterranean in the matter of the Barbary Pirates and the French invasion of Algeria (1830). On this occasion, Muhammad Ali is reported to have said '. . . I am a cultivator, I am essentially a merchant . . . if England and I went hand in hand, and in the event of an American War, she (Great Britain) should call upon me for a quantity (of cotton) to supply all her manufactories, she should have it exclusively . . . I foresaw long ago that I could undertake nothing grand without her permission' (PRO FO: 142/3 part 3, Alexandria to London, 8 March 1830; Lawson 1988).

The details of the Egyptian case help to illuminate the nature of several similar 'para-colonial' states of this period. The Qajars in Iran, the Emirs of Sindh, Ranjit Singh in the Punjab, the new monarchy of Thailand, even some of the protected princely states in India such as Awadh and Hyderabad, sought again to build monopolies. They fostered a greater sense of ethnicity and territoriality, whether the cultural context was Imami Shiism, the Sikh Panth or the closer assimilation of kingship and Buddhist hierarchy. On the face of it, the institutions of government in these states often remained 'traditional', but the context of operation was subtly different. In Qajar Iran, for instance, there was a revival of the civil institutions of the Safavids (Flor 1976). But there were also shifts in social and economic power. Large landlords (some connected with cotton or tea exports to Russia) grew in importance. So too did merchant bodies connected with the Indian trades. Even the rôle of the Shia jurists appears to have revived and become more institutionalised as they put behind them the massive social and religious conflicts of the eighteenth century (Flor 1976). The revenue systems and resources of these para-colonial states varied greatly, but all to a greater or lesser extent pushed forward a policy of settling nomadic populations. They tried to break up concentrations of landed power and deal with complaisant yeoman farmers or small landholders; they built up modern, European-style armies.

The fight-back of indigenous states during the early nineteenth century has been underemphasised because these efforts ended in failure, or at least in the loss of independence over the generations between 1830 and 1880. Egypt was quickly penetrated by European usury capital after 1840; Iran was subjected to stronger British and Russian influences; the Punjab and Sindh lost their independence between 1838 and 1854; in southeast Asia and the archipelago, only Thailand retained autonomy, owing to the conflicts of the British and French.

One reason for the failure was the growing elan of the free trade movement in Britain and the perception among her manufacturers and bankers of an end to the 'barbarism and self-sufficiency' of other peoples. However, indigenous states were unable to banish the spectre of internal economic and ethnic conflict. These conflicts were periodically intensified by international economic fluctuations which now registered more sharply on their economies. Not only did the exercise of monopolies tend once again to increased conflict between state, landowners, peasant and merchant. But the broadening of the ideologies of these states to create royal-sponsored cults and ethnicities continued to call forth a furious response from entrenched communities which had historically defined their own identities according to different principles. So the distance between Turko- Circassians and Arabs weakened Egypt; the tension between Sikh peasant soldier and chieftains tore the Punjab apart after Ranjit Singh's death in 1839. Qajar Iran was bedevilled by revolts of Muslim 'heretics' and suffered in the trade depressions of the 1830s, as influences from the international economy became more powerful.

However, the tensions which arose from these intensified efforts at state-building at the beginning of the nineteenth century spilled over into revolt and decline not only in what we have called 'para-colonies', but in the European colonies themselves. More than this, the conflicts which arose in the British empire, and in the Asian or African kingdoms with which it was uneasily linked, have much in common with the problems faced by neo-absolutist states more generally as they approached the second 'age of revolutions' of 1848.

THE DECLINE OF THE SECOND BRITISH EMPIRE, 1830–60

During the 1830s and 1840s, liberal ideas, and particularly utilitarian liberal ideas, were on the offensive. Domestic and imperial historians have characterised these decades as an 'Age of Reform' in which the Great Reform Act, the extension of municipal government and the repeal of the Corn Laws in Britain were matched by the termination of the East India Company's monopoly, the end of West Indian protection and the patchy beginnings of 'responsible government' in Canada, Australasia and southern Africa (Ward 1976: 209–46).

This came about largely, according to established historiography, because the theoretical basis of the old régime was undermined by the doctrines of liberalism which edged nearer to the sources of power in the 1830s. Utilitarian thought began to influence the activities of Indian settlement officers who were now less solicitous of indigenous aristocracies (Stokes 1959). Dissenting evangelicalism made headway in most colonies, and the victory of the Abolitionists finally came to pass when slavery was outlawed in 1833. Ironically, the ideas of Thomas Malthus, a conservative theorist of the Anglican school were enlisted by proponents of large-scale colonial emigration who argued that this would relieve population pressure, especially in Ireland and the new English cities. The intellectual victory of the political economists (Adam Smith was now joined by David Ricardo and J S Mill) powered the onward rush of free-trade legislation. The vision of the future was one of a free imperial economic association of British trading nations, ushering to the threshold of civilisation a number of dependent races who had been schooled in the English language and modern education. Many of the ideas of this new wave had been in the air for more than a generation, of course, but the defeat of 'Tory' philosophy (what we have seen as Regency aristocratic paternalism) was suddenly overwhelming. The view that there was a significant change in domestic and imperial political economy during these years has worn reasonably well. However, the real impact of ideological and institutional changes in Britain has probably been overstated and the nature of the pressures in the world outside Europe have been underplayed. We will consider both these points in the remainder of the chapter.

British historians, it has been observed, have spent much time of late 'proving that nothing happened', and their colleagues in imperial history have also had a field day challenging earlier simplicities. If an 'Age of Reform' did happen, it now appears to have been much less stirring than the Victorians or the imperial generation of 1931 believed. Moreover, its guiding principles were still pragmatic conservatism rather than liberalism. In Britain, the Great Reform Act did little to challenge aristocratic domination of politics, indeed it may have been designed to perpetuate it. Aristocrats and their professional clients were able to create 'communities of deference' within municipal electorates; and in the countryside the solid bond between tenant, yeoman farmer and landowner was hardly touched by periodic food riots or protests against new machinery. Social status was still based on land. The industrial middle class remained a lowly breed, and if any group began to aspire to political power it was the professional middle class, the financier, rentier and other 'gentleman capitalists'. The Indian summer of the Whig aristocracy in the early nineteenth century thus merges imperceptibly with the *fin de siècle* of the great broad-acred politicians like Lord Salisbury and Lord Rosebery, towards its end. In this interpretation, the age of industry and liberalism was a trick of the light – or perhaps it happened after 1900. Great Britain continued to have much more in common than had been supposed with the rest of Europe where 'the human material of feudal society continued to fill the offices of the state, officer the army, and devise policy' (Schumpeter, cited in Mayer 1981: 11).

The image of an empire of free trade and responsible government has also been dented. Slavery, it is held, was merely succeeded by other forms of bonded labour or by the exploitation of Asian peasantries instead of black slaves. 'Responsible government' was a tactic to shore up imperial defence and it conceded more influence to small cliques of pro-empire speculators rather than signalling the emergence of nations-in-the-making. 'Free trade' was no more than the nostrum of a nation which had achieved superiority by the use of military force to break into others' protected markets; the British could now afford to be free traders. As for reform in Britain's greatest colony, India, this also promised more than it delivered. There were gestures such as the abolition of widow-burning (actually very few widows were ever burned), but little changed. Macaulay's Indian law codes were shelved until the 1870s. Evangelical Christianity foundered on the caution of the civil and military establishment. The 'utilitarian tide' in India was often no more than 'one clerk speaking to another', while James Mill's total assault on Indian culture and society merely underlined an already racist and interventionary strand in imperial policy. Detailed investigation of the localities has further eroded earlier certainties. Very few great Indian land controllers were swept away by the radical rent theory which was supposedly implemented in the interests of a prosperous yeomanry. Generally, *zamindars* managed to reproduce their power or blunt the decisions of the revenue courts. Social bonds between lord and dependent proved even more resilient to administrative fiat than they were in the home country. Even after the abolition of its monopoly of the China trade, the government of India still had a mercantilist heart. It maintained its monopoly of salt and opium and derived its revenue from a heavy land tax distributed according to customary principles of status rather than the imperatives of a free market in land.

The old construct of an Age of Reform, then, was obviously too simplistic. Viewed in the longer term, though, the 1830s and 1840s still seem to represent a watershed in the style of government both in the colonies and Britain, though it would be naive to see this simply as a watershed between the *ancien régime* and liberalism. The decline of what some Canadians called 'Pitt's system' and what with justice could also be called 'the Wellesley system' was a long process marked by savage breaks such as the Canadian rebellion of 1837, the Great Famine in Ireland or the Indian Mutiny of 1857. But many clear signs of decay had appeared by the 1830s. The reasons for this were as much clashes in the periphery as changes in domestic British politics. The main symptoms were the revived problems of financing the greatly extended empire. These were deepened by cyclical depressions operating in a more integrated world economy and by the continuing splutter of local wars which often marked the advance of settler capitalism into indigenous societies. In the empire it is striking how tensions and contradictions which were inherent in the new empire of Pitt's day were becoming intolerable by its third decade. The assaults of Liberals and free traders in Westminster may have pointed up the coming problems, but the underlying malaise was the parlous state of imperial finances and the growing restiveness of colonial élites and peasantries in both the colonies of settlement and the dependent, Asian and African empires.

As in the eighteenth century, the cost of internal and frontier protection proved to be the greatest burden on colonial budgets which were supposed, by the rules of financial orthodoxy prevalent in Britain, to be self-sustaining. The creation of a more elaborate colonial military and administrative apparatus had merely moved the problem of protection into a higher gear. The very presence of large garrisons and their associated trade on colonial frontiers unsettled relations with surviving indigenous states. For instance, in southern Africa, despite Somerset's policy of segregation and the *cordon sanitaire*, the buoyant expansion of the settler frontier reflected the growing population of the Cape colony and its commercial agriculture. Conflict with Xhosa and Bushman became endemic; costly wars were fought in 1811–17, 1834–7 and 1846. Imperial policing of relations between the settlers, English and Dutch, had equally poor results. It was regarded as an intolerable infringement of their communal rights, hastening the rise of Afrikaner separatism, but at the same time adding to the demands on an already straitened financial situation.

In Upper and Lower Canada and in Australasia in the 1840s, the same dilemma revealed itself. The policy of settlement after the Napoleonic Wars and the nudge given to the commercial economy by early nineteenth-century administrations set the frontier of 'settler capitalism' rolling ahead, invading tribal lands, tying down the indigenous labour force, and leading to severe conflicts with the aboriginal populations. In Lower Canada the inrush of new colonists and new capital after 1816 had also intensified conflicts between the old French yeomanry and incoming Anglo-Saxon money. If the British refused to concede protection or arbitration they risked losing control of the settler populations as they had done previously in the Thirteen Colonies. If they accepted responsibility for defence, this implied taxation and control which ensured the hostility of these quasi-republics.

The problem of the expanding frontier and the cost of protecting it was also at the root of the intractable financial problems of the British despotism of Asia. Wellesley's policy of putting Indian princes under 'subsidiary' alliances and making them pay for British troops had been intended as a means of stabilising the East India Company's internal frontiers and ensuring its paramountcy over the Indian states. But as in the eighteenth century, the demands laid on these intricate polities were so severe that conflict over the payment of subsidy, faction and disaffection was almost inevitable. The rolling outward of the British frontier of administration also expanded the scope of capitalists, both British and Indian. Plains Hindu moneylenders invaded the wastes and the hills; logging agents jealously eyed the forests of Indian and Burmese rulers. The very implementation of the 'rule of law', the mesh of constraints and absolute rules imposed by Cornwallis and his successors on Indian government, also tended subtly to draw the British into disputes and conflicts in Indian states which they could not ignore.

The consequence was that the rate of territorial expansion was hardly halted even in those periods when official pronouncements were most fiercely opposed to it, as after Wellesley's recall and during Bentinck's reforming administration of 1828–36. The final war against the Marathas and the Gurkhas was hardly over when Burma was invaded (1824–6) and British ambitions in Malaya were renewed (1826); even during Bentinck's reign, when liberalism and caution were supposed to have ruled, the conditions for the annexation of Sindh and the Punjab were in gestation. At all times, pressures for subsidy payments and 'reform' on the dependent Indian states – Awadh, Hyderabad and Mysore – were unrelenting. The Company viewed with terrible foreboding the loss of its monopoly of the China trade to the pressure of the free-trade lobby, but mainly because its finances were already reeling from its failure to halt frontier wars or devise a system which could tax the Indian peasantry without squeezing it to death. Ceylon proved to be a smaller-scale financial disaster. The cinnamon monopoly did not pay for the administration. But the introduction of white-run plantations had its own risks. After the annexation of Kandy in 1818, the British hoped to maintain internal control by creating a Crown monopoly of waste and forests lands and beginning to sell these off to planters. However, attempts to stop 'encroachments' by Ceylonese farmers led to serious agrarian unrest which culminated in a major revolt in 1848.

To pay for internal control and external conquest, the imperial power was forced to raise the land tax or, in the case of India, to keep an existing land revenue at very high levels. Inevitably, this policy dampened the possibilities of agrarian expansion and stoked up further agrarian tension. These difficulties were compounded by the development of severe problems in external trade which also assumed threatening proportions again by the late 1820s. Many of the export trades which were supposed to vitalise the economies of the component parts of the new empire and tie it to the metropolis were bound to run into trouble because they had flourished in artificial conditions of blockade and economic warfare before 1816. Turning first to the small laboratory of the Mediterranean, it is interesting that the brief attempt to stimulate cotton production on Malta and Gozo after 1802 was virtually snuffed out by 1825 when cheap Egyptian cotton flooded on to the market as Muhammad Ali's production got into its swing. Malta's once-flourishing trade had already been damaged by the international cholera epidemic of the early 1820s. Raisin production, the staple of the Ionian Islands, also suffered badly in the 1830s and 1840s as the production of mainland Greece reasserted itself in the English market once Greek independence was assured. The result was a worsening of the financial problems of the Mediterranean colonial administrations already struggling under a swollen bill for expatriate salaries and a diminution of standards of living among the islanders. The economic downturn provided a context for the intensification of conflicts between the colonial administrations and the islanders. This flared into open revolt in Cefalonia and Zante in 1836–7 and 1842.

World-wide, the unravelling of commercial imbalances arising from the wars damaged both the finances and internal stability of colonies. Cape wine production was hit by the re-entry of Spain and Portugal into the British market after 1818. In the Indies, the dangerous dependence of Indian cotton and opium exports on Chinese markets and Chinese government activity was intensified by the indirect effects of emerging trade cycles in the British cotton industry which affected international demand. Colonial economic problems also began to assume that linked pattern which was characteristic of the more mature empire. The 1833 decision to admit East Indian sugar to the British market, for instance, was a further blow to the sugar economy of the Caribbean which had already suffered two generations of internal crisis as a result of the end of the slave trade and declining yields from exhausted lands. The terminal convulsions of the sugar economy and expectation of emancipation brought about a massive slave revolt in Jamaica in 1831, another sign that the fragile post-Waterloo stability of empire was coming to an end.

Under the surface of these cyclical booms and slumps, a series of more fundamental changes were also beginning to surface. First, in many parts of the world where man–land ratios were poor and population had resumed its upward path despite periodic disease and famine, peasant holdings were already dangerously subdivided. In Ireland, Bengal and Java (which remained partly within the British sphere of influence) signs of overpopulation were beginning to appear, while the fiscal pressures of governments and international economic turbulence made it impossible for farmers to invest enough to push themselves out of the cycle of decline.

Secondly, international supplies of silver dwindled as Latin America was engulfed by rebellions against the Spanish Crown. For eastern countries such as India and China which had silver currencies, this meant that farmers' produce declined in value in relation to specie, and they had difficulty in paying cash land revenues. This was one of the several causes of the depression which hit agriculture in India after 1828. Finally, the industrialisation of England, which had already had consequences in Ireland and continental Europe, had begun to affect more distant markets. Although the surge in imports of twist and yarn, and later of manufactured goods into the Ottoman empire, India and southeast Asia did not lead to the total collapse of rural weaving in these areas, it did undoubtedly destroy specialist production and appears to have led to a general decline in the by-income of weavers' families.

However serious economic problems were for ministers and the Colonial Office, the decline of internal stability was even more worrying. The rash of revolts, peasant disturbances and movements for self-determination which spread during the 1830s and 1840s was particularly embarrassing because it coincided with the debates about parliamentary reform and the emergence of the working class as a political force in Britain. These outbreaks reflected much more than demands for representative government among various élites. In many parts of the empire they had an ethnic or religious character or fed on deep-seated agrarian conflicts. One reason for this was that the more or less subtle assimilationist policies of the new empire had forged firmer bonds between non-Protestants or non-Christian élites and subject populations.

In Ireland the 'Protestant Crusade' of the early years of the century against the Catholic peasantry coincided with the rise of the Orange movement among Episcopalian and Presbyterian gentry and middle classes who had been frightened by the revolution of 1798 and 1799. Agrarian conflict and violence persisted as landlords regained the upper hand during the depression after the end of the Napoleonic Wars. Catholic husbandmen fought back as Protestant landlords tried to turn arable back to pasturage. Rack-renting and eviction by a new breed of capitalist landlords, farmers and factors sustained the 'spirit of '98' in the localities. There were minor revolts in 1810–11, 1813–16 and the 1820s. By the mid-1830s, agrarian bitterness was channelled into random assassinations of landlords and farmers or arson attacks in the Midlands and southern counties. The tithes paid to Protestant churches became a fiercely contested issue among the Catholic peasantry once again. The swelling of the British military and police presence after 1815 had made the 'heretical' churches more obtrusive and tithes seemed a heavier burden when peasant incomes were falling.

Most important of all, resistance in England to Catholic political emancipation until 1829 wasted the political capital which had been generated by Pitt's policy of political assimilation through the Union, just as it rendered useless the policies of reconcilation with Catholic gentry followed by successive viceroys. The imbalance of political and economic power between Anglo-Irish and Celtic society became confounded with the religious suspicion between Protestant and Catholic. The lines were not yet hard drawn, but in Daniel O'Connell's movement for emancipation and against the Union, all the elements of Catholicism, gentry patriotism and rural defence against the outside were coming together. The abolition of anti-Catholic penal laws in 1829 was seen as a victory for mass agitation and an acknowledgement of the ability of the Catholic majority to make Ireland ungovernable if their aspirations were thwarted. Since it was wrested from Britain and the Protestant

Ascendancy by threat, rather than a concession made in the spirit of reason and justice, it was bound to throw doubt on the future of the Union itself. By the mid-1830s, the Young Ireland movement had begun to sow the seeds of a revolutionary Catholic republicanism. So it was the naked incompleteness of Pitt's policy of assimilation which presaged its failure from the beginning (Beckett 1981: 304–5).

The reaction of Catholic farmers and tradesmen to a more aggressive Protestant and English colonial élite also helps explain growing restiveness in Lower Canada. The Canadians and Irish were aware of each other's plight within the Protestant empire, and their fears grew fast in the 1830s. French Canadian arable farming was burdened with poor agricultural techniques and the rapid subdivision of holdings which occurred as population grew. Great English-speaking landlords and timber owners, who were often descendants of beneficiaries of 'Pitt's system', were an obvious target, accused of keeping land out of the hands of the original settlers, the French. Imperial tariff and trade policy was thought to discriminate in favour of the small urban and landlord élite which had a stake in the British connection. Protestant emigration, Protestant schools and official encouragement of the English language seemed to be a plot to isolate and dissolve French culture and the Catholic religion. Colonial nationalists and French *patriotes* such as Louis-Joseph Papineau at first had the support of some English farmers and middle-class people, but his increasingly strident anti-English and revolutionary rhetoric had alienated much of this support by the 1830s. Then peasant radicalism was given a sharp spur by terrible harvests in 1836 and 1837 which left the colony with insufficient grain for local consumption. Since the timber trade was closely dependent on the English market, the 1837 depression in Britain damaged incomes in Canada also as it did over much of the rest of the empire. The scene was set for a full-scale rebellion in the Trois-Rivieres region in the following years (Ouellet 1976: 276–331) which was suppressed not so much because of the efficiency of the British army as because republican radicalism alienated the Catholic Church and important conservative elements among the French population. Only the British Cabinet's concession of virtual full responsible government within a new Canadian Federation over the following fifteen years was to restore stability to the Canadas.

In South Africa the critical issue was the struggle between the Dutch farmers and the colonial government over the control of land on the fringes of the settlement. But cultural tensions were beginning to envenom the agrarian conflict. The dwindling influence of the Dutch in major towns and the expansion of Anglican or Scottish Presbyterian colonists in the later 1820s and 1830s was a powerful stimulus to the creole patriotism of the Boers which had already cut its teeth against the Dutch Company and felt itself permanently embattled by Khoikoi and Xhosa. The 'injustifiable odium' heaped on the Dutch settlers by the new generation of colonial officials after 1806 further alienated them. The Great Trek out of the domain of the British was only one manifestation of an economic battle which was being significantly reinforced by religious and cultural animosities. As A H Potgeiter wrote in 1841, 'I do not want to subject myself to any Briton nor in justice to any other power in the world; and I am no Briton . . . nor I hope and trust ever become one. I pray to the Almighty for this, not only for me but for the whole United Society of Burghers' (du Toit and Giliomee 1983: 217).

In Asia too, peasant protest and the restiveness of the élites of the colonial cities took on forms which reflected a cultural reaction to the anglicist and assimilationist character of colonial government. Some have argued that the adoption of the practice of widow-burning as a sign of purity and respectability even in the environs of a city such as Calcutta was a form of concealed protest against the steady encroachment of colonial rule on Indian custom. Certainly, the neo-orthodox revival throughout India and among both Hindus and Muslims was well underway by 1820 and drew strength from the widespread feeling that colonial government was closely allied with Christian missions and that the rulers were establishing a new social hierarchy in which the respectable and revered classes of the pre-colonial order were being treated with indignity. Resistance movements among tribal people and peasants nearly always embodied appeals against infidel rule as well as purely agrarian programmes. There was great hostility to revenue surveys and house taxation, not only because they were expected to lead to further taxation, but because they seemed to bring Christian rule nearer to the hearth. In Ceylon too, a 'new party of Gooroos' had emerged among the Hindus of Jaffna which combined a revived and aggressive Shaivism with elements taken from Christianity (Tennent 1850: 171–2). Its leaders were trying to build a new identity within colonial society. In the Buddhist south and centre of the island, meanwhile, the revival which had taken root in the eighteenth century prospered despite the fall of the Kingdom of Kandy. Even in Java, the aggressive policies of Raffles and Crawfurd towards

Javanese nobility and religion provided some of the deepest grievances for a growing sense of resentment which erupted in the great war against the Dutch of 1825–30. Movements such as this had deep roots in Asian society. Ethnic and religious identities had been sharpened by the political practice of the pre-colonial states, while international economic changes created new ranges of social conflict. These were much more than the stirrings of newly 'westernised' élites or 'post-pacification revolts'.

The response of the British to the decline of the 'Second Empire' was piecemeal and often confused. But overall the arrangements that had begun to emerge in the 1830s heralded significant departures from the style of rule which had held sway during the Regency years in the 'colonies of settlement' as well as in the dependent Asian empire. In India, Bentinck's 'Age of Reform' attempted to tackle the Company's parlous financial position by paring salaries, restricting expense and withdrawing the swollen bureaucracy which had been the legacy of the Wellesley years and further expansion under the Marquess of Hastings. Under conditions of financial stringency, cheap Indian officials were reintroduced at the lower end of both the judicial and revenue services. This was a move away from the discrimination against Indians instituted by Cornwallis, and its implications were that a new English-educated cadre of native administrators would be required. Indians were not to be included in political decision making in the new age, but they were to be associated with empire through cultural (and if possible) religious assimilation. Public works and free internal trade were to tie the sub-continent to Great Britain's booming capitalist economy, and an improved peasantry was to replace paternalist landlords over much of India as the preferred agent of economic revitalisation. Crude attempts to extract the Mughal revenue at its maximum gave way in the 1840s to more 'scientific' surveys of revenue, which in the longer run did in fact improve the state's financial position. In Ceylon and even Malaya as well as India, the rigid opposition to white settlement was somewhat modified. The Arcadian tone of the despatches of men like Sir Thomas Munro gave way to a more rigorous discourse on modernisation. These moves were only fitfully implemented before the rebellion of 1857, but after the troubles of the later 1820s and 1830s no-one could doubt that change was needed.

In the 'colonies of settlement' the change was as clear, but the response almost as varied. Anglo-Saxon colonisation and free trade without the perils of state intervention were the new nostrums. In Canada and Australasia, full 'responsible government' with electorates choosing their own ministries under the Crown were implemented over the generation after 1830. Constitutional government emerged in parallel with developments in Britain where the rôle of the Crown declined further while the Great Reform Act and the rise of municipal government opened politics to new influences. Problems of control in Australia and the revolts in Canada, like growing working-class restiveness in the English towns, counselled new methods of political control.

However, there were some colonies where these moves were tempered or even aborted by the severity of social tensions. In Jamaica and other Caribbean colonies, persistent slave revolt before emancipation and brutal attempts by planters to maintain control over labour after 1834 gradually drew the British government into more direct control. The Colonial Office finally achieved its long-prized goal of direct control in the islands. By 1863 the Caribbean islands had become a series of Crown colonies and the vestiges of white self-government had been eliminated. Similarly in southern Africa, the conflict of Afrikaner, Briton and indigenous people if anything intensified. The separatist movement in the eastern Cape gathered pace in the 1840s while in 1851 a new Kaffir (Xhosa) war broke out. The Cape therefore received representative institutions, but not responsible government (Ward 1976: 311). Finally, the move towards local self-government on the British mainland was not fully reflected in an Ireland now devastated by famine. In 1840, when the Irish Municipal Corporations Act was finally steered past fierce Conservative opposition in Parliament, it turned out to be much more restrictive than its English counterpart (Beckett 1981: 322). Meanwhile, the authority of resident magistrates was maintained in the countryside and Irish Catholic legislative aspirations were frustrated by their representatives' minority status in Westminster. The Age of Reform worked remarkably unevenly throughout the empire. But in all of these cases it was social change and local conflicts in the colonies as much as the new wind from Britain which determined the form of colonial political economy in the later nineteenth century.

The 'Second British Empire' had been created quite rapidly in the context of war, revolt and the international ideological challenge of Republican France. It fell apart more slowly under the pressure of financial crisis, free trade pressures and, again, revolt and tension in the colonies themselves. Some features of 'Pitt's system', such as the East India Company's army or the veranda autocracy in the Mediterranean islands, lingered on into the Victorian empire. However, the change of style and emphasis was clear. Aristocracy, agrarian paternalism, Anglican assimilation and the philosophical interpretation of racial difference faded in importance. New forms of labour control replaced slavery and forced labour while the state retreated from the central position which it had held in the economy. Scientific and biological theories of racial energy began to oust the brusque chauvinist ideas of the Cornwallis era. The emphasis in economic development now lay on trade, steam, railways and canals. There was less faith in the unsullied industry of yeomen and peasants protected by their natural leaders.

Conclusion

The massive expansion of British imperial power which accompanied the French Revolutionary and Napoleonic Wars has never attracted the interest accorded to the Elizabethan plantations, the Partition of Africa or the Transfer of Power after 1945. Partly, this is because British historians have been particularly skilful here at showing that 'nothing happened'. Vincent Harlow's attempt to demonstrate the emergence of a Second British Empire, especially in the East, and to predate the rise of a free-trade imperialism appropriate to an industrialised state has received only a muted reaction from scholars, compared with the fierce disagreements which have raged around the occupation of Egypt in 1882 or the Partition of India. It is often asserted now that the industrial revolution had only a limited effect on the pattern of Britain's foreign and colonial trade before 1830 and, some Celtic prophesyings by Dundas apart, there is not much evidence that statesmen saw the promotion of industrial exports or securing imports for these industries as major objectives of state power. New markets came as a result of war and empire; they did not apparently cause it. And if British mercantile horizons were broadened, it was not, at least superficially, the 'swing to the East' hailed by Harlow which deserves notice, but the rapid development of markets in North and South America. In the same way, the general acceptance that the abolition of the slave trade in 1807 did, in fact, represent the victory of a moral crusade rather than the outward manifestation of fundamental change in the form of capitalist accumulation has tended to diminish the importance of the period.

The huge new conquests which occurred during the administration of Pitt the Younger and Lord Liverpool therefore have continued to be treated almost as aberrations of war, quickly forgotten after 1816 when the Congress of Vienna ushered in an age which was 'not imperialistic' (Parry and Sherlock 1963: 437–47; *cf.* 1961 Koebner). Yet many of Great Britain's institutions and the greater part of her empire have been forged during wars, and it has always seemed peculiar that domestic and imperial historians have both implied that what the British do during wars should not be taken too seriously.

This fit of absence of mind on the part of historians has allowed a myth of British uniqueness to develop in imperial history that mirrors the myth of English uniqueness in domestic history. England had no state, only administration; it had no nationalism, only patriotism. Its colonial policy was pacific, pragmatic and economically determined; from time to time events took place which forced the English to become colonialists against their will. This was a view so powerfully expounded by liberal statesmen of the nineteenth century that it impressed otherwise sceptical foreigners such as Joseph Schumpeter, whose entire problematic in *Imperialism and Social Classes* was distorted by the distinction between 'pacific' British colonial policy and the aggressive imperialism of the continental powers. Ironically, the thesis was given a new lease of life by Robinson and Gallagher who argued that African empire was a 'bondage' unwillingly entered into by liberal statesmen who wanted nothing better than a quiet life, but were haunted by the spectre of 'local crises' happening in the periphery.

The myth could then be pushed on into the twentieth century. The French were assimilationist, ideological, militaristic and repressive; the Dutch were similar despite being Protestants and having an ethical policy. The French, in particular, executed nationalists because of 'la gloire' while the British gave them light prison terms because the path was already open to 'responsible government', perhaps even as early as 1783. The British found it easy to retreat from empire because they never had much emotional investment in their colonies and because empire was in any case little more than an expensive *cordon sanitaire* for the trading posts and financial centres which they were really interested in.

It has been useful to caricature the liberal Anglican view (as Ronald Robinson calls it), and its unlikely bedfellows, Robinson and Gallagher, because myths, after all, are part-truths. For much of imperial history including, as we have seen, much of the eighteenth century, colonial policy was indeed reactive and pragmatic, seeking to pre-empt rather than to colonise and, above all, to save money.

However, the picture is too lacking in contrast; it explains too much and too little. There was another strand, a constructive authoritarian and ideological British imperialism which explains many other themes, events and policies pushed to the margins by the dominant view. These include the colonisation and settlement of the Highlands of Scotland and Ireland; the savage wars of repression against the Ceylonese, Burmese, Maori, or Indian rebels of 1857; and the many imperial police actions of the present century against Afghans, Malayan Chinese, or even Argentinians. It explains Curzon, Milner and Churchill better than Cobden, Gladstone or Attlee. It explains the speed and efficiency with which civil government and local representation in the colonies were swept away in time of war or disturbance throughout the nineteenth and twentieth centuries. It illuminates the tight, caste-like and racially exclusive form of colonial social life and the sense of Christian mission, less theatrical but no less pervasive than that of the French, Belgians or Portuguese, which has subtly informed so much British imperial decision making.

This form of British imperialism came of age in the years between 1783 and 1820. During this period, commercial aims and the need for financial stability were assimilated into, and supercharged by, an altogether sharper sense of national identity, expressed in the need to override class and regional divisions in Britain and to subordinate subject races overseas. While Pitt and Dundas sought to create a 'British Empire in Europe', Lord Minto's aim was 'to purge the eastern side of the globe of every hostile or rival European establishment' and 'with patriot zeal' to bring wisdom and reason to Asia's people.

This book has traced some of the institutions and ideologies which flourished in Pitt's Britain and were then modified and exported to the new empire. These ideologies and institutions were, of course, buckled and compromised by the conditions of the societies into which they were introduced. But even if the consequences of their introduction were often unintended, the impulse cannot be ignored, for they affected not only Europeans overseas, but also the particular histories of African, Asian and American societies. 'Economical reform' of corrupt government reinforced the financial basis of the state in Great Britain and Ireland; its parallel in Asia and Africa was the creation of a new administrative corps d'élite separated from European tradesmen and 'native depravity'. 'Agrarian patriotism' and its paraphernalia of statistical surveys and improving landlords was exported both in its English and Scottish form to the colonies where it had great influence even though buckled by the pressures of indigenous social change. 'Anti-slavery' and the missionary projects of both the Anglican and Scottish Churches embraced attempts to discipline and settle which were formative influences on colonial societies even though direct proselytisation and assimilation were much less overt than in the case of the Catholic powers.

The vitality and elan of these institutions and ideologies were derived from a response to the rapid and alarming social changes which were affecting the home country. The 'gentlemen' were 'thoroughly frightened'. Church, property and Crown seemed under assault not only from the republican menace outside but also from the 'rise and growth of popular disaffection', and from Catholic peasant rebellion in Ireland. The foundations seemed to be shifting as rapid social change consequent on uneven economic growth created the impression that morality and social discipline were breaking down. Wesleyans, libertines and republicans might fill the ensuing vacuum unless patriotism, anglicanism and sobriety became active powers in the state and the cities rather than passive gentilities of the shires. The project of reinforcing social control was aided by the fact that the gentry, buoyed up by profits from land, coal and turnpike trusts, seemed once again to be in the ascendant, returning to local government and reinforcing their position in the boroughs. Long years of war revived their rôle as a *noblesse d'épée* and provided them openings in the military, naval and colonial services. Since some of the most successful of this revived aristocracy were from Ireland, Scotland and outlying parts of England and Wales, the careers open (more or less) to the talents helped assimilate new élites and created a reinvented style of patriotism centred on Crown, Church and empire. Its emblems and tokens both classical and romantic were remarkably similar to those of contemporary imperial France. British military impotence in Europe directed much of this new energy and the collective mind of this new 'imperial consensus' to the world outside Europe.

If we look beyond the question of narrowly-defined 'origins of empire' to the form that the new imperial provinces took and to the assumptions and prejudices which held sway in them, the Regency empire was in an important sense an extension of domestic social change overseas, an example of social imperialism. Of course, there was no crude sense in the mind of statesmen that picking up a Caribbean island here or an Indian province there would help discipline the working class and provide a field for the emigration of pauper Highlanders or disaffected Irish peasants. It was more that the sense of national mission, forged out of conflict and unease in Britain, and spread particularly by a newly militarised gentry, spilled overseas and regenerated the sleepy ambitions of complaisant governors in colonial outposts. A telling moment here was the arrival of Richard Wellesley in Madras in 1798, stirring the slumbering settlement with a puritanical drive for efficiency and morality, displaying disdain for corrupt natives and orientalised Britons alike.

A new urgency in the drive for dominion infected the old debates about paying for the East India Company's army or keeping the French off the trade routes. Nor can we vulgarise Schumpeter's tangled arguments and assert that the creation of the new empire was an example of aristocratic atavism forced on an unwilling and pacific bourgeoisie. The important feature of this period was that class interest and the perception of profit were both transcended in the explosion of a new nationalist energy which largely identified law, religion and commerce as the highest national goods and perceived them to be threatened at a universal level. This was in some places an era of the 'imperialism of free trade', but there are as many examples of the 'imperialism of monopoly' or simple chauvinist appropriation. Many thought that the best thing to do with the Dutch establishments in Java was just to extirpate them, but the shame of destroying Christian rule over pagans more than perceptions of marginal profit counselled against this. The search for the economic origins of empire is by no means redundant. Yet it has been overplayed by a reductionist and empirical historiography which always saw nationalism as a dubious enthusiasm to which foreigners were prone.

This study has therefore supported Vincent Harlow in his view that there was a 'Second British Empire' emerging more rapidly after 1783, and that it differed in important respects from the earlier empire of colonies. Except during the immediate aftermath of the Seven Years' War, the pace of imperial expansion had earlier been governed by change outside England. In Asia the consequences of commercialisation and the formation of new states had indirectly drawn the servants of the East India Company into great acquisitions in Bengal and Arcot. The pace of British expansion was related to the slow 'crisis of proto-capitalism' in the great Muslim empires. In the West Indies and Canada wars of monopoly and mercantilism had given opportunities to creoles to hamstring their French or Spanish enemies. After 1783, however, the role of England in empire-building was strongly reasserted. We would agree with Hopkins and Cain that the economic value of empire to Britain continued to lay much more in its contribution to finance and services than to the emerging industrial economy. However, empire itself transcended the confines of 'gentlemanly capitalism', becoming for the critical span of years up to 1830 a patriotic and godly project forged in the context of international ideological and social conflict. And while Anglicanism did indeed inform this empire at important junctures (Clark 1985) it was in the context of a reinvented and refounded consensus of national élites, not the persistence of an ancient absolutist tradition.

The aim of this book, however, is not simply to enshrine the 'metropolitan element' once again, whether this be gentlemanly capitalism or aristocratic militarism. Empire by definition was a dialogue between metropolitan impulses and the history of the colonised societies. Neither a 'Eurocentric' nor an 'excentric' 'theory of imperialism' could ever be logically sufficient. The assumption from the start was that empire in a world-historical sense could only be understood by examining social change in the areas colonised as an essential component of an imperial system. This aim would not be served by giving a few examples of 'collaborators' or local crises, but would have to proceed from an understanding of the broader direction of political change and class formation outside England and in a world which was not yet divided into regions and provinces. The direction of change in Asia or North Africa in the seventeenth and eighteenth centuries is a matter of the greatest technical complexity and attempts to generalise are perilous. Nevertheless, the genre of 'imperial history' or of 'European expansion' has no future unless it can draw on the growing body of studies of the extra-European world to illuminate the development of social institutions and ideologies which were as formative of the nineteenth-century colonial world as were the policies of European governments or the profit-hunger of their merchants. Equally, there is little value in a picture of the development of a European capitalist world system which cannot provide an explanation of the great diversity within it.

The approach adopted in this study was already in some respects familiar. Rather than seeing the eighteenth century in greater Eurasia as the culmination of a process of degeneration in stagnant empires, it was the very vitality of markets in land, produce and royal rights stimulated by the expansion of those empires which accounts for the sharp escalation of conflicts between states and internal social disorder which gave pre-colonial Asia its gloomy reputation. In this sense, multifarious forms of Asian (or North African) 'capitalism' were struggling to accommodate themselves to institutions and ideologies which had been generated out of an earlier period of military expansion. These events took place in very different material and social conditions from the contemporary struggles to confine early 'settler capitalism' within the integument of weak imperial states or chartered companies in European colonies of settlement. However, they are analytically comparable, the more so because European free merchants and entrepreneurs of the chartered companies were active in both spheres. In Eurasia the consequence of widened social and political conflict was the creation of new regional states which represented an alliance between imperial officials, provincial élites and mercantile capitalists. These new political formations faced expanding European trading corporations in Eurasia with severe challenges, both economic and political, and speeded their transformation into military and political powers. They also forged new relations with peasants, literate men and mercantile élites which persisted into, in some cases underpinned, the colonial empires of the nineteenth century.

There is a danger here of constructing a set of arguments which is too mechanical and too economic in nature. The Asian social conflicts which heralded and accompanied the rise of European domination were not simply the results of the corrosive effects of indigenous capitalism eating into the social structure of Islamic, Hindu or Buddhist kingdoms. The very unity of the greater Islamic world, or of the Chinese and Indian diasporas had also spread ideas, aspirations and styles of transcendent political or religious authority. Institutions and communities which might have begun as outgrowths of economic expansion – western Indian village communities or trade routes in south-western Arabia, for instance – could become 'ideological', embodying the expectations and pride of élites in conflict or a sense of neighbourhood reacting against the outside world. The puritanical movements of Muslims in Arabia and west Sumatra or of Christians in the Ottoman Balkans or of Sikhs in northern India must all be set in the context of state, commerce and élite conflict, but in all cases the imperatives of community and belief gained autonomy from these origins.

This is particularly true of the events of the world crisis of the 1790s and 1800s which were characterised by an astonishing range of interlocking resistances and conflicts. The export of the European revolutionary wars and the new radical ideologies played their part, of course. But internal changes in and conflicts within Buddhist, Islamic or Hindu society and struggles by the last indigenous states to control their peasantries or external opponents had also set free movements which were as formative of the modern world order as Liberty, Equality and Fraternity. There is no simple teleology which connects eighteenth-century Islamic revivalism with the events of Muslim Asia today, or Ranjit Singh's Sikhs with the militants of the Golden Temple. Nevertheless, the sharper sense of ethnic or regional identities which characterised the later eighteenth century in some areas must at least be seen as a precondition for modern communal or national movements, and as a store of legends and myths which could be drawn upon by later religious or secular leaders.

In the medium term, the reaction of colonial governments and indigenous élites to these challenges to their position determined the form of the early nineteenth-century world order as surely as did the vigorous nationalisms of Europe. Colonial governments aided landed élites and commercial people in the restoration of control over 'their' peasantries, or at the very least provided a basic structure of coercive power with which to arbitrate these dangerous social tensions. The contemporary European notions of law, property and the moral hierarchy of cultures were sometimes appropriated by the emergent colonial régimes. Outside the formally colonial world, régimes like that of Muhammad Ali in Egypt or the new Thailand ('para-colonies' they have been called here) played a similar rôle. In the longer term, the Far East and sub-Saharan Africa were also to become spheres in which the same sort of conflict which erupted in south and west Asia in the eighteenth century was to be played out once again in the mid-nineteenth century. The monarchies of China and Japan had sought to close themselves, to enforce what Europeans saw as 'monopolies' in an attempt to control internal political and economic changes which threatened to pull them apart. Those tensions revived again in the vigorous commercial conditions after 1830. The east Asian monarchies sought to limit the access of European traders and reimpose order in the commercial 'fringe' of their domains. The result was the Opium Wars of 1838–42 and the opening up of Japan in the 1850s.

Finally, and beyond the question of 'formal' or 'informal' colonial rule, the period between the end of the American War and the Western-inspired Tanzimat reforms in Turkey during the 1830s seem to stand as a watershed in the creation and consolidation of new forms of power. Universal kingship as embodied in the claims of the Safavids, Mughals and old Ottoman empire, and perhaps also in the court of Versailles and the Papacy, had suffered epochal defeats, retreating to its last bastion in China. Legitimacy and territory, legitimacy and ethnicity or nationhood had been much more closely aligned not only in Europe but in Asia and Africa. Administration and economy had consolidated themselves further at the expense of tribute-taking and gifting. The magical element in authority persisted, represented now in a more concentrated form in the rituals of the central state. Police and regulation had further diminished the scope for the self-organisation of lineages, groupings of villages and other corporations, not only in Asia, Africa and the Pacific but in Europe itself.

Over much of the world the alliance between the state, the commercial classes and controllers of land was now more overt than it had been at the beginning of the eighteenth century. In turn, the representation of these events in histories helped consolidate them. Eighteenth-century philosophy had commonly tried to explain the evolution of human society at a universal level, paying particular attention to China and 'oriental despotism'. Increasingly, as the nineteenth century progressed, the history of the world came to be fragmented. There was the history of Europe, the history of colonies and, to encompass the social and cultural life of the non-West, Orientalism. The project of future histories will be to fit the fragments together once again. This book has been written in the spirit of that project.

Select Bibliography

MANUSCRIPT SOURCES

Public Record Office: CO 48, 54, 55; FO 24, 78, 142.
India Office Library, London: Board's Collections,1790–1810, Canton Diaries and Consultations, 1795–8, Home Miscellaneous Collections, 475–7, 479, 481, 605, 607, Raffles Papers, MSS Eur. D 34 and 35; MSS Eur. D 199; MSS Eur. E 104.

CONTEMPORARY JOURNALS

Annals of Agriculture and other Useful Arts
Asiatick Annual Register
Blackwood's Edinburgh Magazine
Quarterly Review

UNPUBLISHED DISSERTATIONS AND PAPERS

Al-Juhany, J., 1983. 'Trade and Society in Najd, 1200–1750'. Ph D, UCLA.

Chander, S., 1987. 'From pre-colonial order to princely state, Hyderabad, 1740–1860'. Ph D, Cambridge.

Cole, J R I., 1984. 'Imami Shi'ism from Iran to north India'. Ph D, UCLA.

Gilmore, G T., 1985. 'Episcopacy, Emancipation and Evangelisation.

257

Aspects of the History of the Church of England in the British West Indies'. Ph D, Cambridge.

Grove, R., 1988. 'Conservation and colonialism. Aspects of the development of environmental attitudes . . . in the colonial context'. Ph D, Cambridge.

Nizami, F A., 1983. 'Madrasahs, scholars and saints. The Muslim community of U.P., 1800–57'. D Phil, Oxford.

Singh, D., 1975. 'Local and land-revenue administration in eastern Rajasthan, c. 1750–1800'. Ph D, Jawaharlal Nehru University, New Delhi.

Stokes, E T., 1976. 'Bentinck to Dalhousie. The Rationale of Indian Empire'. Paper presented to the Director's Study Group on 'Policy and Practice under Bentinck and Dalhousie'.

Subramanian, L., 1984. 'The West Coast of India: the Eighteenth Century', Ph D, Visva Bharati University, Calcutta.

Subrahmanyam, S., 1986. 'Trade and the regional economy of South India, *c.* 1550–1650'. Ph D, Delhi University.

BOOKS AND ARTICLES

Alam, M., 1986. *The Crisis of Empire in Mughal North India. Awadh and the Punjab, 1707–1748*. Delhi.

Albion, R G., 1926. *Forests and Seapower*. Cambridge, Mass.

Algar, H., 1969. *Religion and State in Iran, 1785–1906*. Berkeley.

Al-Sayyid Marsot, A L., 1977. 'The wealth of the *ulama* in late eighteenth-century Cairo', in Naff and Owen, 1977.

Al-Sayyid Marsot, A L., 1984. *Egypt in the reign of Muhammad Ali*. Cambridge.

Anderson, P., 1974. *Lineages of the absolutist state*. London.

Anon., 1782. *Political Observations on the Population of Countries*. London.

Anon., 1799. *An Essay on the Present State of Manners and Education among the People of Ireland and the Means of Improving Them*. Watson, Dublin.

Anon., 1810. *A Refutation of the Second Part of the Book Entitled A Statement of the Penal Laws which aggrieve the Catholics of Ireland*. Dublin.

Anon. (Binny and Co.), 1969. *The House of Binny*. Madras.

Anstey, R., 1975. *The Atlantic Slave Trade and British Abolition, 1760–1810*. London.

Appadurai, A., 1981. *Worship and conflict under colonial rule. A south Indian case.* Cambridge.

Arjomand, S A., 1984. *The Shadow of God and the Hidden Imam.* Chicago.

Aspinall, A., 1971. *The Correspondence of George Prince of Wales, 1770–1812,* 8 vols. London.

Athar Ali, M., 1968. *The Mughal Nobility under Aurangzeb.* Bombay.

Atiyah, P S., 1979. *The Rise and Fall of Freedom of Contract.* Oxford.

Baer, G., 1968.'Social change in Egypt, 1800–1914' in Holt, P. M. (ed), *Political and Social Change in the Middle East.* London.

Bailyn, B., 1967. *The Ideological Origins of the American Revolution.* Cambridge, Mass.

Baker, N., 1973. 'Changing attitudes towards government in eighteenth century Britain', in Whiteman, A., Bromley, J. S. and Dickson, P. G. (eds), *Statesmen, Scholars and Merchants. Essays in Eighteenth-Century History presented to Dame Lucy Sutherland.* Oxford.

Barnett, R B., 1980. *North India between Empires. Awadh, the Mughals and the British, 1720–1801.* Berkeley.

Bartless, C J., 1966. *Castlereagh.* London.

Bastin, J., 1957. *The Native Policies of Sir Stamford Raffles in Java and Sumatra.* Oxford.

Bayly, C A., 1988. *Indian Society and the Making of the British Empire. New Cambridge History of India,* ii, 1. Cambridge.

Bayly, S B., forthcoming. *Saints, Goddesses and Kings. Muslims and Christians in South Indian Society, 1700–1900.* Cambridge.

Beaglehole, T H., 1966. *Thomas Munro and the development of administrative policy in Madras, 1792–1816.* Cambridge.

Beckett, J C., 1981. *The Making of Modern Ireland, 1603–1923.* London.

Beattie, J M., 1986. *Crime and the courts in England, 1660–1800.* Oxford.

Bezzina, J., 1985. *Religion and Politics in a Crown Colony. The Gozo–Malta Story, 1798–1864.* Valetta.

Blackburn, Robin, 1988. *The overthrow of Colonial Slavery, 1776–1848.* London.

Blake, S., 1987. 'The urban economy in pre-modern Muslim India: Shahjahanabad, 1639–1739', *Modern Asian Studies,* 21, 3.

Blussé, L., 1979. 'Japanese historiography and European sources', in Wesseling, H. and Emmer, P. (eds), *Reappraisals in Overseas History.* Leiden.

Blussé, L. 1984. 'Labour takes root. Mobilisation and immobilisation of Javanese rural society under the cultivation system', *Itinerario*, Leiden, 8, i.

Blussé, L., 1986. *Strange Company. Chinese settlers, mestizo women and the Dutch in VOC Batavia*. Dordrecht.

Boahen, A., 1968. *Britain, the Sahara and the western Sudan, 1788–1861*. Oxford.

Bolt, C., 1971. *Victorian Attitudes to Race*. London.

Bosworth, E. and Hellenbrand, E., 1983. *Qajar Iran. Studies presented to Professor L P Elwell Sutton*. Edinburgh.

Boustany, S. (ed.), 1971. *The Journals of Bonaparte in Egypt, 1798–1801*, vol. viii. Cairo.

Bowen, D., 1971. *The Protestant Crusade in Ireland, 1800–70*. Dublin.

Braithwaite, E., 1971. *The Development of Creole Society in Jamaica, 1770–1820*, Oxford.

Breen, T H., 1988. 'Baubles of Britain. The American and Consumer revolutions of the eighteenth century'. *Past and Present*, 119.

Breman, J C., 1980. *The Village on Java and the Early Colonial State*. Rotterdam.

Breman, J C., 1983. *Control of Land and Labour in Colonial Java*. Leiden and Dordrecht.

Brereton, B., 1981. *A History of Modern Trinidad, 1783–1962*. Kingston.

Bridges, G W., 1827. *The Annals of Jamaica*, 2 vols. London.

Bristow, E., 1977. *Vice and Vigilance. Purity Movements in Britain from 1700*. Dublin.

Brydges, H J (tr. ed.) 1833. *The Dynasty of the Kajars. A Manuscript of Fateh Ali Shah*. London.

Brynn, E., 1978. *Crown and Castle. British Rule in Ireland, 1800–30*. Dublin.

Buchanan, C., 1812. *Sketch of an Ecclesiastical Establishment for British India*. London.

Buchanan, C., 1813. *Colonial Ecclesiastical Establishments . . .* London.

Burckhardt, J L., 1831. *Notes on the Bedouins and Wahabys collected during his tours in the East by the late J L Burkhardt*, 2 vols. London.

Burn, W L., 1937. *Emancipation and Apprenticeship in the British West Indies*. London.

Cadell, Sir P., 1949–53. 'Irish Soldiers in India', *The Irish Sword*, i.

Cage, R A., 1985. *The Scots Abroad. Labour, Capital, Enterprise, 1750–1914*. London.

Campbell, A J., 1930. *Two Centuries of the Church of Scotland*. Paisley.

Campbell, R H., 1977. 'Scottish Improvers and the course of

change in the eighteenth century', in Cullen and Smout, 1977.

Cannadine, D N., forthcoming. *The British Landed Establishment, 1780–1980. An Economic, Political and Social History.* Princeton.

Cannon, J., 1984. *Aristocratic Century. The Peerage of Eighteenth Century England.* Cambridge.

Canny, N. and Pagden, A., 1987. *Colonial Elites, 1500–1800.* Princeton.

Carey, P B R., 1986a. 'The British in Java. A Javanese Account', in van Goor, J. (ed.), *Trading Companies in Asia, 1600–1830.* Utrecht.

Carey, P B R., 1986b. 'Waiting for the Ratu Adil: the Javanese Village Community on the Eve of the Java War', *Modern Asian Studies*, xx, i.

Carmichael, Mrs, 1833. *Domestic Manners and Social Conditions of the White, Coloured and Negro Population of the West Indies*, 2 vols. London.

Chandavarkar, R S., forthcoming. *Labour and Society in Bombay.* Cambridge.

Chandra, S., 1959. *Parties and Politics at the Mughal Court, 1707–40.* Delhi.

Chaudhuri, K N., 1978. *The Trading World of Asia and the English East India Company, 1660–1760.* Cambridge.

Chaudhuri, K N., 1985. *Trade and Civilisation in the Indian Ocean. An Economic History from the Rise of Islam to 1750.* Cambridge.

Chinnian, P., 1982. *The Vellore Mutiny, 1806.* Madras.

Christie, I. and Labaree, B., 1976. *Empire or Independence, 1760–76.* London.

Clapham, Sir John, 1944. *The Bank of England*, 2 vols. Cambridge.

Clark, J C D., 1985. *English Society, 1688–1832.* Cambridge.

Clark, S. and Donnelly, J S (eds), 1983. *Irish Peasants. Violence and Political Unrest, 1780–1914.* Madison.

Clowes, W M., 1897. *The Royal Navy. A history*, 8 vols. London.

Cohen, A., 1973. *Palestine in the Eighteenth Century.* Jerusalem.

Colley, L., 1984. 'The Apotheosis of George III: Loyalty, Royalty and the English Nation', *Past and Present*, 102.

Colley, L., 1986. 'Whose Nation? Class and National Consciousness in Britain, 1750–1830', *Past and Present*, 113.

Colquhoun, P., 1815. *A Treatise on the Wealth, Power and Resources of the British Empire in every quarter of the Globe.* London.

Cory, G E., 1910. *The Rise of South Africa*, 2 vols. London.

Craig, G M., 1963. *Upper Canada, 1784–1841.* Toronto.

Crawfurd, J., 1820. *History of the Indian Archipelago*, 3 vols. Edinburgh.

Cullen, L M and Smout T C. (eds), 1977. *Comparative Aspects of Scottish and Irish Economic History, 1600–1900*. Edinburgh.

Cullen, L M., 1977. 'Merchant communities, the navigation acts and Irish and Scottish responses', in Cullen and Smout, 1977.

Curtin, P D., 1964. *The Image of Africa*. Madison.

Curtin, P D., 1984. *Cross cultural trade in world history*. Cambridge.

Danmon, D., 1982. *The Judicial Bench in England, 1727–1875. The reshaping of a professional elite*. London.

Das Gupta, A., 1967. *Malabar in Asian Trade, 1740–1800*. Cambridge.

Das Gupta, A., 1979. *Indian Merchants and the decline of Surat*. Wiesbaden.

Davies, L T and Edwards, A., 1939. *Welsh Life in the Eighteenth Century*. London.

Davy, J., 1969. *An Account of the Interior of Ceylon and of its Inhabitants with travels in that Island*. London, 1821, reprint, Colombo.

de la Tour, N M., 1784. *History of Ayder Ali Khan Nebab Bahadur*. London.

'Demerara Planter', 1816. *To Lord Bathurst and the Colonial Department*. London.

van Deventer, M L., 1891. *Het Nederlandsch Gezag over Java*, i, *1811–20*. S'gravenhage.

Dewaraja, L S., 1972. *The Kandyan Kingdom of Ceylon 1707–60*. Colombo.

Dickson, D., 1983. 'Taxation and Disaffection in late Eighteenth century Ireland', in Clark, S and Donnelly, J S., *Irish Peasants*. Madison.

Dixon, C W., 1939. *The Colonial Administrations of Sir Thomas Maitland*. London.

Dobbin, C., 1983. *Islamic Revivalism in a Changing Peasant Economy. Central Sumatra, 1784–1847*. London.

Donnelly, J S Jr, 1983. 'Pastorini and Captain Rock: millenarianism and sectarianism in the Rockite Movement of 1821–4, in Clark, S and Donnelly, J S (eds), *Irish Peasants*. Madison.

Dowell, S., 1884. *History of Taxation and Taxes in England*, 2 vols. London.

Duly, L C., 1968. *British Land Policy at the Cape, 1795–1844*. Durham, North Carolina.

Dundas, Henry, 1799. *Substance of the Speech of the Rt Hon Henry Dundas in the House of Commons, 7 February, 1799, on the Subject of the Legislative Union with Ireland*. London.

du Toit, A and Giliomee, H., 1983. *Afrikaner Political Thought Analysis and Documents, 1780–1850*. Berkeley.

East India Company, 1793. *Three Reports of the Select Committee appointed by the Court of Directors to take into account the export trade from Great Britain to the East Indies, China, Japan and Persia.* London.

Ehrman, J., 1969. *The Younger Pitt*, vol. i, *The Years of Acclaim.* London.

Ehrman, J., 1983. *The Younger Pitt*, vol. ii, *The Reluctant Transition.* London.

Elphick P., and Giliomee, H., 1983. *The Shaping of South African Society. 1600–1850.* London.

Elphinstone, M., 1815. *An Account of the Kingdom of Caubul*, 2 vols. London.

Embree, A., 1962. *Charles Grant and British Rule in India.* London.

Emsley, C., 1979. *British Society and the French Wars, 1793–1815.* London.

Encyclopaedia of Islam, vol. iii. Leiden and London, 1972.

Evans, E J., 1983. *The Forging of the Modern State. Early Industrial Britain, 1783–1870.* London.

Faroqhi, S., 1985. *Towns and Townsmen of Ottoman Anatolia.* Cambridge.

Flor, W M., 1976. 'The merchants (*tujjar*) in Qajar Iran', *Zeitshrift der Deutschen Morgenländischen Gesellshaft*, 126.

Floud, R. and McCloskey (eds), 1981. *The Economic History of England since 1700*, 2 vols. Cambridge.

Fortescue, Sir J 1910–30. *History of the British Army*, 7 vols. London.

Furber, H., 1976. *Rival Empires of Trade in the Orient, 1620–1750.* Minneapolis.

Furneaux, R., 1974. *William Wilberforce.* London.

Gardner, W J., 1971. *A History of Jamaica.* London.

Garthwaite, G R., 1983. *Khans and Shahs. A documentary analysis of the Bakhtiari in Iran.* Cambridge.

Garwood, Lt. Col. (ed.), 1934–9. *Despatches of the Duke of Wellington*, 13 vols. London.

Gash, N., 1984. *Lord Liverpool . . . 1770–1823.* London.

Gellner, E., 1983. *Muslim Society.* Cambridge.

Gellner, E., 1983b. *Nations and Nationalism.* Cambridge.

Gill, C., 1925. *The Rise of the Irish Linen Industry.* Oxford.

Glover, R., 1963. *Peninsular Preparation. The Reform of the British Army, 1795–1809.* Cambridge.

Gordon, S., 1977. 'The Slow Conquest. The administrative integration of Malwa into the Maratha Empire, 1720–60', *Modern Asian Studies*, 11, 1.

Graham, G., 1930. *British Policy and Canada, 1774–1791*. London.

Gran, P., 1978. *The Islamic Roots of Capitalism. Egypt, 1760–1840*. Austin, Texas.

Grant, C., 1797. *Observations on the state of society among the Asiatick subjects of Great Britain*. London.

Grewal, J S., forthcoming. *The Sikhs in the Punjab. New Cambridge History of India*, ii, 6. Cambridge.

Gross, I., 1980. 'The Abolition of Negro Slavery and British Parliamentary Politics, 1832–3', *Historical Journal*, xxiii, 1.

Gupta, S P., 1986. *The Agrarian System of Eastern Rajasthan*. Delhi.

Habib, I., 1963. *The Agrarian System of Mughal India, 1556–1707*. Bombay.

Halls, J J., 1834. *Life and Correspondance of Henry Salt Esq., Late Consul-General in Egypt*, 2 vols. London.

Halstead, J P., 1983. *The Second British Empire. Trade Philanthropy and Good Government*. Westport.

Hamilton, C., 1787. *An Historical Relation of the Origins, Progress and Final Dissolution of the Government of the Rohilla Afghans in the Northern Provinces of Hindustan*. London.

Hamilton, H., 1963. *An Economic History of Scotland in the Eighteenth Century*. Oxford.

Harlow, V T., 1940. 'The new imperial system. 1783–1815', in Holland Rose, J., Newton, A P and Benians, E A (eds), *The Cambridge History of the British Empire, 1783–1870*, ii, *The Growth of the New Empire*. Cambridge.

Harlow, V T., 1952 and 1964. *The Founding of the Second British Empire, 1763–1793*, 2 vols. London.

Headrick, D., 1981. *The Tools of Empire. Technology and European Imperialism in the Nineteenth Century*. Oxford.

Hechter, M., 1975. *Internal Colonialism*. London.

Hetherington, W M., 1843. *A History of the Church of Scotland*. London.

Hewat, E., 1960. *Vision and Achievement, 1796–1856. A History of the Foreign Missions of the Churches united in the Church of Scotland*. London.

Hill, J R., 1984. 'National festivals, the state and Protestant ascendancy in Ireland, 1790–1829', *Irish Historical Studies*, 29, 93.

Hilton, B., 1977. *Corn Cash and Commerce: The Economic Policies of the Tory Government, 1815–30*. Oxford.

Hilton, B., 1988. *The Age of Atonement, 1780–1860*. Oxford.

Hinde, W., 1981. *Castlereagh*. London.

Hobsbawn, E J., 1968. *Industry and Empire*. London.

Hodgson, M G S., 1974. *The Venture of Islam*, 3 vols. Chicago.

Hodgson, R., 1821. *The Life of the Rt. Revd. Beilby Porteus*, 5th edn, 2 vols. London.

Holland Rose, J., Newton, A P and Benians, E A., 1940. *The Cambridge History of the British Empire*, ii, *The Growth of the New Empire, 1783–1870*. Cambridge.

Holt, P M (ed.), 1968. *Political and Social Change in Modern Egypt*. London.

Holt, P M., 1973. *Studies in the History of the Near East*. London.

Holt, P M., Lambton, A K and Lewis, B., 1970. *Cambridge History of Islam*, vol. ia. Cambridge.

Hopkins, A G and Cain, P J., 1986. 'Gentlemanly Capitalism and British expansion overseas. 1. The Old Colonial System, 1688–1850', *Economic History Review*, 2nd series xxxix, 4.

Horton, Sir R W., 1838. *Exposition and Defence of Lord Bathurst's Administration of the Affairs of Canada when Colonial Secretary*. London.

Hourani, A., 1961. *A Vision of History*. London.

Hourani, A., 1962. *Arabic Thought in the Liberal Age, 1798–1839*. Oxford.

Howse, E M., 1953. *Saints in Politics*. London.

Huart, C., 1901. *Histoire de Bagdad dans les Temps Modernes*. Paris.

Hudson, K., 1973. *Patriotism with Profit*. London.

Hunt, Lynn, 1984. *Politics, Culture and Class in the French Revolution*. Berkeley.

Hyam, R., 1976. *Britain's Imperial Century, 1815–1914*. London.

Hyam, R and Martin, G., 1975. *Reappraisals in British Imperial History*. London.

Inalcik, H., 1973. 'Capital Formation in the Ottoman Empire', *Journal of Economic History*, xix, 9.

Inalcik, H., 1977. 'Centralisation and decentralisation in Ottoman administration', in Naff and Owen, 1977.

Inalcik, H., 1987. 'When and how British cotton goods invaded the Levant markets', in Islamoglu-Inan, H (ed.), *The Ottoman Empire and the World-Economy*. Cambridge.

Ingram, E (ed.), 1970. *Two Views of British India. The Private Correspondence of Mr. Dundas and Lord Wellesley, 1798–1801*. Bath.

Ingram, E., 1981. *Commitment to Empire. Prophecies of the Great Game in Asia*. Oxford.

Ingram, E., 1984. *In defence of British India. Great Britain in the Middle East, 1775–1842*. London.

Innes, J., 1987. 'Jonathan Clark, Social History and England's Ancien Regime', *Past and Present*, 115.

Islamoglu-Inan, H., 1987. *The Ottoman Empire and the World-Economy*. Cambridge.

Issawi, C., 1971. *Economic History of Iran, 1800–1914*. Chicago.

James, C., 1938. *The Black Jacobins. Toussaint Louverture and the San Domingo Revolution*. London.

Jones, G E., 1984. *Modern Wales. A Concise History, c. 1485–1979*. Cambridge.

Jones, Sir William (ed. Cannon, G), 1970. *Letters of Sir William Jones*, 2 vols. Oxford.

Kames, Lord (Henry Hume), 1774. *Sketches of the History of Man*, 2 vols. London.

Kames, Lord, 1776. *The Gentleman Farmer*. London.

Kelly, J B., 1980. *Britain and the Persian Gulf, 1795–1880*. Oxford.

Kennedy, P., 1988. *The Rise and Decline of Great Powers*. London.

Kennedy, W., 1964. *English Taxation, 1640–1799*. London, 1913, reprinted.

Kirmani, H A K (ed. tr. Miles, W), 1834. *Kirmani's History of Hyder Ali and Tipoo Sultaun*. London.

Knot, J W., 1984. 'Land Kinship and Identity. The cultural roots of agrarian agitation in eighteenth and nineteenth century Ireland', *Journal of Peasant Studies*, xii.

Knox, J., 1784. *A view of the British Empire, more especially Scotland, with some proposals for the improvement of that country, the extention of its fisheries and the religion of the people*. London.

Koebner, R., 1961. *Empire*, Cambridge.

Kunt, I M., 1983. *The Sultan's Servants. The Transformation of Ottoman Provincial Government, 1550–1650*. Columbia.

Laferla, A V., 1938. *British Malta, i, 1880–72*. Malta.

Lambrick, H T., 1952. *Sir Charles Napier and Sindh*. Oxford.

Lambton, A., 1953. *Landlord and Peasant in Persia*. London.

Lambton, H K S., 1977. 'The tribal resurgence and the decline of the bureaucracy in eighteenth-century Persia', in Naff and Owen, 1977.

Langford, P., 1976. *The Eighteenth Century, 1688–1815*. London.

Lawson, F H., 1988. 'Economic and Social Foundations of Egyptian Expansionism: the Invasion of Syria, 1831', *International History Review*, x, 3.

Leckie, G F., 1808. *An Historical Survey of the Foreign Affairs of Great Britain with a view to explain the causes of the late and present wars*. London.

Lehman, W C., 1971. *Lord Kames and the Scottish Enlightenment.* The Hague.

Lenman, B., 1981. *Integration, Enlightenment and Industrialisation. Scotland, 1746–1832.* London.

van Leur, J C., 1955. *Indonesian Trade and Society. Essays in Asian Social and Economic History.* The Hague.

Lewin-Robinson, A M (ed.), 1973. *Letters of Lady Anne Barnard to Henry Dundas from the Cape and Elsewhere.* Cape Town.

Lewis, B., 1961. *The Emergence of Modern Turkey.* Oxford.

Lewis, N N., 1987. *Nomads and settlers in Syria and Jordan, 1800–1980.* Cambridge.

Linklater, E and A., 1977. *The Black Watch.* London.

Lockhart, L., 1958. *The Fall of the Safavi Dynasty and the Afghan Occupation of Persia.* Cambridge.

Longrigg, S H., 1925. *Four Centuries of Modern Iraq.* Oxford.

Lord, W F., 1935. *Sir Thomas Maitland.* London.

MacDonagh, O., 1961. *The Pattern of Irish History.* London.

MacDonagh, O., 1977. *Ireland. The Union and its Aftermath.* London.

MacDonagh, O., 1984. *The Inspector General. Sir J. Fitzpatrick and the Process of Social Reform.* London.

McDowell, R B., 1979. *Ireland in the Age of Imperialism and Revolution, 1760–1801.* Oxford.

McGilvray, D., 1982. 'Dutch burghers and Portuguese mechanics. Eurasian ethnicity in Sri Lanka', *Comparative Studies in Society and History,* 24.

McGowan, B., 1981. *Economic Life in Ottoman Europe.* Cambridge.

McKendrick, N., Brewer, J and Plumb, J H (eds), 1982. *The Birth of a Consumer Society. The Commercialisation of Eighteenth Century England.* London.

Madden, F W (with Fieldhouse, D K), 1987. *Imperial Reconstruction, 1763–1840, Select Documents on the Constitutional History of the British Empire and Commonwealth,* iii. New York.

Malcolm, Sir J., 1815. *The History of Persia from the most early period to the present time,* 2 vols. London.

Malik, Z U., 1977. *The Reign of Muhammad Shah, 1709–48.* Bombay.

Manning, H T., 1933. *British Colonial Government after the American Revolution.* Hamden, Conn.

Manning, H T., 1962. *The Revolt of French Canada. 1800–35.* London.

Marais, J S., 1939. *The Cape Coloured People.* London.

Marshall, H., 1969. *A General Description of the Island of Ceylon and of its Inhabitants.* London, 1846, reprinted Colombo.

Marshall, P J., 1964. 'The First and Second British Empire: a

Question of Demarcation', *History*, xlix.

Marshall, P J., 1965. *The Impeachment of Warren Hastings*. Oxford.

Marshall, P J., 1975a, 'British expansion in India in the eighteenth century: a historical revision', *History*, 60.

Marshall, P J., 1975b. 'Economic and Political Expansion. The Case of Oudh, 1765–1804', *Modern Asian Studies*, 9, 4.

Marshall, P J., 1976. *East Indian Fortunes. The British in Bengal in the Eighteenth Century*. Oxford.

Marshall, P J., 1981. 'A free though conquering people: Britain and Asia in the eighteenth century'. Inaugural lecture, King's College, London.

Marshall, P J., 1987. 'Empire and authority in the later eighteenth century', *The Journal of Imperial and Commonwealth History*, xv.

Marshall, P J., 1988. *Bengal the British Bridgehead, The New Cambridge History of India*, 2.2. Cambridge.

Marshall, P J., forthcoming. 'British attitudes to the Dutch in the eighteenth century', *Itinerario*.

Martin, R M (ed.), 1936–7. *The Despatches, Minutes and Correspondence of the Marquess Wellesley during his administration in India*, 5 vols. London.

Martin, R M., 1843. *History of the Colonies of the British Empire*, 2 parts. London.

Matheson, C., 1933. *Life of Henry Dundas*. London.

Mathieson, W L., 1916. *Church and Reform in Scotland. A History from 1797 to 1843*. Glasgow.

Mayer, A., 1981. *The Persistence of the Old Regime*. London.

Metcalf, B., 1982. *Islamic Revival in British India. Deoband, 1860–1900*. Princeton.

Millar, A K., 1965. *Plantagenet in Africa. Lord Charles Somerset*. Cape Town.

Minto, Lord, 1799. *Speech by Lord Minto in the House of Lords on the Subject of the Legislative Union with Ireland, 11 April 1799*. London.

Minto, Countess of, 1834. *Lord Minto in India. Life and Letters of Gilbert Elliot, First Earl of Minto, 1807 to 1814*. London.

Mitchison, R., 1962. *Agricultural Sir John. The Life of Sir John Sinclair of Ulbester 1754–1835*. London.

Morton, W L., 1963. *The Kingdom of Canada*. Toronto.

Mukherjee, R., 1982. 'Trade and Empire in Awadh, 1765–1804', *Past and Present*, 94.

Murray, D J., 1965. *The West Indies and the Development of Colonial Government, 1801–34*. Oxford.

Murrin, J M., 1980. 'The Great Inversion; or Court *versus* Country' in Pocock, J G A (ed.), 1980.

Mutafçieva, V P., 1965. 'L'institution de l'ayanlik pendant les dernières decennies du xiiième siècle'. *Études Balkaniques*. Sofia, 2–3.

Nachtegaal, L., 1986. 'The Dutch East India Company and the relations between Kartasura and the Javanese North Coast c.1690–1740', in van Goor, J., *Trading Companies in Asia c. 1690–c.1740*. Utrecht.

Naff, T and Owen, R (eds), 1977. *Studies in Eighteenth-century Islamic History*. Cambridge.

Napier, Sir C., 1833. *The Colonies, treating of their value generally and of the Ionian Islands in particular*. London.

Napier, Sir C., 1835. *Colonization, Particularly in South Australia, with some remarks on small farms and overpopulation*. London.

Naquin, S and Rawski, E., 1987. *Chinese Society in the Eighteenth Century*. New Haven.

National Theatre, 1984. *Venice Preserved* (programme note).

Neatby, H., 1966. *Quebec. The Revolutionary Age, 1760–91*. Toronto.

Newham, Gerald, 1987. *The Rise of English Nationalism*. London.

Nightingale, P., 1970. *Trade and Empire in Western India, 1784–1806*. Cambridge.

Norman, E., 1976. *Church and Society in England, 1770–1970*. Oxford.

Norris, J., 1963. *Shelburne and Reform*. London.

O'Brien, P K., 1982. 'European economic development; the contribution of the periphery', *Economic History Review*, 35.

Olson, A G., 1980. 'Parliament, Empire and Parliamentary Law, 1776' in Pocock, J G A (ed.), 1980.

Ouellet, F., 1976. *Lower Canada, 1792–1841*. Toronto.

Owen, R., 1981. *The Middle East and the World Economy, 1800–1914*. London.

Palmer, S H., 1975. 'The Irish Police Experiment: the beginnings of modern police in the British Isles, 1788–95', *Social Science Quarterly*, lvi, Dec.

Pamuk, S., 1987. *The Ottoman Empire and European Capitalism, 1820–1913*. Cambridge.

Papers relative to Tipoo Sultan, Madras, n.d. Connemara Library, Madras.

Parry, J H and Sherlock, P M., 1963. *A Short History of the West Indies*. London.

Percival, R., 1803, *An Account of the Island of Ceylon*. London.

Percival, R., 1806. *An Account of the Cape of Good Hope*. London.

Perkin, H., 1969. *The Origins of Modern English Society, 1780–1880*. London.

Perlin, F., 1983. 'Proto-industrialisation and pre-colonial South Asia', *Past and Present*, 98.

Perry, J R., 1979. *Karim Khan Zand*. Chicago.

Philips, C H (ed.), 1977. *The Correspondence of Lord William Bentinck*. 2 vols. Oxford.

Phillipson, N., 1974. 'Edinburgh and the Scottish Enlightenment', in L Stone (ed.), *The University in Society*, ii. Princeton.

Philpin, C H E (ed.), 1987. *Nationalism and Popular Protest in Ireland*. Cambridge.

Pieris, P E., 1918. *Ceylon and the Hollanders, 1658–1796*. Tellippalai.

Platt, D C M., 1968. *Finance, Trade and Politics in British Foreign Policy, 1815–1914*. Oxford.

Platt, D C M., 1973. 'The national economy and British imperial expansion before 1914', *Journal of Imperial and Commonwealth History*, ii, i.

Pocock, J G A., 1971. *Politics, Language and Time*. New York.

Pocock, J G A (ed.), 1980. *Three British Revolutions, 1641, 1688, 1776*. Princeton.

Pocock, J G A., 1985. *Virtue, Commerce and History, Essays on Political Thought and History chiefly in the Eighteenth Century*. Cambridge.

Porter, R., 1982. *English Society in the Eighteenth Century*. London.

Potts, E D., 1967. *British Baptist Missionaries in India, 1793–1836*. Cambridge.

Pratt, M., 1978. *Britain's Greek Empire*. London.

Pryde, G S., 1962. *Scotland from 1603 to the Present Day*. London.

Rafeq, A., 1977. 'Changes in the relationship between the Ottoman central administration and the Syrian provinces from the sixteenth to the eighteenth centuries', in Naff and Owen, 1977.

Raffles, T S., 1817. *The History of Java*, 2 vols. London.

Ragatz, L J., 1928. *The Fall of the Planter Class in the British Caribbean, 1763–1833*. Washington.

Raychaudhuri, T and Habib I., 1982. *The Cambridge Economic History of India*, vol. i, *1200–c. 1650*. Cambridge.

Raymond, A., 1968. 'Quartiers et Mouvements Populaires au Caire au xiiième siècle', in Holt, P M (ed.), *Political and Social Change in Modern Egypt*. London.

Raymond, A., 1973. *Artisans et Commerçants au Caire au xviiième siecle*. 2 vols. Damascus.

Reid, A., 1975. 'Trade and the Problem of Royal Power in Aceh', in Reid, A and Castles, L (eds), 1975. *Pre-Colonial State Systems in South-East Asia*. Kuala Lumpur.

Richards, J F., 1981. 'Mughal state finance and the premodern world economy', *Comparative Studies in Society and History*, 23.

Richardson, J., 1777. *A Dissertation on the Languages, Literature and Manners of the Eastern Nations*. Oxford.

Richardson, P., 1968. *Empire and Slavery*. London.

Ricklefs, M C., *A History of Modern Indonesia*. London.

Ritchie, J., 1986. *Lachlan Macquarie*. Melbourne.

Rizvi, S A A., 1982. *Shah Abd-al Aziz, Puritanism, Sectarian Politics and Jihad*. Canberra.

Robinson, F., 1979. *An Atlas of the Islamic World since 1600*. London.

Robinson, R and Gallagher, J., 1953. 'The Imperialism of Free Trade, 1814–1915', *Economic History Review*, 2nd series, vi, 2.

Robinson, R., 1972. 'Non-European foundations of European imperialism', in Owen, R and Sutcliffe, B (eds), *Studies in the Theory of Imperialism*. London.

Roseveare, H., 1969. *The Treasury*. London.

Rosselli, J., 1974. *Lord William Bentinck. The Making of a Liberal Imperialist, 1774–1839*. London.

Rothblatt, S., 1974. 'Student Culture and the Examination System', in Stone L (ed.), *The University in Society*, i. Princeton.

Rousseau, J., 1802. *Description du Pachalik de Baghdad*. Paris.

Rubinstein, W D., 1983. 'The End of the Old Corruption, 1790–1860', *Past and Present*.

Savory, R M., 1980. *Iran under the Safavids*. Cambridge.

Schumpeter, J., 1951. *Imperialism and Social Classes*. New York.

Sen, A., 1977. 'A pre-British economic formation in India of the late eighteenth century', in De, B. (ed.), *Perspectives in the Social Sciences, i, Historical Dimensions*. Calcutta.

Sen, S., 1928. *The military system of the Marathas*. Calcutta.

Senior, H., 1966. *Orangism in Ireland and Britain, 1795–1836*. London.

Shaw, S J and Shaw, E K., 1977. *The History of the Ottoman Empire and Modern Turkey*, 2 vols. Cambridge.

Sheffield, John, Lord, 1785. *Observations on the Manufacture, Trade and Present State of Ireland*. Dublin.

Siddiqi, N A., 1970. *Land Revenue Administration under the Mughals, 1700–1750*. Bombay.

Siegfried, A., 1960. *Itinéraires de Contagion. Epidémies et Idéologies*. Paris.

Sinclair, Sir J., 1814. *General Report of the Agricultural State and Political Circumstances of Scotland, drawn up for the Consideration of the Board of Agriculture and Internal Improvement*, 21 vols. Edinburgh.

Singapore National Museum, 1978. *National Monuments of Singapore*. Singapore.

Singaravelu, S., 1982. 'The Rama Story in the Thai cultural tradition', *Journal of the Siam Society*, 70, i.

Singh, C., 1988. 'Centre and periphery in the Mughal state: the case of the seventeenth century Punjab', *Modern Asian Studies*, 22, 2.

Smith, A M., 1982. *Jacobite Estates of the Forty-five*. Edinburgh.

Smith, M G., 1965. *The Plural Society in the British West Indies*. Berkeley.

Southey, T., 1827. *Chronological History of the West Indies*, 3 vols. London.

Spiers, E M., 1980. *The Army and Society*. London.

Stafford, W., 1982. 'Religion and the doctrine of nationalism in England at the time of the French Revolution and Napoleonic Wars', in Mews, S (ed.), *Religion and National Identity*. Oxford.

Stein, B., 1985. 'State formation and economy reconsidered', *Modern Asian Studies*, 19, 3.

Stein, B., forthcoming. *Sir Thomas Munro and the British construction of south India*. Delhi.

Stock, E., 1899. *The History of the Church Missionary Society*, i. London.

Stokes, E T., 1959. *The English Utilitarians and India*. Oxford.

Stokes, E T., 1980. 'Bureaucracy and Ideology: Britain and India in the nineteenth century', *Transactions of the Royal Historical Society*, 5th Series, xxx.

Stone, L and Stone, J F., 1984. *An Open Elite? England 1540–1880*. Oxford.

Sutherland, H., 1979. *The Making of a Bureaucratic Elite. The Colonial Transformation of the Javanese Priyayi*. Singapore.

Tarling, N., 1969. *British Policy in the Malay Peninsula and Archipelago, 1824–71*. Oxford.

Tate, D J., 1971. *The Making of Modern Southeast Asia*, vol. i, *The European Conquest*. Kuala Lumpur.

Temperley, H., 1966. *The Foreign Policy of Canning, 1822–7*, 2nd edn. London.

Tennent, Sir J E., 1850. *Christianity in Ceylon*. London.

Tennant, W., 1804. *Indian Recreations. Consisting chiefly of strictures on the domestic and rural economy of the Mahomedans and Hindoos*, 2nd edn, 2 vols. London.

Theal, G M., 1898–1905. *Records of the Cape Colony*. 36 vols. Cape Town.

Thirsk, J (ed.), 1984. *The Agrarian History of England and Wales*, vol. v. Cambridge.

Thompson, E and Garratt, G T., 1934. *The Rise and Fulfilment of British Rule in India*. London.

Tilly, C., 1975. *The Formation of National States in Western Europe*. Princeton.

Tinker, H., 1974. *A New System of Slavery. The export of Indian Labour overseas, 1830–1920*. London.

Valensi, L., 1977a. *Fellahs Tunisiens. L'économie rurale et la vie des campagnes au xviiième et xixème siecles*. Paris.

Valensi, L., 1977b. *On the Eve of Colonialism*. London.

Valentia, Viscount George, 1809. *Voyages and Travels in India, Ceylon, the Red Sea, Abyssinia and Egypt . . .* 3 vols. London.

Vicziany, M., 1986. 'Imperialism, botany and statistics in early nineteenth century India. The surveys of Francis Buchanan', *Modern Asian Studies*, 20, 4.

Villiers, J., 1981. 'Trade and society in the Banda islands during the sixteenth century', *Modern Asian Studies*, 15, 4.

Wallerstein, I., 1980. *The Modern World System II. The Consolidation of the European World Economy, 1600–1750*. New York.

Walsh, T., 1803. *Journal of the late Campaign in Egypt*. London.

Ward, J M., 1976. *Colonial Self-Government. The British Experience, 1759–1856*. London.

Washbrook, D A., 1988. 'Progress and Problems. South Asian Economic and Social History, c.1720–1860', *Modern Asian Studies*, xxii, 1.

Wellington, Duke of, 1867–80. *Despatches, Correspondence and Memoranda*, ed. by his son, 8 vols. London.

Wilberforce, William, 1798. *A Practical View of the Prevailing Religious System of Professed Christians in the Higher and Middle Classes of the Country contrasted with Real Christianity*. London.

Williams, E., 1964. *Capitalism and Slavery*. London.

Williams, G and Marshall, P., 1980. *The British Atlantic Empire before the American Revolution*. London.

Wink, A., 1986. *Land and Sovereignty in India. Agrarian Society and Politics under the Eighteenth Century Maratha Svarajya*. Cambridge.

Young, Arthur, 1892. *Arthur Young's Tours in Ireland*, 2 vols, ed. Hutton, A W. London.

Young, G A., 1839. *The Canadian Question*. London.

Young, D M., 1962. *The Colonial Office in the Early Nineteenth Century*. London.

Maps

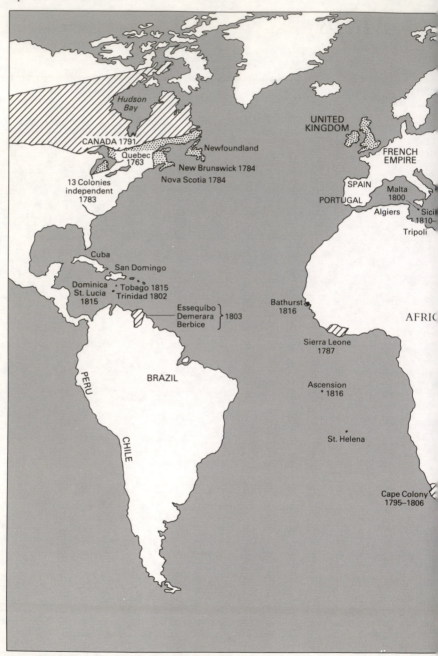

Map 1   The expansion of British control, 1750–1830

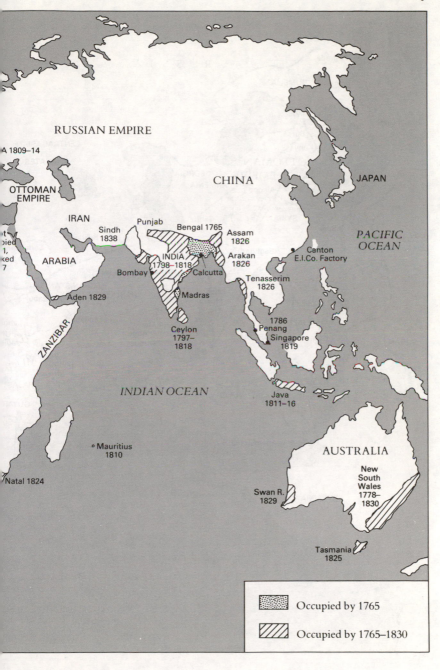

RUSSIAN EMPIRE

A 1809–14

OTTOMAN
EMPIRE

CHINA

JAPAN

IRAN

Punjab

Sindh
1838

Bengal 1765

Assam
1826

*PACIFIC
OCEAN*

ARABIA

INDIA
1798–1818

Arakan
1826

Canton
E.I.Co. Factory

Bombay

Calcutta

Aden 1829

Madras

Tenasserim
1826

pied
1,
ked
7

ZANZIBAR

Ceylon
1797–
1818

1786
Penang

Singapore
1819

INDIAN OCEAN

Java
1811–16

Mauritius
1810

AUSTRALIA

Natal 1824

New
South
Wales
1778–
1830

Swan R.
1829

Tasmania
1825

	Occupied by 1765
	Occupied by 1765–1830

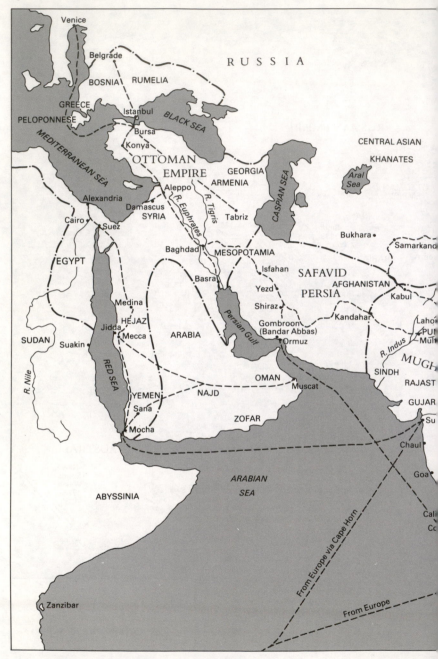

Map 2   The Muslim empires

Trade routes
Boundaries of Empires

The Great Silk Road

JAPAN
KOREA
Peking

CHINA

R. Hwang Ho

TIBET
R. Salween
R. Yangtze Kiang
Foochow
TAIWAN

Canton
Macao
PHILIPPINES

SOUTH
CHINA
SEA

Patna Murshidabad
BENGAL
Hugli Chittagong
R. Irrawaddy

PIRE
R. Ganga
rbada

BAY OF
BENGAL

BURMA
Pegu

SIAM
(THAILAND)
Ayuthia

R. Mekong

ROMANDEL
Masulipatam
yderabad
ras
Tanjore
Tenasserim

CEYLON
(SRI LANKA)
Kandy
mbo

MALAYA

BORNEO

Kedah
Penang
Malacca
Johore-
Riau

SUMATRA

To Spice Islands
MATARAM
JAVA
Jogjakarta

INDIAN OCEAN

Bencoolen
From Europe
Bantam Batavia

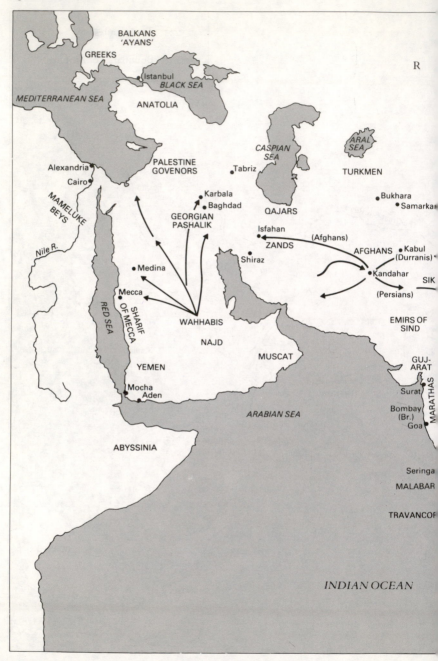

Map 3 The regional states of eighteenth-century Asia

S I A

JAPAN

Peking

R. Hwang Ho

C H I N A

TIBET

TAIWAN

elhi
Agra

AWADH

PHILIPPINES

(Marathas)

Murshidabad
Dacca

R. Irrawaddy

R. Salween

R. Yangtze Kiang

SOUTH
CHINA
SEA

BENGAL
Hugli

Calcutta
(Br.)

CAN

BURMA

THAILAND

R. Mekong

DERABAD

Masulipatam

ARCOT

*BAY
OF BENGAL*

Madras (Br.)

KEDAH

DUTCH
CEYLON

Kandy

Penang (Br.)

Malacca

Johore-Riau

NJORE

PADRI

SURAKARTA

SUMATRA

Bencoolen
(Br.)

Batavia

Bantam
(DUTCH)

JOGYAKARTA

281

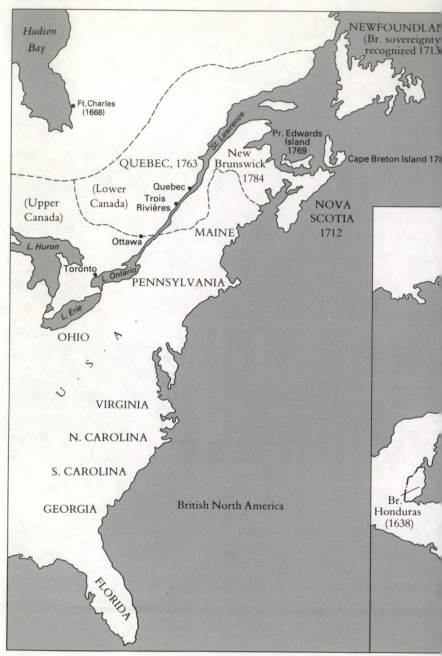

Map 4 The Americas

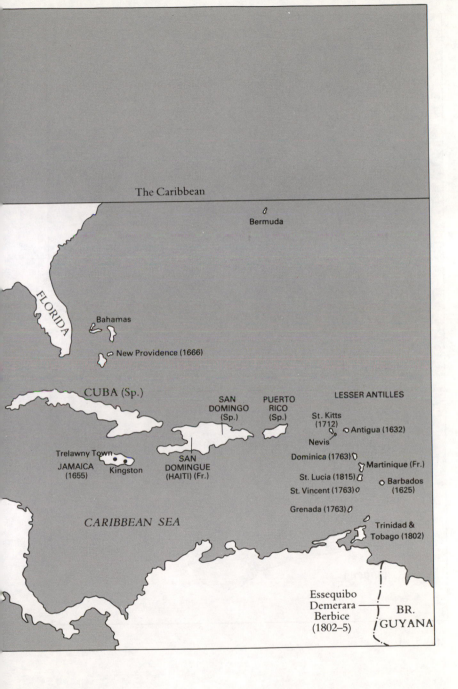

The Caribbean

Bermuda

FLORIDA

Bahamas

New Providence (1666)

CUBA (Sp.)

SAN DOMINGO (Sp.)

PUERTO RICO (Sp.)

LESSER ANTILLES

St. Kitts (1712)

Antigua (1632)

Nevis

Trelawny Town

JAMAICA (1655)

Kingston

SAN DOMINGUE (HAITI) (Fr.)

Dominica (1763)

Martinique (Fr.)

St. Lucia (1815)

Barbados (1625)

St. Vincent (1763)

Grenada (1763)

CARIBBEAN SEA

Trinidad & Tobago (1802)

Essequibo Demerara Berbice (1802–5)

BR. GUYANA

Map 5   Ionia

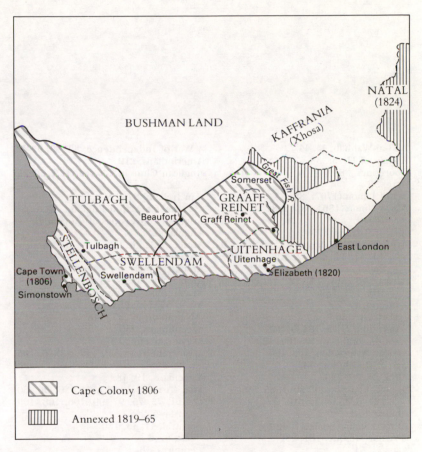

Map 6 The Cape

Index

Index

Haileybury College, 6, 115, 142, 150
Haiti, 'black emperors' of, 176
haj, the, 232
Haldane, John Alexander, 145
Hamdad Pasha, 187
Hamilton, Walter, 39–40
Harlow, Vincent, 8, 9, 12, 248, 252
Hastings, Marquess of, 106, 186, 245
Hastings, Warren, 147, 148, 149, 156
Hawkesbury, Lord, 209
Hejaz, the, 36, 43, 54, 180
Highland Clearances, 101
Highland Society, the, 123
Hinduism, 22, 45, 146, 152–3, 210, 212-3, 222
Holland
    Liberator Party, 175
    Patriot Party, 175
Holy Alliance, 8, 195
Home, Henry, *see* Kames, Lord
Hottentot Code, 203–4, 222
Hottentots (Khoikoi), 153, 167, 203–4, 209, 219, 222, 244
Hudson Bay Company, 94
Hume, David, 84, 110
Hume, Joseph, 199
Huskisson, William, 121
Hyderabad, 40, 42, 47, 106, 229, 230, 234, 239

Iberia, 3
Iberian Peninsula, 178
iltizam/ijarah, 30
imperialism
    ecological, 76, 130
    economic, 1, 102–7
    free trade, 9–10, 252
    historiography, 1–2, 73–6, 137, 248–9, 253
    ideologies, 7–8, 11, 59, 103–9, 111, 147–55, 237
    proto-capitalism, 73–6, 252
    rituals, 111–3, 199
    social, 251–2
Inca empire, 64
income tax, 116
indenture contracts, 221
India, 4, 8, 10, 15, 18, 24, 25, 26, 27, 29, 30, 32, 33, 36, 39, 46, 47, 50, 52, 54, 55, 58–60, 63, 98, 99, 102, 105–6, 113, 116–7, 119–21, 148–9, 159, 173–4, 180, 182, 186, 188, 221, 224, 230, 241, 248, 250
Indian Mutiny, 136, 238

Indian Ocean, 3, 18, 37, 43
Indo-Muslim gentlemen, 26
Indonesia, 15, 18, 64, 180, 182
Indonesian Archipelago, 99, 182
Insurrection Act, 119
Ionian Islands, 8, 20, 103, 104, 198–202, 240
Iran, 4, 14, 15, 24, 26, 30, 31, 32, 36, 37, 38, 43, 44, 46, 47, 48, 50, 52, 54, 55, 60, 165, 170–1, 181–2, 186, 188, 229, 234
    see also Qajar Iran
Iraq, 36, 43, 46, 54, 186
Ireland, Irish, 5, 6, 8, 12, 77, 81–2, 85, 86–9, 91, 95, 98, 99, 101–2, 109, 113, 115, 118–9, 122, 124–5, 162, 177, 196, 215, 241
    Chief secretary, 196
    Constabulary, 131, 190–1
    Lieutenant Governors, 196
    Municipal Corporations Act, 24–6
    Police Act (1887), 119
    Prisons Amendment Act, 118
    revolts (1797, 1798), 166
    Settlement (1782), 94
    Union, 6, 12, 81–2, 101–2, 193
Isfahan, 19, 22, 23, 26, 50, 189, 191
Islam, 19–21, 44–6, 152, 153–4
    revival, 36, 44–6, 65, 179–84, 232–3
    Shias, 22, 38, 45, 50–1, 171, 234
    Sunnis, 38, 39, 45, 51
Istanbul, 19, 20, 26, 35, 50, 57, 61, 170, 191, 230, 232
Italy, 103, 232

'Jacobinism', 115, 164, 167, 208, 214
Jaffna, 179
jagirdari system, 29
jagirs, 20
Jamaica, 15, 77, 90, 91, 92, 208, 221
    slave revolts in, 241, 246
Japan, 229, 255
Jats, 39
Java, 6, 7, 10, 14, 16, 64, 65, 67, 68, 69, 73, 105, 111, 149, 157, 162, 168, 173, 175, 181, 182, 187, 190, 202, 211–2, 213, 225, 241, 244
Jerusalem, 181
Jews, 19
Jezzar Ahmed, 56–7, 58, 98, 231
Jogjakarta, 64, 191, 211
Johore-Riau, 69–70
Jones, Sir William, 131–2, 147–8

Kames, Lord, 85, 155, 156

Index